Praise for the Fifth Edi

Letting Go

"As the perspectives of students and their parents have changed and evolved through the years, this new edition of *Letting Go* continues to enrich our understanding of the college student experience. It has always been at the top of the recommended reading list that I give to parents during new student orientation and is truly one of the best resources for parents and educational administrators." —Lori White, Vice President for Student Affairs, Southern Methodist University

"A sensitive, informative, and well-written guide to let parents know what their children are getting into when they leave for college. Full of practical advice and psychological insight, it's a better antidote than Valium for the anxieties parents feel as they prepare to let their children go."

—Ben Lieber, Dean of Students, Amherst College

"As someone who works with stressed-out high school seniors and their anxious parents, I especially appreciate their honesty about, and their obvious affection for, the complexities of college life. The book is not only extremely informative and timely; it is also warmly reassuring. I think it belongs on the bookshelves of parents, teachers, and college counselors alike."

—James Alan Astman, Ph.D., Headmaster, Oakwood School, Los Angeles

"*Letting Go* provides valuable insight to help parents successfully navigate the challenges, surprises, and excitement of the transition into the college years. Coburn and Treeger open a window for parents to glimpse into contemporary college life, helping parents to maintain healthy relationships with their children. I have given *Letting Go* as a graduation gift to every parent of a graduating senior I know!" —Ronnie Mae Weiss, Work/Life Liaison, Harvard School of Public Health

"Sensible, thorough, comforting. The authors offer a wealth of helpful information to guide parents through an important family transition." —Parker J. Beverage, Dean of Admissions and Financial Aid, Colby College

"*Letting Go* unscrambles the exhilarating, confusing, and anxiety-producing experience of launching a child in the world of higher education. With sensitivity, humor, and wisdom, Karen Coburn and Madge Treeger provide sound advice, good counsel, and practical strategies to help parents navigate the experience."
—Sheila Murphy, Dean for Student Life, Simmons College

"A thoughtful, well-written, and comprehensive guide for parents. It describes in understandable terms the major changes that have taken place on the American college campus over the last twenty to thirty years."
—Lattie F. Coor, President Emeritus, Arizona State University

"This is certainly the best treatment I have read on this subject. It is intelligent, thorough, and researched with great professionalism and care. The discussion of the impact of technology is superb."
—Stephen Singer, Director of College Counseling, Horace Mann, New York

"Very practical, with lots of nuts-and-bolts illustrations of how to deal with concrete situations that arise for freshman college students." —John N. Gardner, Executive Director, Policy Center on the First Year of College, Brevard, North Carolina

"*Letting Go* continues to be a must-read for parents of college-bound students. The enduring value of *Letting Go* is that you can go back to it periodically to find those sections that resonate to your own experiences with kids in college. After you read it, you'll want to write your son or daughter a letter full of understanding about the richness and turmoil of college life."
—Mark Govoni, Dean of Students, Philadelphia University

"Filled with practical and up-to-date information, *Letting Go* is must-reading for parents embarking on this next stage of life with their soon-to-be college students. Undoubtedly, the best guide available today."
—Dr. Patricia A. Whitely, Vice President for Student Affairs, University of Miami

"As a high school principal, I find *Letting Go* to be an invaluable resource. Written in a humorous and accessible style, it answers the questions 'What happens next and how can you deal with it?'"
—Louise Losos, Principal, Clayton High School, Clayton, Missouri

"A seminal source of information for families and their college-bound children!"
—Larry Moneta, Vice President for Student Affairs, Duke University

"*Letting Go* should be considered required homework for the education that parents receive when their children go to college! As deans (and one of us the parent of six college graduates), we have found *Letting Go* an invaluable resource for providing perspective and thoughtful advice on the ups and downs, joys and trials, and patterns of college life. It also highlights the challenges and rewards of parenting college students. We will continue to recommend it to Smith parents and to use it ourselves."
—Tom Riddell, Associate Dean of the College; Dean of the First-Year Class, and Rae-Anne Butera, Associate Dean of Students, Smith College

"*Letting Go* sheds light on the rapidly changing dynamics of the American family and the powerful impact this is having on the transition to college for parents and their children. Clever, anecdotal, and insightful, this book is a wonderful resource for families navigating through an exciting, yet challenging, period of adjustment."
—David Mahler, Head of School, Open Door Academy, Sarasota, Florida

"After more than a dozen years as a dean of first-year students, of routinely advising parents on how to 'let go,' I sent my own first child off to college, as nervous and tearful as my 'lay' friends. My own professional experience proved less than useful; *Letting Go* helped to assure and reassure me. A practical reference tool, it kept me on track in the challenging and complex transition to being the parent of a college student."

—Dorothy Denburg, Dean of the College, Barnard College

"*Letting Go* should be a required text for any college parent. It reflects today's college students' reality and helps prepare parents for the exciting journey that awaits both them and their sons and daughters."

—Marc Wais, Vice President for Student Affairs,
New York University

David Kilper, Washington University Photographic Services

About the Authors

Karen Levin Coburn (left), coauthor of *The New Assertive Woman* and *Hitting Our Stride*, is Senior Consultant in Residence and longtime Assistant Vice Chancellor/Associate Dean at Washington University in St. Louis. Madge Lawrence Treeger is a psychotherapist and former member of the Washington University Counseling Service. Coburn and Treeger, two of the country's leading experts on the college experience, are popular speakers at educational institutions and conferences and have aided thousands of parents and students nationwide.

LETTING GO

A PARENTS' GUIDE TO UNDERSTANDING THE COLLEGE YEARS

FIFTH EDITION

KAREN LEVIN COBURN
& MADGE LAWRENCE TREEGER

HARPER

NEW YORK • LONDON • TORONTO • SYDNEY

HARPER

A previous edition of this book was published in 1997 by HarperPerennial, an imprint of HarperCollins Publishers.

FIRST QUILL EDITION PUBLISHED 2003.
FIRST HARPER PAPERBACK PUBLISHED 2009.

Designed by Elina D. Nudelman

The Library of Congress has catalogued the Quill edition as follows:

Coburn, Karen Levin.
Letting go : a parents' guide to understanding the college years / Karen Levin Coburn and Madge Lawrence Treeger.
Includes bibliographical references and index.
ISBN 0-06-052126-0
1. College students—United States—Psychology. 2. Parenting—United States. 3. Parent and child—United States. 4. Universities and colleges—United States. I. Treeger, Madge Lawrence. II. Title.

LA229 .C53 2003
378.1'98—dc21 2002031785

ISBN 978-0-06-166573-8 (Harper paperback)

09 10 11 12 13 OV/RRD 10 9 8 7 6 5 4 3 2

For Stephen and Tom, our loving partners;
Alison, Andrew, Anne, and Jennie,
who continue to teach us about letting go;
and Ayanna, Carly, August, Gus, Charlie,
Delilah, and Clementine—the next generation

CONTENTS

PREFACE TO THE FIFTH EDITION

FOR US, RETURNING TO *LETTING GO* TO WRITE the fifth edition is like opening an old family photo album—full of nostalgia, with warm memories of the time when our own children were venturing forth on this college journey. With each new edition, we have "filled our album" with the new students, parents, faculty, and administrators who have generously contributed their experiences and insights.

Each time we have come together to write, we have been amazed at the easy cadence of our partnership. The stimulation of delving into new data, research, and reports, the fascination with the rapid changes, the liveliness of new interviews and perspectives have sparked our enthusiasm, generated new bursts of energy, and landed us in a place of déjà vu—surrounded by the sights and sounds and emotional landscape of the ever-fascinating transition to college and the years that follow.

As we stroll the university pathways—our senses heightened—we are acutely aware of the changes that have become commonplace in our everyday lives. The images of students connected to their MP3 players, texting and chatting on iPhones; the jarring sound of a "Crank That" ringtone interrupting an otherwise peaceful morning walk; the beeps and clicks of laptops in the dining hall and library and coffee shop—all are simply part of the milieu of today's students. Bulletin boards and kiosks are covered with new signs of new times . . . visual indications of the many environmental, social action and multicultural groups: V.E.R.D.E. (Volunteers for Environmental Restoration, Development and Education), Engineers Without Borders, Niños (mentoring and tutoring Hispanic elementary school students), Staam (Jewish a cappella group).

And there are many changes that are not visible but that affect the climate of the campus and those engaged in life there: demographic changes, economic shifts, and a magnified sense of anxiety in our culture. All have caused profound challenges for students, their families, and the whole academic enterprise. We see these challenges in the increasingly frantic and competitive press to "get in" by students, and the parallel race of the institutions to position themselves on the top of prestigious lists; in the reports of student-loan scandals and the financial burden on families as children leave for college at an economically shaky time; in the pressure on the institutions themselves to keep up with the technological and global imperatives; in the enormous increases in numbers of students seen at counseling centers; in new security measures and emergency procedures and challenges to privacy.

These realities have influenced today's parents, who are more involved in their children's lives than generations of the past. Many are justly proud of the fact that their college-age children are closer to them than they had been to their own parents. But how close? How involved? The so-called helicopter parents—parents who hover—have become the target of the media and many college administrators. How do parents walk this balance beam, enjoying the closeness of their relationship with their adolescent children while encouraging them to become increasingly confident and competent during their college years? In our world of instant and ubiquitous communication, how can a parent enjoy sharing the joys and sorrows of a daughter or son, providing support without hovering, resisting the urge to solve problems and rescue from afar? This is the daunting task facing today's college parent.

Twenty-first-century colleges and universities are tackling these challenges as well. Recognizing that students may not need the "*in loco parentis*" oversight of yesteryear—but acknowledging that they do need the wisdom of experienced adults available to them as guides, counselors, and mentors—more faculty and staff are involved in the daily lives of students, some even living right on campus. Many schools are forming a partnership with parents, creating comprehensive parent websites and special parent programs that provide information about the college and its resources for students. The goal is to ward off hovering and help parents find appropriate and effective ways to respond so that they can support their child's growing independence.

We do much of our research and writing in Karen's office, situated in a building that is a hub of activity, housing sorority suites, a formal lounge for academic and social gatherings, and a drama and dance studio. As we write about diversity, we experience it firsthand. Across the hall, the insistent drumming from an African dance class draws our attention; we look into the studio filled with white, black, and Asian young men and women of varying size and ability, clad in colorful sarongs, stomping their feet and leaping through space. On St. Patrick's Day, we glance out the window to see a young man striding across campus with collar-length green hair flowing out from under his yarmulke. Sounds of the Visions Gospel Choir practicing in the chapel mingle with the polite applause coming from the nearby formal lounge during a lecture on "Justice and the Feminization of Global Poverty." On one evening, after several hours at the computer, we are reminded that it is time for dinner as we smell the sweet aroma of the Korean Student Association's barbecue wafting through our open window.

Each day or night is different, all reverberating with the college scene and reflecting the time of year and the state of the weather. The unrelenting drilling noise from yet one more construction site across the lawn competes with the distant cheering from an IM soccer game. Students—men and women—celebrate the first hot day of the year with a full-fledged water fight; they toss water-filled balloons at each other until all collapse, soaking wet, laughing and exhausted. The Quad is filled with a stage and massive sound equipment as students rehearse *Cabaret* wrapped in ski jackets on an unseasonably cold spring evening.

We are often enchanted as we listen to these sounds, see the sights, and catch occasional vignettes that tell a story of their own: the iambic rhythms of Shakespeare recited by a student practicing in the hall outside the office before the *Hamlet* dress rehearsal is interrupted by the ring of his cell phone, which he answers instantly with a booming, "Hey, dude, what's up?"; the ongoing parade of admissions tour guides stopping under our window with a captive audience of questioning parents and prospective students to explain what goes on in this building, each exuberant variation a reflection of the tour guide's own special interest—sorority meetings; campus radio station; dance studio; poetry readings.

The daily and nightly interruptions are for the most part welcomed as they add grist to our mill, embodying the life that we write of. A parent calls seeking advice about a proposed visit to a homesick daughter. A sophomore stops by to get a signature for a summer program in Kenya. A proud senior comes by with a poster advertising his upcoming art exhibit. In mid-August, a student orientation leader "Facebooks" Karen to invite her to a gathering of new students. Though we are well aware that today's students spend countless hours connecting online, we are, nevertheless, astonished when we notice that more than 1200 students (out of Washington University's 1400 entering freshmen) have joined the Class of 2012 Facebook group before ever setting foot on campus! The chapel bells ring on the quarter hour—a sonorous reminder of fleeting time. We don't have to imagine the heartbeat of campus life; we feel it.

This is but a glimpse of the captivating world your child is about to enter. There is much in today's college experience that has a distinctly new flavor, and we aim to give you an insider's view. Though the rate of change in many dimensions of college life has accelerated dramatically, much of what we wrote in the original edition of *Letting Go* remains the same. It is the soul of our book: the ongoing but changing relationship between parents and their about-to-be-adult children during the college years.

Karen Levin Coburn and Madge Lawrence Treeger

St. Louis, Missouri, 2009

Part I

THE COLLEGE EXPERIENCE

1

LETTING GO

"I'M NOT GETTING OUT."

I sat behind the wheel of the car; Jennie sat beside me with her tattered stuffed teddy bear at her side, and we looked out at the line of young men and women laughing and chatting as they waited for the doors of the freshman dormitory to open.

"I'm not getting out," she repeated.

I panicked. My mind flashed back to the first day of nursery school. "Don't leave me," were her words then.

"But you wanted to get here early to get the best bed," I reminded her.

"I've changed my mind," she replied. That was evident.

We had just traveled for seventeen hours, over two days. Jennie was beginning her freshman year at college—our first child to leave home. Was I going to have to turn around and go back to St. Louis with her still beside me?

"Suppose we get out and just stand next to the car." She agreed reluctantly. I was relieved to see her leave the teddy bear in the car.

Jennie made it to the line of seemingly relaxed, happy freshmen—and was swept along by an overanxious young woman who handled her anxiety by hyperactivity instead of shyness. I looked over and saw Jennie blending in and looking just as relaxed as the others and let out a sigh of relief.

Within a half hour, I was excess baggage. Now it was my turn to separate. "Why don't you wander around campus and stop back in a few hours," Jennie suggested diplomatically.

(What about all my fantasies of helping you fix up your room, chat with your roommates a bit, and see what coed living looks like? Of course, I kept these thoughts to myself.)

I smiled diplomatically in return, said good-bye, and began a somewhat aimless tour of the campus, passing other parents along the way who looked as lost as I felt. When I returned to the dorm, I found out Jennie had arranged for me to have dinner with another parent since she already had plans. I graciously bowed out, returned to the motel, and had a good cry.

Two days earlier, as a part of freshman orientation at Washington University, I had stood on a stage before hundreds of parents who had come to hear my professional words of wisdom as a member of the Student Counseling Service. The topic was "Letting Go."

And now *I* had begun.

■

The process of "letting go" actually starts in the first years of life. As parents, we can remember the struggles of the early years, especially between the ages of 1½ and 3, when our children seesawed back and forth between acts of independence—a toddling strut accompanied by a "world is my oyster" smile—and clinging, whining periods of hanging on. Although this separation process continues throughout our children's growing years, it is especially evident as they move through adolescence and begin to leave home, when we once again see their ambivalence acted out in puzzling ways. We were often more patient and understanding of the process when our children were small. We were also better informed. The "terrible twos" may not have been pleasant, but we all knew they were coming, and we knew they would end. Information and reassurance were readily available if we felt uncertain about our children's development or our roles as parents. But when we send our sons and daughters off to college, there are no *What to Expect* books to reassure us, no guidelines for moving through this time of transition.

Some parents don't see this as a time of transition at all. It is simply the end of childrearing for them and of childhood for their sons and daughters. "You're an adult now; start acting like one," they admonish. Others have trouble giving up their role. They still see themselves as necessary protectors and their sons and daughters as immature children rather than self-reliant young adults. "Don't you worry about it, dear. I'll call your Dean and take care of it for you."

Most of us flounder somewhere in between. We send our children off with a mixture of anticipation and anxiety, a sense of loneliness and freedom, fantasy and reality. Our childrearing days are ending. Our children are launched. We anticipate dealing with our own reactions to their leaving—loss of companionship, financial belt-tightening, a quiet house—but we are caught off guard by the continuing demands and concerns that we discover as each week and month goes by *after* the launching. As they struggle to be independent and separate once again, as in their toddler years, they venture forth with bravado and periods of newfound confidence and wisdom, only to retreat into times of anxiety and hanging on. They want Mom or Dad to be there *when* they want them. They call and pour out fears and hurts, hoping to be understood, or they withdraw into silence; advice and parental concerns become intrusions.

We shift gears constantly as we meet our offspring in an elusive dance of change. We find ourselves relentlessly retracing old patterns one week and discovering new ways of getting along the next. The temptation to tell our children *how* to be independent is a compelling one. The contradictory, but all too familiar, parental message is "It's about time you were grown up and on your own, so follow my advice." Translated, this painfully becomes "It's time for you to be independent, but I don't trust your judgment."

As our sons and daughters enter these college years, we have to come to terms with their strengths *and* their limitations. At the same time we realize that we too are at a watershed, entering into a new phase of our lives—growing older. We may find ourselves taking a new look at our marriage or career—our own limitations. And so as they struggle with a turmoil of conflicting emotions about leaving, we often are flooded with conflicting feelings of our own about being left.

It is common for parents who were eager to see their children leave, to lament their departure later. "Somehow there must be a biological process at work; my son is so impossible this year it makes it easy to see him go—in fact I can't wait," becomes, three months later, "It's quieter in the house; I have to hold back from wanting to call him and find out how his day went"—the same parents wanting to stay connected and wanting to let go.

A parent, whose daughter struggled through several rebellious years in high school and emerged at 17 as a delightful young woman and close companion to her mother, confessed, "I dreaded her leaving; we had just begun to enjoy each other again. But now that she's gone, I have to admit I love the simplicity and freedom of living as a couple again."

We all know intellectually that this is a time for our children to separate and assert their independence. But long after they have become taller or stronger than we are, our primal protective feelings are easily unleashed. We carry images in our heads of the curly-haired toddler, the gap-toothed 6-year-old, and times when a caress or a hug could make their world all better. As they get older the problems they face have increasingly greater consequences. The stakes get higher. The mature, rational part of us wants them to solve their own problems and believes they can, but another part of us wants to stay connected, be in control, feel needed, and protect them from any pain they will have to face.

We tend to see the years of college as the calm before the storm—a time within a safe bastion of learning that will provide a protected environment for our children as they prepare for the "real world." Though college provides a unique opportunity for learning, the college years are no more a calm than all the years that follow are necessarily a storm. College students are confronted with a host of the pressures and societal constraints that are part of the *ongoing* process of human experience.

Our expectations of college life are often large-scale and grandiose. They are born of many factors: our own hopes and dreams, images from the media, a need to justify the large financial investment we are making. The fire is fanned by the big buildup—years of planning and positioning so that our children can compete in the furor of "getting in." We are courted with a marketing blitz from the institutions themselves, all promising dreams fulfilled, horizons waiting to be discovered, unencumbered bliss. The effect of all this is to raise the college years to a larger-than-life, once-in-a-lifetime opportunity that will make or break our children's future. Both parents and students feel the pressure and push to make this myth their reality.

Most of us have the same hopes and goals for our children as they have for themselves. We want them to be happy and successful, self-confident and self-reliant. The trouble is that the specific notion of what constitutes success or self-reliance is often very different for a parent than it is for his or her offspring. Although independence is valued as a goal, actual steps toward independence are likely to make parents nervous. Intellectual exploration may threaten established family values and ideas about life's meaning. Sudden shifts in behavior and ideas are confusing, and sometimes exasperating, to even the most patient, understanding parents. Too often, parents inhibit their children's growth without realizing how their good intentions are backfiring. It doesn't have to be that way, but as educators, we've seen it happen again and again, and as parents, we have felt this dilemma ourselves.

Students talk to us about their parents—about pressures and misunderstandings and their longing to be accepted by their parents as separate adults. We listen; we probe; we empathize, and then we recall conversations with our own college-age children who recited variations on the same themes. Except that with them, *we* were the ones who didn't understand, who were putting on too much pressure, who were overprotective or not around when we were needed. Our experience as parents broadened our perspectives and brought new insights to our professional work.

We both have spent much of our adult lives working on college and university campuses. We have listened to countless students as they have struggled with the disparity between their parents' expectations and their own; with broken romances and disappointing grades; with the excitement and the confusion of expanding intellectual horizons and new values. As we look out our windows at the ivy-covered Gothic buildings and the Frisbee game in the quad, all may look idyllic, but when we listen to what students have too say, it is clear that their lives are complex and often unsettling. No matter how fraught with complications and responsibilities our own adult lives may seem, we can't simply retreat to "the good old college days" refrain sung by many of our peers. Our students give us daily reminders that youth is not synonymous with simplicity or freedom from responsibility.

The college years are a time of transition for young people and their parents. There is no way to move through such an important passage without some feelings of dislocation and loss. But information and insight can help parents negotiate this significant and often neglected phase of their children's lives.

As professionals immersed in the daily routine of life on the college campus, we hope to offer a realistic view of the many facets of this experience—one that reflects the trials and tribulations as well as the excitement, opportunity, and promise of these years. We will focus on the experience of traditional-age college students who go to school away from home, but much of the material will be relevant to parents of commuter students as well.

Part I of this book, "The College Experience," begins with information about late adolescent development, so that our children's behavior can be viewed in the broader context of normal growth. We will explain how *all* college students struggle with developing a sense of their own identity, with becoming independent, and with establishing intimacy. Each young person finds his or her own way to express these struggles, often to the consternation and confusion of concerned parents. But knowing that a certain amount of experimenting and exploring is, in fact, healthy can be reassuring. Insight into normal development enables parents to discriminate between the universal problems of college students and those that require parental or professional intervention. With this understanding, parents can respond more appropriately and with more assurance to the signals their children send them.

We will look also at the changes in the larger contemporary society, and at its campus reflections in high-tech classrooms, multicultural activities and courses, complex security systems, and a proliferation of choices. Although we all went through our own versions of young adult confusion and self-discovery, the world in which we grew up was clearly different from the one our children are grappling with today. Perhaps no place is that more evident than on college campuses.

This chapter opened with the story of Jennie, clutching her childhood teddy bear. Her tenuous approach to the freshman dormitory and subsequent dismissal of her mother a few hours later was not an unusual sequence of events. What she needed most at that point was nothing more than her mother's willingness to let go.

Other freshmen find different ways to begin. One departs from his hometown airport, guitar slung casually over his shoulder, barely stopping to wave good-bye as he walks out to the plane. Then he calls his mother every day for two weeks. What does he need? Probably just a reassuring adult voice from home, someone who understands and tolerates his temporary need to return to familiar territory while he adjusts to an alien one. A flashback to his toddler years as he rushed off with gusto only to check back and make contact will help us to understand—he is still in the ongoing process of separating.

Another young woman drives off to college only a few hours from home. She doesn't communicate or come home for weeks. Her parents worry and feel hurt. She too is separating; perhaps she needs to "go cold turkey"—to sever the ties abruptly, at least for a while—so that she isn't pulled back to the close, secure home that is so easily accessible.

The theme of separation is the same for all these young people. The variations are uniquely their own. An understanding of separation, the thematic cornerstone of every chapter of this book, enables parents to engage in that process more productively.

Part II, "A Parents' Guide: From Start to Finish," provides a chronological guide to the college experience from senior year in high school through college graduation. We'll look at the way the separation process evolves, and the predictable rhythm it takes throughout the first academic year and the years that follow. Above all, we will listen to what college students and their parents have to say as they move through this exciting, sometimes turbulent phase of life. They will tell us what has worked for them and what hasn't.

Understanding what we and our children are going through reduces our anxiety and validates our reality. It opens our eyes so that we can see what our children's world is like; it allows us to listen and communicate more effectively. It frees us to help our children become themselves.

2

SOME THINGS NEVER CHANGE

The Search for Identity, Independence, and Intimacy

"WHO AM I, APART FROM MY FAMILY, MY COMMUNITY, my school?" This question is what young people ask themselves over and over again. It is a question replayed by every generation, each in its own context. We, their parents, struggled with the same question years ago as we tried to find our own way on the road to adulthood. The context may have changed, the choices may be different, but the theme is the same—the theme of self-definition. This is the curriculum not spelled out in college catalogs, and yet much of the college experience is devoted to it.

I'm going to let my hair grow; I'm going to cut out drinking and smoking and be quiet and subdued—the way I was when I came here. They say a girl can't be like that and "get by," but I always loathed the typical college girl anyway. The main trouble is that whenever I am or claim to be different, I'm accused of posing—people can't conceive of how anyone can have any individualism. Damn it all, I'm going to change and be me.

JOURNAL ENTRY, SOPHOMORE, SMITH COLLEGE, 1924

I feel like I can't be myself. I try to pretend everything's fine, but who am I kidding? I feel lonely and isolated even from my family and best friends at home. Part of that's my fault, because every time I try to write a letter or talk on the phone, I catch myself trying to impress people with how great things are. I don't want to admit to anyone that I'm having problems adjusting, so I try to overcompensate and act as if everything's wonderful and then I sound fake and I feel fake. I can't be natural—I'm not even sure what that is.

Journal entry, sophomore, University of Vermont, 1984

It's been a month into college and I've met lots of new people, but the group of friends I have now seems like a temporary comfort for being lonely. Fact is, I don't enjoy hanging out with them that much. Everyone else also seems very different and unrelating to my personality and it seems like no one enjoys my company other than maybe this group of friends I don't really like.

I constantly feel lonely even when surrounded by people I've met. I was at a party on Friday and got rather drunk and had fun, but the second I woke up this morning, I felt alone again and hating college.

I know this is another sob story and I've read other threads that say that loneliness and homesickness take time, but things aren't getting any better and it's been a month already. Should I transfer? But even if I did, I don't think things will be any different.

Entry posted on college discussion forum, 2008

These reflections from three generations of college students span eighty-four years. Yet all of these students are grappling with issues of identity, with who they are and how to integrate this sense of themselves with the world in which they live.

Unlike students of the past whose personal thoughts were guarded under lock and key in diaries and private journals, today's students are just as likely to broadcast their struggles and musings in the public forum of an online blog or message board.

Becoming a unique and individual person doesn't happen at any one particular time. Hallmark has yet to design a card for the universal celebration of "being an adult." Graduation days, 18th birthdays, bar mitzvahs, quinceañeras, have all been adopted as dates to mark entry into so-called adulthood. The fact that one ritual takes place at 13 or 15, another at 18 or 21 tells us that our notion of what adulthood is varies by religion, culture, and individual family.

Many young men and women leave their homes to work, marry, or go away to college. But to become separate in a psychological sense is a lifelong process of becoming—continually building on, reaffirming, refining a sense of self. This process begins in the first months of life.

Although the seeds of their own identity exist from the start, infants are totally dependent on the person who cares for them, usually their mother. Before they can discover their separateness, they must establish the boundaries between their parents and themselves. Understanding the complexities of that earlier time helps put in perspective the often puzzling transitions of the college years.

SEPARATION IN EARLY CHILDHOOD AND ADOLESCENCE

The separation that begins in the first year of life is a prototype for later separations, in particular for the turbulent years of adolescence and young adulthood. Separation is not isolation from others, but is instead a bridge that helps us cross from dependence to interdependence. Parents' memories and photograph albums carry images of their children's early attempts at separation: a baby tugging on his mother's nose, yanking at her hair, peering out from behind chubby spread fingers to play peekaboo; a 7-month-old, creeping across the floor, pausing to glance back at her father before scurrying on; a toddler walking like a drunken sailor, building up speed as he giggles exuberantly running away from his mother; the same toddler, as his mood shifts, waddling along, thumb in mouth, dragging a blanket behind him; a 2-year-old throwing herself on the floor in the supermarket, screaming "no" furiously, her face red with rage and frustration, wanting to do it herself one minute and whiningly asking for help the next—all of these are the images of young children struggling with the confusion and ambivalence of separation.[1]

The images of separation in adolescence are as vivid and familiar to all parents as those of our children's early days. They are new images, reminiscent of old struggles: the teenager chafing at his parent's simplest words of advice; the 17-year-old, heady with a sense of her own high school success, flying off to college unaccompanied and secure, coming home six weeks later for refueling, her wings clipped with the discovery that she is no longer special; the 19-year-old, calling home depressed and frightened; an anxious high school senior asking her parents for advice one day and snapping, "It's my life" the next. All of these efforts to move away echo earlier times from our children's first three years of life. And they reawaken our own ambivalence about separation and may make it more difficult for us to let go.[2]

IDENTITY

To separate psychologically is to know oneself. The core of identity, of one's uniqueness, is what makes it possible to tolerate the inevitable feeling of aloneness that we all experience. Despite moving across the country or the world, despite dramatic changes in emotions or physical feelings or interactions with a variety of people, we develop a sense of continuity, a consistent sense of who we are. It is this self-knowledge that makes it possible to move into truly intimate relationships with others without the fear of losing oneself or one's own integrity. Indeed, this search for a cohesive and integrated self is one of the major tasks of the college student.

Why now? Why does the concern for identity become so all-consuming during the college years? We know that our children have had distinct personalities for as long as we can remember. We speak of them in phrases that encapsulate characteristics that are so uniquely theirs. "Ellen's our organizer. She's been organized since she was a toddler." Or, "Peter's very easy-going. He's always marched to the beat of a different drummer." Our children have been building since birth an inner core that is exclusively theirs, identifying with significant people in their lives, developing talents, internalizing notions of right and wrong.

But puberty arrives and shakes their foundations; bodies shift so that their tall and rounded selves no longer reflect the inner image of themselves as a small and fragile child. Tenors turn into basses and with the change may lose a special singing talent. The "braininess" that was scorned at 8 is valued at 16, but the feeling of being an outsider—the one who was picked last for the kickball game—lingers. Sexual yearnings are new and unpredictable. With the onslaught of puberty, our children lose the sense of continuity that they had; confusion sets in; change becomes the norm. The spontaneity and creativity of childhood become the self-conscious inhibition of early adolescence.

To assure stability, some illusion of identity, adolescent boys and girls often attach themselves to a group or an idol to show the world who they are—"a jock," "a goth," "a geek," an "emo kid." And somewhere in the process of discovering who they are, they leave for college. Not all will have reached the same developmental point at the same time or with the same intensity. All the variables that influence development—genetic factors, ethnicity, gender, societal influences, personal experiences—are brought to bear.

For some the transition to college is a smooth and gradual one; it may be the time for consolidation after a rocky adolescence. For others, the distance in miles that the freshman travels may represent the only separation that takes place as the student holds on tightly and brings his parents with him in spirit, if not in body. Their identity is his; he defines himself according to their guidelines. Still another freshman may plunge headfirst into the new environment, cutting loose the ties in an impulsive and sometimes desperate manner, attaching herself quickly in a mutually dependent romance, jumping into a new lifestyle, or running frantically from one new activity to another. She may join the rugby club one day, the literary society the next, and hang out in the alternative coffee houses on the weekends, bouncing back and forth between groups searching for a new identity in this new place.

Some students create ever-changing images of themselves on Facebook, MySpace, or other social networking sites to tell others who they are or who they want to be. Students who feel insecure or have low self-esteem may use the Internet to create alternate identities. In chat rooms, online games, virtual realities, they can present themselves as any persona they choose.[3]

Often students find themselves burdened with guilt, wanting to remain loyal to their families' traditional values, but also wanting to chart their own courses. The young man who is still tied to home and places his parents in the center of his thoughts and decisions, who says, "I can't major in Art History; my parents would be so disappointed in me," is struggling with the same dependency as the scientifically talented but belligerent young woman who proclaims, "I wouldn't consider medicine if it were the last profession on earth. I've had it shoved down my throat all my life. I wouldn't give them the satisfaction." Both are having trouble letting go, unable to make choices of their own.

As our children move through the college years, most of them will be wrestling with the question, "Who am I?" They will be trying to integrate what they've learned about themselves in earlier stages with the demands of the adult world. Some will defer to those demands so completely that they will conform to expectations of family and society at the expense of a sense of self. For others, their identity is so precious that they will ignore social norms entirely and become alienated from the mainstream.

In late adolescence, the time is ripe to focus on self-definition; our children are ready physically, cognitively, and socially. Colleges and universities offer a breather after the dependency of childhood and before the commitments of adulthood. During this time, students may explore, take risks, test, and "try on" new ways of being, and make mistakes without drastic consequences. Many of us look back to our own youth and recall such times of uncertainty, excitement, and turmoil.

When our children cast about in search of this sometimes elusive identity, their behavior is often misunderstood. At times, in their exuberant discovery of new worlds, they test extremes and hang on tight to them for a while as their fragile sense of self regains enough equilibrium to settle on a more balanced view. The tighter the psychological knot that ties them to their parents, the more abrasive and rebellious the testing may be. A perplexed mother from New Jersey describes her daughter on her first visit home from college.

> Cindy—she's asked us to call her by her full name, Cynthia—has the most beautiful hair; she's always worn it long to show off its natural thickness and

> shininess. It was her badge, her emblem. Her motions, the way she would peek out from that wavy, raven mop, the way she would toss it around—a sort of exclamation point to emphasize whatever she was saying—it would be both irritating and ingratiating. And now it's gone, at least on one side of her head. She's practically shaved one side and the other is cut in a severe line which falls over one eye—only she doesn't toss it anymore. It just sort of hangs there. I'm not sure how she sees, and I'm not sure what it means.

Another exasperated parent from a conservative midwestern community lamented, "I'm still trying to explain to myself, and to other people, why Brian came home from his first year of college wearing an earring."

One thing their parents can be sure of, Brian and Cindy are "trying on" a new identity, one that may or may not fit. They cling to their new looks, which may be quite different from the conservative wardrobe they left for school with. Does this mean Brian is gay? Is this the beginning of a permanent punk look for Cindy? Perhaps they're both on drugs. The mind of a worried parent knows no bounds. Parental imagination may run rampant to explain a new hairstyle or a tiny dot of gold in a son's ear. But it is best if parents refrain from jumping in and creating a chasm between themselves and their experimenting offspring. They might do well to recall themselves or their peers at 18 or 19 decked out in Doc Martens, pegged jeans, or tons of jelly bracelets. One mother commented with amusement:

> Every time Maggie came home to visit she had a new persona. We sent her off freshman year in the proverbial polo shirt and conservative matching shorts. She prided herself on her neatness, never a hair out of

> place. We used to laugh about how long she spent taking showers and joked about finally being able to use the bathroom again when she went to college. Her first trip home, we barely recognized her at the airport. She was wearing a thrift-shop version of a Garbo hat, and a lot of somebody else's much-too-large and very dirty clothes. She explained that she hadn't done laundry during finals. Our trips to pick her up at the airport became filled with "what next" jokes between John and me. She never failed to surprise us.

And from another mother:

> Tanya got home from school this week, sporting a pierced eyebrow. I haven't mentioned it, on the basis of the old school playground advice, "If you can't say anything nice, don't say anything at all." Actually, I think the fact that I haven't mentioned it might bug her. Damned if you do and damned if you don't.

But these are just the external signs of exploration. Young men and women during their college years are defining everything from their sexual orientation to their place in the world of work. They wrestle with the same questions—What do I want to be like as a sexual being? How do I want to define myself as a man or woman? How does my racial, ethnic or religious heritage fit into who I am? What do I believe in? What will I fight for? What do I want to do with my life?

INTELLECTUAL DEVELOPMENT: NEW WAYS OF THINKING

How do students go about making these important decisions? Along with the dramatic onslaught of hormonal and physical changes, adolescents undergo a more subtle but equally important intellectual growth. During their college years, students develop the capacity to engage in more complex and abstract thinking.[4]

At the time they enter college, many students see the world in black and white, clear-cut, and often rigid terms—a dichotomous view in which answers are simply right or wrong. They view their professors as authorities, the source of right answers, and assume that their own role is to learn and retain these right answers. For the student who sees the world in this way, absolute truths prevail outside of the classroom as well—right or wrong answers to moral dilemmas, to career choices—and as a result they are often seeking *the* right answer and are impatient and judgmental of compromises: "All jocks are idiots"; "My Dad sold out when he became a banker"; "I can't seem to find the right career for me."

As students become exposed to the diversity of ideas and people at college, their world no longer looks quite so simple. They gradually move from their clearly defined black-and-white view of the world to one of stimulating, but often blinding, color—a kaleidoscope of possibilities. Absolute truths no longer prevail. Many points of view seem to have equal value.

From the day they arrive at their residence hall, they are confronted by the diverse population of their fellow students. Students who have been brought up in homogeneous environments—whether in small towns revolving around a single church or political point of view or sheltered segments of a larger city bound by social and economic norms—are often overwhelmed and confused by the variety of people, values, and ideas they encounter in the first months on a college campus.

An 18-year-old freshman from the Bible Belt exclaimed:

> I had never met anyone Jewish before. I always felt kind of sorry for them, because they hadn't accepted Jesus and were sinners in our church. My roommate's

> a really observant Jew, and we've talked for hours late at night. He believes in his religion as much as I do and he's a really great guy. It confusing; it's a whole new world here.

In their classrooms, too, professors encourage varying opinions and ideas. Revered professors disagree with each other. Students see more than one "authority" with opposing viewpoints. While doing research, students find sources with different credible answers to the same question. They can no longer rely simply on the dogma of an authority. Numerous possibilities become evident. For many, this is unsettling and often overwhelming. So many choices may lead to a kind of paralysis. "If all opinions have validity, how do I decide?" "How do I make sense of my world?" Sophomores, suitably named from the Greek roots for *wise* and *fool*, often find themselves at this precarious point, recognizing the complexity of the world and their vulnerability in it.

As they move through their four years, students are increasingly expected to analyze and give evidence to support their opinions, and gradually most of them begin to understand that valid answers depend on the context in which they are viewed. Students are challenged by professors to back up their opinions with cogent arguments and relevant data. The same professor who might have been seen as arbitrary and confusing by a freshman may be valued as a catalyst for individual critical thinking by a junior or senior who has begun to wrestle with the complexity of making personal and intellectual commitments.

Intellectual growth often fosters a new sense of community, as students share ideas in exhilarating late-night debates with friends who hold divergent opinions. The lens that was focused so narrowly when students saw the world in dualistic terms, and then became wide-angled and expansive, begins to focus again.

As they see that many dilemmas can't be reduced to simple right or wrong answers, they weigh each situation, let go of the lesser alternatives, and take a personal stance.

Many students leave college before they have made sustained choices of life direction, values, and relationships. Most don't change evenly in their intellectual growth. Some, in fact, pause or retreat or may choose to avoid responsibility altogether by letting the chips fall where they may. But most students will not leave college without making impressive strides in their ability to think critically.

For many parents, the commitments that they made as young adults have become so familiar and so much a part of them that their beliefs begin to look rigid and arbitrary to their children. The questions that arise when their children challenge their values often unsettle, even threaten, parents of college students. Parents are forced to look at their earlier decisions in today's context—decisions that may range from the place of sex in relationships to the value of intensive hard work. Through their college years, students confront their parents' values, lifestyle, and relationships. A student's developing identity brings his or her parents face to face with their own.

None of this maturing exists in a vacuum, of course. Growth is nourished by an environment that is both supportive and challenging. Colleges and universities offer students opportunities to stretch themselves, but within safe boundaries. Parents can join university personnel as partners in encouraging their children to explore and take those risks, to discover their multifaceted world, and in so doing to discover themselves.

INDEPENDENCE

Talk about our children's identity formation or intellectual development is not part of our common parlance. We do talk often, however, about their growing independence.

Independence is part of our children's vernacular as well, a word bandied about among friends and family. What does it really mean? Probably different things to them than to us, at least initially. For many of our children, it means "I can do it by myself, thank you very much!"—an updated version of earlier attempts at getting dressed, crossing streets, and the like. It is the badge of separateness. In high school, the car was the symbol of independence for many students. "I can get away from you—take charge of where I'm going." A car is freedom; it provides an opportunity to explore and experiment with time and space away from home. It is associated with control and power. "I don't need you to drive me" is a metaphor for "I don't need to depend on you anymore."

In addition to the car, many high school students have access to a new financial freedom as they earn their own money working after school or during the summers. Ironically, for those who go away to college to live, these symbols of independence become less accessible. Cars are not permitted for freshmen on many college campuses, and the prohibitive costs of a college education often place students in a dependency bind—reconnected to parents through a powerful monetary umbilical cord.

College students do learn to take care of themselves in important new ways, however. Handling the humdrum details of everyday life that many of us take for granted is an important step on the road to a growing independence. They have to do laundry, to get themselves up in the morning, to decide when to come home at night or if they will come home at all; they manage their money; decide where and if to study, when and what to eat; they take care of their contact lenses, their acne, and their stomach flu. As they move on to become upperclassmen, they may have a car to take care of or may move off-campus and assume the added responsibility of apartment living. To care for themselves as their parents have cared for them brings feelings of confidence and strength, a self-reliance that can't be taught, only learned through experience.

Management of money often becomes an arena for the independence struggle. The reality is that for most students, financial dependence of some sort is a fact of life. In relationships with mutual respect, the conflict should be minimal. But most parents worry about the return on the huge financial investment that they are making in their child's education. The cost seems preposterous. Will it enable their child to become a successful professional, financially solvent, able to live comfortably on his or her own? Will their investment be worth it? As their worry grows and their resources dwindle, even the most well-intentioned parents may feel the need to take control as they would with any other investment. They may try to direct, to point out how to do it better, to orchestrate their children's college years—which courses to take, how to spend their time, and perhaps even with whom to spend it.

Technology has presented new challenges to a student's developing independence. The availability of affordable instant access to parents via cell phones, text messaging, IMing, and webcams offers the enticing possibility of consulting with Mom or Dad about multiple decisions each day. It is so easy for parents to succumb to the temptation to micromanage—to check up on a son or daughter's daily activities and emotional state. In doing so, of course, they deprive their children of the most long-lasting knowledge they can gain: the knowledge of how to live independently, form their own opinions, make their own decisions and mistakes, and ultimately make their own commitments to personal and political values, a vocation, and another human being.

The freedom that students enjoy with this sense of independence is often coupled with fears, especially about the change in their relationship with their parents. "Will my parents still care *about* me if they're not caring *for* me?" "Will they still love me even though they don't approve of my choices?" "Will I be abandoning them if I don't need them anymore?" They fear the responsibility inherent in their new self-reliance and the sense that the buck stops here.

Part of their discomfort comes from the false notion that independence means never asking for help. Many students, intent on asserting their autonomy, do so with a bravado and insistence that belies the feeling of tenuousness underneath. Teetering on the edge of separation, they turn away help and advice, fearing that they will be pulled back into the safety of the fold. One poised young woman, a Middlebury sophomore from Illinois, looks back at her freshman year:

> I had always prided myself on my independence, so I went to school alone. That was dumb. I was so unfamiliar with the area. I lost all perspective those first few weeks.
>
> I wasn't nervous at all when I went. I took a cab from Burlington—shared a ride with a guy who was also a freshman. I was very friendly, and he was very cold. That started it. People seemed cold in general. The more people seemed turned off to me, the more uptight I became. Then people were really turned off by me. I was very intimidated. I had never had problems meeting people before. I began to think, it must be because I'm from the Midwest. I'm not cool. I'd try to talk to people but I felt so self-conscious and got more and more withdrawn and nervous. People didn't want to be with me. I didn't blame them. I didn't want to be with me either.
>
> My parents didn't know too much about how miserable I was those first few months. I think I was always fighting dependence on my parents so I didn't say much. The one time I really broke down and

> called about ten times in one week, my father got angry. For me to be weak was hard for them to see. They counted on me to be strong and independent.

Balancing autonomy and closeness to parents and others is an ongoing theme that intertwines with a developing sense of self. In the comings and goings of vacations and summers during their college years, students often describe a gradual change—a redefinition of their relationship with their parents. One senior at Rice recalls a shift in perspective:

> It was winter break of my junior year. I was exhausted from some all nighters to finish up papers and study for finals. In the past, I had often felt mixed emotions about going home. I was usually looking forward to it—anything after the craziness of the end-of-the-semester crunch—but shortly after I got there, my mom and I would be at it, and I'd just want to get away someplace where I wouldn't be treated like a kid.
>
> But this year was different. I remember saying on the way home from the airport, "I'm really exhausted; I just want to be pampered and taken care of." And I was! My parents were great. I could never let myself admit that was what I wanted before, but somehow, now I felt different. I knew that I wasn't going to become a baby just because I wanted a little tender loving care. I wasn't fighting it anymore, because I guess I just felt generally more in charge of things.

INTIMACY

The issues of identity and intimacy are bound together in a dynamic interplay that encourages the growth of each.[5] Throughout their college years, young men and women experiment with a variety of relationships. These may include intense new friendships with the same or the opposite sex, sexual play and exploration and, for many, falling in love. As students continue to refine aspects of their own identity through these relationships, they become more self-confident and allow themselves the vulnerability to enter into increasingly open and mature partnerships. Over and over again, students describe their relationships with friends and lovers as critical to the learning and growth that takes place during the college years.

A young woman, in her final year at Washington University, traces the evolution of her developing sexual identity and her increasing capacity to enter into close relationships:

> Freshman year I developed some very close friends. We really played a lot. It's kind of hard to describe. Maybe it's easier to describe what it wasn't. I wasn't going out on dates or to parties. It was just two guys and another girl, and we spent a lot of time hanging out talking, going to the zoo and the park. It was a very happy time.
>
> I had a really close relationship with one of the guys. We were together all the time. We even slept in the same room a lot, but it was never sexual. He had a girlfriend at home, and even after I started going with someone, we still spent a lot of time together. This was a big change for me. I wasn't even allowed to have guys come upstairs at home.
>
> Second semester, I started going out with Jim. Our first date was the spring formal. Until then, he was just a guy I knew in the dorm. It was my first real relationship, and it definitely was his. It was a very intense relationship—symbiotic, actually.
>
> We spent about a third of the summer together. He

was my life; I was his life—for a whole year. My parents were kind of cool about it. My dad just said it wouldn't last, and my mom didn't say much of anything—or if she did, I don't remember.

We spent most of our sophomore year together. We were with each other all the time—slept in each other's rooms. That was never any problem. Our roommates were very flexible. We always worked it out easily. We weren't like the kids who kick their roommates out or leave secret codes on the door that mean "stay out."

We took a couple of classes together, but mostly we were together outside of classes. It was real good for both of us. We both grew a lot, and became a lot more confident. We each began to see each other through the other person's eyes, which I know did incredible things for my self-image, and it did for his also. And it's funny that the basic reason we broke up was that we both needed to spend time with other people, and we couldn't adjust our relationship to do that. We were used to having each other available whenever we wanted. We ended up spending September to March of junior year breaking up and getting together over and over again. When I think of college, junior year was spent breaking up with Jim. Without us becoming aware of it we had come to expect total availability of the other person. We were an incredible support system to each other. But we just couldn't make the transition to staying together, while moving out to be with other people also.

It was a time of separation from my mother. Up till then, my mom knew everything that happened to me that had any significance, but last summer I decided I

> didn't want to tell her everything. I didn't want her to know all about us.
>
> My relationship with Jim was an important time of my life; it affects how I am now too. I'm more open. I'm more conscious of what's going on in my relationships, of taking risks and making commitments.

Throughout the college years, the pendulum continues to swing back and forth between separateness and union. Many relationships during these years of learning and experimentation will have the look of intimacy, but may be well-disguised attempts at fulfilling other needs. Often during the freshman year, especially in the first semester, students pair up, substituting new dependent relationships for old ones. As the Washington University senior above related, even though there are difficulties with such a relationship, this kind of bond may serve to help students grow, reassuring them of their self-worth as they discover their sexuality, learn to be open, and separate from close, perhaps too close, families.

In a campus culture that has replaced dating with hooking up, an increasing number of students may postpone committed relationships for a variety of reasons—to conform to the college "scene," to focus on school and career, or perhaps just to avoid commitment. Some students substitute sexual relationships for emotional closeness, a pseudo-intimacy that provides temporary release but often a gnawing sense of emptiness and isolation as well. Others who open up and trust before they have a sense of their own identity may become frightened as they begin to feel themselves engulfed by another's demands.

Students who do enter serious relationships during the college years discover that mutual trust is essential—trust that one's friend or partner will respect and appreciate one's separateness, trust in one's own capacity to "let go" temporarily and remain intact. To be intimate is to expose one's vulnerabilities to another. To be intimate is to balance one's own needs with someone else's and to resolve conflict together. Students learn that to give is not to give in—compromise is part of the partnership.

CHANGE

Students come to us in such different packages. I often say my job is to get all of the students close to the emotional age of 22 when they graduate. Some come to us emotionally at 14—others are at the emotional age of 32. That's the difficulty in a nutshell, isn't it? Emotional 14-year-olds are living with emotional 32-year-olds. We try to get the "32-year-olds" to loosen up and the "14-year-olds" to grow up!

Wendy Bashant, Dean of Students, New College of Florida

There is no way to predict exactly how our children will move through the continuing ebb and flow of their growth and development during their college years. For a number of students, college prolongs adolescence and is just the beginning of their search for identity, independence, and intimacy. For others, the progress in these arenas from freshman to senior year is staggering. We *can* predict, however, that change will occur, that it is an inevitable byproduct of the college experience. With change, even positive change, adjustment is necessary and stress unavoidable. For most students, many of the disruptions will lead to opportunities for growth, and they will continue to learn how to think more critically and to take responsibility for their own opinions and actions. For these same students, there will be times of stagnation and regression.

Along the way, the road is often a rocky one for parents as well as children. The inconsistencies of a student's behavior may leave parents breathless. How could someone who acted with such mature deliberation one day resort to such ill-conceived impulsiveness the next? Should we respond with amusement or concern?

One mother of a Bates freshman, her first child to go to college, offers a familiar refrain:

> When he was a toddler, I used to worry that Eric would never give up his bottle. I remember my pediatrician telling me with a wry smile to stop worrying, that he would not go to college with it. Now I worry that he will never be organized enough to hold a responsible job. And when I worry, I start barging in on his life and try to tell him once more what he already knows. Won't I ever learn that my perspective as a 45-year-old is not his at 19? I keep thinking that I will have really matured when I can get that wry smile on my face, and stop worrying.

Understanding some of the underpinnings of normal development may alleviate parents' anxiety. It is easier to be supportive when we can see the broader view. Our children may rebuff our advice, but they will appreciate our acknowledgment of their distress—a listening ear that doesn't judge even if we disagree, a sense of confidence that doesn't crumble when they do, an adult anchor who provides perspective on the predictable but often painful changes that they are bound to go through.

3

SOME THINGS DO CHANGE

College Life Today

STROLLING ONTO A COLLEGE CAMPUS, WE ARE STRUCK by a sense of history and continuity. Who walked these paths before? Who will walk them in the years to come? For some of us, there is a dizzying nostalgia. For almost all of us there are feelings of respect, even awe.

Imposing rectangular structures of red granite or limestone; Georgian brick residences with symmetrical columns; ivy-covered Gothic lecture halls with leaded windows and vaulted archways announce that this place commands attention. Our eyes glance past the modern glass and steel additions, lighting on the older, more traditional centers, the quadrangles, the plazas, the courtyards. Giant oaks and elms attest to the passing of time. Latin phrases over doorways remind us of the scholarship that is carried on here. This oasis of learning, separated from the cacophony of the workaday world just beyond its gates, lulls us into tranquility, perhaps even reverie.

So it is with a jolt that we come upon a bulletin board layered with recent posters and notices askew—a collage of ink and paper—a jarring reminder that time has not stood still:

"Bulimia Support Group," "Gay, Lesbian, Bisexual and Transgender Alliance," "Black Women; Jewish Women," "Alcohol Peer Educators," "Wanted: Roommate to share apartment. Male or female, non-smoker, no drugs," "Brown Sugar Masala: Best Indian A Cappella Group," "AIDS Symposium," "Tryouts for *Vagina Monologues*," "Sustainability Forum." Sandwiched between these announcements are notices of recitals and colloquia on more orthodox scholarly topics; of art exhibits and plays and poetry readings; of pep rallies and tailgate parties. But these traditional cultural and social events of the campus scene are overshadowed by the contemporary reflections of today's world.

The social transformations of the past thirty years, which have touched all of our lives, have invaded the seemingly tranquil campus as well. Changes in technology, curriculum, security measures, institutional policies, co-curricular offerings—even the very makeup of the student population—confirm that today's college is neither rarefied nor unaffected by the rapidly changing society of which it is a part.

WHO ARE TODAY'S STUDENTS AND WHAT DO THEY BELIEVE?

Impressionistic portraits of today's students range from conservative, hardworking Babbitts to materialistic, freewheeling Gatsbys—from focused careerists to statement-making demonstrators—from '40s-style swing dancers to proud and active supporters of gay rights. Personal impressions such as these are important to keep in mind as a backdrop for the profile drawn by specific data and statistics. Both contribute to our understanding of today's college students.

Perhaps the most comprehensive storehouse of information about college freshmen is *The American Freshman: National Norms*, an ongoing survey of representative samples of college freshmen conducted annually since 1966 by the Cooperative Institutional Research Program at UCLA. Commonly referred to as the CIRP Freshman Survey, these annual reports present a vivid picture of changes in the "nature of students' characteristics, aspirations, values, attitudes, expectations, and behaviors."[1] Much of the data that follow are culled from this important research project.[2]

No longer the elite bastion of affluent, white 18-to-22-year-olds, today's college campus is home to students from an increasing diversity of backgrounds. In 1971, 94 percent of college students were white, and approximately 55 percent were men. Colleges and universities began to open their doors to a wider spectrum of students in the late 1960s and early 1970s. The percentage of minorities in entering freshman classes nearly doubled between the mid-1960s and mid-1970s, and these students became a notable presence on campuses that had formerly excluded them. By 1996, more than 21 percent of college freshmen were students of color, and by 2006, that number had increased to slightly more than 23 percent.[3] Perhaps most noticeable of all is the growth in the number of multiracial students today. In 1971 few students—slightly more than one percent—categorized themselves in more than one racial group, but by 2006 more than seven percent did so.

The women's movement has also influenced campus demographics. After a steady increase of women's enrollments throughout the 1970s, there are now more women than men in college. They earn better grades, and a higher percentage of them graduate. Although the small number of remaining women's colleges still play an important role and provide a unique experience, women have been an integral part of the most prestigious, formerly all-male Ivys and their small, liberal arts counterparts for two generations.

The number of international students enrolling in American colleges and universities has made a powerful impact on many campuses. According to the Institute of International Education, in 2006 there were approximately 236,000 undergraduate international students enrolled on U.S. campuses. Although international students can be found on campuses nationwide, most are concentrated in 200 to 250 colleges and universities that actively recruit them. The largest percentage come from Asia. The leading countries of origin are India, China, Korea, and Japan, comprising 42 percent of international students in the U.S. The "graying" of the campus has also become a common phenomenon, particularly at community and other commuter colleges that court older students.

Today's students come from a broad range of economic backgrounds. An increasing number of them are concerned about having adequate funds for college. Most students have to help finance their education; they spend their college years trying to maintain the delicate balance among part-time jobs, academic demands, co-curricular activities, and time with friends. College costs have continued to rise, and in spite of efforts by well-endowed colleges to meet full need for low and middle income students, the number of students who will graduate with extensive debt has increased substantially. Financial aid officers try to educate students, both when they arrive as freshmen and before they graduate, about the realities of taking on huge debt from loans, and the implications it may have for their career options when they graduate. According to the American Council on Education, the number of students borrowing money for college and the size of the loans they take out are both continuing to soar. In 2007, more than 70 percent graduated with loan debt. The average student inflation adjusted debt has soared over 50 percent in the past decade.[4] Though these numbers may seem daunting, there is a large variation in college costs and many potential options for financing an education.

The economic polarities on campus are striking. Students whose financial worries are part of their daily consciousness live side by side with those who arrive on campus with a sense of entitlement and an alphabet soup of expensive equipment—TVs, PCs, MP3s and Wiis. Reflecting nationwide changing family patterns, more students are coming to college from divorced, single-parent, same-gender, and so-called blended families formed through remarriage. In 1955, 60 percent of American households were of the "Leave It to Beaver" genre—working father, stay-at-home mother, and two or more school-age children. Today only a small percentage of the population belongs to this type of family unit.

American family life is in flux, and a substantial number of today's college students have paid a price. Many have been overscheduled with enrichment classes, music lessons, athletic practices and games, leaving little free time to make choices of their own. Others come from families that provided them with little structure while they were growing up. It is common to hear students lament the loss of their childhood as they describe taking on the role of friend and confidant to a distraught parent, or the role of surrogate parent to a needy younger sibling. University personnel are concerned about the high percentage of students who come from families with an alcoholic member. And campus psychologists and counselors serve an increasing number of students who report incidents of childhood physical and sexual abuse.

Some students have struggled with alcohol problems of their own and have participated in residential treatment programs while still in high school. Some arrive on campus with a substantial drug habit or an eating disorder. Many of these students are unable to deal with the stress in their lives; they resort to destructive coping mechanisms that temporarily relieve their pain or provide them with the illusion of control that they desperately seek. The proportion of entering college freshmen who reported feeling "frequently overwhelmed by all I have to do" rose from approximately 20 percent in the 1986 CIRP Freshman

Survey to almost 30 percent in 2006. Gender does make a difference; women reported this twice as much as men.

Some students enter college with well-developed, constructive coping skills. Many of today's freshmen have a healthy respect for exercise, and they are intent upon enhancing both their physical and emotional well-being. They bike, jog, lift weights and join aerobics classes; they participate in intramural sports, practice yoga and tai chi, or take dance to keep in shape. These health-conscious students are concerned about eating well and favor salads and stir fry dishes over Big Macs and fries.

Though today's students enter college with higher high school grades than ever before, the percentage who reported studying at least six hours a week in high school has reached the all-time low of 33 percent. As a result of grade inflation, many freshmen are optimistic about their academic performance, but ill-equipped to succeed. They come to college expecting a great deal of themselves, the institution, and the whole academic enterprise.

One way to better appreciate and understand this generation of college students is to view them within the context of the world of their parents and the world that has shaped them. Their parents—who wear the Boomer or Gen-X labels—grew up in an environment informed by the economic malaise of the Carter years and the hostage crisis, the conservative renewal of the Reagan revolution, the war on drugs and "just say no." They majored in business in unprecedented numbers, conducted their research *inside* the library, and protested apartheid and investments in South Africa. They gathered together around the TV with friends for reports on the Chernobyl disaster and the Challenger explosion. The outbreak of AIDS tempered the sexual revolution of the '60s, MTV was in its infancy, home computers were still a novelty, phones were connected to walls, and security on campus was a given.

Most of today's students find it hard to imagine such a time. Their realities are the threats of national and international terrorism, environmental devastation and climate change, campus emergency warning systems and omnipresent security cameras, genetic engineering, and worldwide economic and political upheaval. They take for granted instant access to information and each other. Their facility with technology leaves their parents shaking their heads in wonder. They are environmentally conscious and are concerned about the future of the planet.

When asked to choose the most important reasons for going to college, the two top reasons cited by the 2006 crop of freshmen were "to learn things that interest me," and "to get a better job." There is no doubt that these young people have been affected by the economic and political uncertainties of recent years. Many of them are seeking a safe route that will lead them to the diminishing number of career slots that may provide high compensation and a sense of security. More and more of them have seen their parents in traditionally secure professions face downsizing or uncertainty about their futures. Whether or not this generation actually will have fewer opportunities for success and career fulfillment remains to be seen. However, students appear to be making decisions about their majors and their futures based on this assumption.

After many years of little attention to politics, an increasing number of students are indicating an interest in political affairs. Fewer of today's entering college students define themselves as politically "middle of the road." When it comes to politics, the numbers who define themselves as liberal or conservative are increasing. More than 28 percent label themselves as liberal—the highest point since the mid-1970s; likewise, the percentage identifying as conservative reached an all-time high in 2006 at almost 24 percent. The increased interest in politics is most evident among those who identified themselves with the "far left" or the "far right."

It is not surprising then that there is a widening rift between students on opposite ends of the spectrum. Isolated ugly incidents shatter an image of harmony on usually peaceful campuses: the president of the Jewish Student Alliance receives a barrage of anti-Semitic slogans and hate messages via e-mail; the Muslim student prayer room is vandalized; a poster announcing a program sponsored by the university's Gay, Lesbian, Bisexual, Transgender Coalition is defaced with obscenities; the African-American students' center is spray painted with graffiti.

The data from the CIRP Freshman Survey indicate that there is a strong endorsement for a number of liberal social and political issues such as support for gay rights and opposition to the death penalty and drug testing. A record high 61 percent believe that "same sex couples should have the right to legal marital status." Although the majority of college students support legalized abortion, the percentage of support declined from a high of 64.9 percent in 1990 to approximately 57 percent in 2007.

Student attitudes toward gender roles have changed dramatically over the last thirty years, though differences between male and female attitudes are still apparent. When asked whether they support the traditional notion that "the activities of married women are best confined to the home and family," 26 percent of today's male freshmen answered yes as opposed to 66.5 percent in 1970. The support for this view among women in the freshman survey declined from 44.3 percent to 15.5 percent in the same time period. About 34 percent of freshmen women approve of sex between two people who have known each other a short while; 58 percent of men support it.

Issues such as American military involvement in foreign conflicts, reproductive rights, or affirmative action stir up vocal groups of politically active students. Concerns closer to home—an admired professor being turned down for tenure, low wages for groundskeepers and food service workers or rising tuition costs—mobilize students, even those typically uninterested in political affairs.

Record numbers of college students are devoting time to community service. Fund raising and volunteer service projects are part of the tradition of the fraternities and sororities that are a strong presence on many campuses. Community service organizations such as the Morgridge Center for Public Service at the University of Wisconsin, and Student Volunteers Council at Princeton are thriving. In 1986, 125 college presidents, including those from Georgetown, Brown, and Stanford, formed a consortium, Campus Compact, to promote community service. By 2008, the number of member institutions had increased to 1100, representing over six million students. Reflecting the growing campus interest, Campus Compact has joined with other advocates in exploring the notion of "service-learning," linking the curriculum with community concerns and bringing the concept of community service into the mainstream of the academy.

The media have labeled today's youth as "the Millennial Generation." In their book, *Millennials Rising: The Next Generation*, William Strauss and Neil Howe described this cohort of students as more sheltered and protected than recent generations—and as a result, they feel special; more pressured and stressed; more achieving and directed—doers rather than talkers; more confident and optimistic. The Millennials, also dubbed by the popular press as "Digital Natives" or "GenM"—the media and multitasking generation—came of age with the personal computer and the cell phone. They tend to be more conventional, more connected to their parents, and more responsive to adult interaction than those who preceded them.

Jill E. Carnaghi, Assistant Vice Chancellor for Students and Director of Campus Life at Washington University notes:

> I am continually amazed at how trusting students are and how much information they're willing to provide

> with very little prodding. On more than one occasion and at more than one institution, when students wanted to stage a protest, they came to me and asked for permission: What do they need to do to not get in trouble? Whom do they need to keep informed as to what they are planning to do? One student group went so far as to include the chancellor and vice chancellor in their march.

Although today's students seem to look to adults for guidance in ways that were alien to their parents' generation, many professors complain that students are disrespectful of those in authority. One professor of French language and literature reports:

> In the past ten years, students are much more aware of their time, and seem to feel they are the absolute equals of the people teaching them. I believe technology has added to this sense of omnipotence—at least a certain independence . . . and a lack of deference.

As an example, she cited an incident of a student calling her at home at 10 p.m., and, after identifying herself, asking her professor to hold while she took another call. "I have run into phones going off in my classes with increasing frequency," this professor continued. "This is nothing shocking really, when you consider that these students are the children my generation always wanted to empower by giving them infinite choices, always listening to their ideas, not wanting to daunt their self-esteem."

An academic advisor recounts: "One of my freshman advisees left me a voice mail message imploring me to call her back right away. I was totally astonished when she answered the phone and whispered, 'I can't talk to you right now. I'm at the movies.' I just couldn't believe it. What have we come to?"

This generation was introduced to education via Sesame Street's thirty-second segments and to problem solving through popular sitcoms in which conflicts are resolved in thirty minutes. Many of their professors comment that their students are used to constant stimulation and want to be entertained. They want simple answers to complex questions and often seek formulas for success rather than opportunities for exploration and risk taking.

Larry Moneta, Vice President for Student Affairs at Duke, expresses a view that's echoed by many of today's educators:

> These students are true multi-taskers, ever engaged with overlapping, competing and multimedia applications. Therefore, they display corresponding characteristics: short attention span, hectic pace, intensity and materialism. They've also been influenced by a growing distrust in public officials and have a relativistic attitude toward rules and laws. Speed limits are relative, alcohol consumption laws are relative, and academic integrity is relative. Rules are simply the starting point for negotiations (for them and their parents!). On the other hand, they also display a need to engage in service and do so in record numbers. They are increasingly concerned about the environment and engage in creative social (and commercial) entrepreneurial endeavors. They are family oriented and seem to have more positive relationships with parents and extended families than has been true for a while. Sprituality is cool for many (though not so much through organized religion), and they expect value for the dollar they, or their parents, are spending.

Sylvia Hoffert, Professor of History at Texas A&M University, offers another point of view:

> The students in my Women's History classes are interested in social issues, particularly those relating to changing gender roles. Most of them work hard in class. Many of them are involved in community service projects and some of them have jobs as well. They're earnest, and they want to make connections between what they're studying and their own lives. But there are other students who are not particularly focused on either education or service. They make poor judgments about their social life, immersing themselves in the party and drinking culture. Unfortunately, they're the ones that get all of the media attention.

Listening to faculty and administrators share their perceptions of this generation reminds us that in spite of broad-scale studies and statistical reports of trends, students differ from campus to campus, as well as within each school. One seasoned dean of students provides a perspective:

> Student populations are a lot like real communities; they have their doers and their loafers, their leaders and their followers, their heroes and their low-lifes.

In her book, *Campus Life*, historian Helen Lefkowitz Horowitz challenges her readers to look beyond the stereotypes that characterize each generation of college students:

> In any decade since 1920, single images of collegians have dominated the public consciousness; it is implic-

> itly assumed that no other kinds of students have existed. Thus all students in the 1920s are seen to wear raccoon coats and carry hip flasks, while those of the 1930s march in demonstrations against war. The problem has been the failure to recognize that undergraduates have been divided into contending cultures. In any one era, one of these appears to be dominant and catches the public eye.[5]

The students who dominate today's campuses share many characteristics with the group Horowitz calls the "grim professionals," cramming for tests, and driven by a desire for success and security. But sharing the campus with them are political activists, carefree hedonists, and the students she calls "the quiet rebels," who see college not as a pre-professional hurdle but as a time to experiment, to struggle with new ideas and take intellectual risks.

WHAT IS HAPPENING ON TODAY'S CAMPUS?

Colleges and universities have come under scrutiny recently for everything from student loan scandals and rampant alcohol abuse, to debate about the academic canon and grade inflation. But colleges and universities have always been works in progress, and campus dialogue about the future of education has never been more lively. The hot topics on most campuses include: sustainability; internationalization of the university and preparing students to live in a global society; enhancement of undergraduate education with special attention to advising, residential life and a core curriculum; commitment to a unified sense of community and personal contact within an increasingly technologically informed campus.

Academic Life

Academics remain at the core of the college experience. But the world of scholarly pursuits has a whole new look.

"Popular Kabbalah and Contemporary Culture? The Mathematics and Politics of Secure Digital Communication?" queried a puzzled father after his daughter called home to report on the classes she planned to take. Like many parents he was more than a little suspicious of courses with such esoteric titles, courses he wouldn't have found in a college catalogue when he was his daughter's age.

The course listings in contemporary catalogues include a legacy from the 1960s and 1970s, when universities opened their doors to diverse populations and the civil rights and women's movements made their mark. "At that time colleges and universities began to give students a variety of lenses through which to view a problem," comments Thomas Ehrlich, Senior Scholar at the Carnegie Foundation. He adds:

> We began to ask, "What about women and minorities?" The structure of the curriculum became more open, and courses began to cut across disciplines. We developed a much more variegated academic set of inquiries.

The influence of black and women's studies programs that were created more than thirty-five years ago reaches beyond departmental boundaries. Feminist theory and research have changed the face of contemporary psychology, and history departments have incorporated scholarship on women and gender, gay culture, and race and ethnicity into the curriculum. Most English departments no longer divide their courses simply by centuries and literary periods. "Gender and Genre in Shakespeare's Plays" and "Native American Expressive

Traditions" join the more traditional fare of "Elizabethan Drama" and "Nineteenth-Century Poetry."

In recent years, there's been a notable movement towards interdisciplinary studies. Faculty in psychology, neuroscience and philosophy are working together to explore and study the brain. Environmental Studies brings together biologists, anthropologists, economists and political scientists. Professors of medicine, biochemistry, and molecular biophysics join colleagues in engineering to create courses and do research in the increasingly popular field of Biomedical Engineering. And many educators stress the importance of integrating new technology, social sciences, and the humanities. The Values and Science/Technology (VAST) courses at Lafayette College are interdisciplinary seminars challenging students to address the values issues of our technological age with titles such as "The Human Genome Project: Benefits and Costs" or "Scientific Prospects and Societal Implications of Genetic Engineering."

Some courses have made their way into the contemporary curriculum because they meet new marketplace demands—courses such as "Entrepreneurial Skills for the Digital Age," "Webportfolio Design" and "Negotiation and Conflict Resolution." Others reflect a growing interest in international affairs and an increasing awareness on the part of the faculty that we are truly members of a global village. Along with an increased interest in Islamic Studies and Asian and Near Eastern Studies, students are taking courses with titles such as "Globalization in the Middle East and North Africa" and "Arms Control and Global Security."

The decline in foreign language studies that occurred in the 1960s now appears to be reversed. In many schools today the language laboratories are high-tech wonders. Students use interactive programs to help them improve their pronunciation; and TV shows via satellite and online videos allow them to watch news and entertainment in the language they are studying. The majority of colleges and universities offer opportunities for study abroad; many encourage all students to participate in some kind of international experience during their undergraduate years.

Even in schools that don't require foreign language study, students are flocking to these courses. The popularity of any given language ebbs and flows with changes in the political and economic landscape. After the Berlin Wall came down, German classes were in vogue; in the aftermath of September 11th, classes in Arabic were in high demand. Language study often takes a vocational slant, as students sign up for classes entitled "Legal and Business Chinese" and "Medical Spanish."

Enrollment in the liberal arts dropped precipitously in the '70s, but there is evidence that the pendulum is swinging back. The word is out that although technical skills are important, employers are demonstrating increased interest in students with a liberal arts background. They are sending messages that they value critical thinking and writing skills and the ability to be flexible, Today's workforce, above all, has to be adaptable to change. The globalization of the workplace calls for an awareness and comfort level with other cultures, often gained through humanities and social science courses as well as study abroad and international internship programs.

Today's liberal arts students are computer savvy, and often choose to supplement their major studies with a minor in business or technology. An increasing number choose to double major, often combining a liberal arts and technical or pre-professional discipline. They talk about "keeping their options open" and "hedging their bets"—in case the job market shifts or they don't get admitted to a professional or graduate school. Moreover, students enrolled in undergraduate professional programs such as business and engineering are taking more liberal arts courses than they used to. For example, MIT has broadened its acclaimed engineering program to include more course work in the arts, humanities, and social sciences. There is more crossover in general.

On campuses across America, curriculum reform is the order of the day. Much of the recent criticism of higher education has been leveled from within. The '60s concern for egalitarianism has been replaced today by a concern with quality, accountability and cohesion.

Almost all institutions are introducing students to the ideas and arts of non-Western cultures. They are developing new general education requirements and are examining more closely the actual skills students are acquiring. They are concerned about competencies in writing, quantitative analysis and technology. They are grappling with questions of assessment, and discussing ways to measure their effectiveness with an eye toward using that information in planning for the future.

More and more faculty and academic deans are expressing concern about academic over-specialization, the division between the liberal arts and pre-professional education, and a lack of common goals. They are claiming that it is not enough merely to reinstate a hodgepodge of distribution requirements, but that it is essential to come to some cohesive view of what should constitute the core experience of education today. The trend is definitely toward establishment of a core academic experience for undergraduates. Just what should be included in this core curriculum is the subject of endless debate among deans and faculty, but there is no doubt that the content of college catalogues is changing.

High-Tech Ivy

Today's faculty and administrators are grappling with the challenges of maintaining the best of scholarly tradition and university life, while attending to the ever-accelerating pace of change of the technological revolution. Technology has transformed today's campuses, affecting all aspects of life from admissions and registration to classroom methodology, to the digitization of the library and the very concept of community.

Although the ultimate benefits of these evolving technologies are beyond the scope of our imaginations, they have already significantly influenced the academic enterprise and methods of scholarly research. Almost all campuses have wireless capability. The library of yesteryear has been enhanced by a sophisticated central information retrieval network, with an electronic catalog and links throughout the campus and the world. Libraries are spending an increasing portion of their budgets on digital materials. Professors put materials on reserve electronically, and students can sit in their residence hall rooms, a local coffee shop, or under a tree on the campus green and search multiple online databases for a research project. Students at a computer terminal in Boston can compare the same page of two different editions of Proust—one from a library in Paris and another from the University of Virginia.

In multimedia classrooms, professors supplement traditional texts with a rich array of computer graphics, virtual tours, and links to worldwide resources, bringing an astounding depth and breadth to any subject. Lectures are available on websites or podcasts, allowing students to make up classes or review materials while exercising or eating lunch in the cafeteria.

The access to instant information online is exciting, pragmatic and seductive, but this transformation raises profound questions about the nature of the university as we have known it. Universities are steeped in tradition, and radical change brings with it fears of technology run amok. How do students discriminate between the useful and the trivial, between the accurate and inaccurate, with this barrage of information? It's easy to waste time surfing the Web. With the growth of distance learning, will campuses of the future be virtual universities without the need for a physical plant? How much will all of this cost, and how will this shift the allocation of financial resources? And what about the human element? How can faculty use these new resources to enhance the dialogue between professor and student?

Neil Rudenstine, former President of Harvard University, devoted an entire commencement speech to the enormous technological transformation in higher education. He described the fast-paced and far-reaching changes in information processing as the most significant since the latter part of the 19th century. At that time, university research libraries came into their own and the explosion of information-processing caused cries of concern—cries that have a familiar ring among today's technology dissidents. Rudenstine related former Harvard president Charles Eliot's musings on information overload in 1876:

> What was to prevent students (and even faculty) from disappearing into the stacks for days on end pursuing a subject from book to book, shelf to shelf, unable to discriminate easily among the limited number of volumes, or to absorb more than a small fraction of the information available on a given topic? And what could possibly prevent less industrious students from simply browsing their lives away in sweet procrastination?

Rudenstine puts today's accelerated changes into an historical context:

> Some of these fears were not completely new. As early as the 18th century, Diderot remarked that "a time will come when . . . the printing press, which never rests, [will fill] huge buildings with books (in which readers) will not do very much reading. . . .

> [Eventually] the world of learning . . . our world . . . will drown in books."

Rudenstine also referred to a 1795 German treatise on public health, which warned people that too much reading might lead to a long list of physical maladies and, most troublesome of all, replace human contact. Some of today's educators have the same concerns; to lose the human contact is to lose the soul of the university. As they struggle with these issues, however, most faculty and administrators applaud the uses of these new technologies as opportunities to supplement and enrich the traditional academic experience, not to replace it.

With today's computer technology, learning extends beyond the formal classroom in new ways. Students communicate online at all hours and across time zones, debating and questioning their professors and other students in small electronic chat rooms, study groups, and one-on-one conversations. Some undergraduates say that they have more student-professor contact in cyberspace than they do in a traditional classroom bound by the limits of the lectern and the clock.

These new modes of communication encourage students to be active participants in the learning process, not just passive listeners and note-takers. As Mark Yim, Professor of Mechanical Engineering and Applied Mathematics at the University of Pennsylvania, writes in the *Pennsylvania Gazette*:

> When I went to school, I watched TV. You went to lectures. You learned things by someone telling you. It's what I call the push model: teachers just push the information into you. Students don't do that now. They grew up on the Internet, on video games. . . . They go on the Web and click something. . . . This is called the pull model: students pull what they want.

> So we have to change the way we teach. . . . The old ways don't work as well.[6]

Through technology, faculty can foster vibrant interaction and collaboration; they can create an environment that encourages thoughtful questions, reasoned debate, and problem solving. And they can now expand the notion of community beyond the bricks and mortar of their campus buildings to include a worldwide virtual community of students actively engaged in discourse about a common intellectual pursuit.

A range of innovative technology spaces can be found across the U.S. landscape of higher educational institutions, large and small—from Emory University's Cox Center in Georgia to San Jose State's Academic Success Center in California. George Mason University's Student Technology Assistance and Resource Center (STAR) includes media resources, technology training and student mentors who staff the labs and provide technical support for their fellow students.

A vision of today's creative possibilities, the Duderstadt Center at the University of Michigan is a state-of-the-art 250,000-square-foot environment for learning, teaching and performing. Open 24 hours a day, 7 days a week, the center houses traditional and digital libraries, virtual reality labs, performance and design studios and interactive multimedia classrooms. The building offers a vivid glimpse into the world of emerging technologies with a lively mix of artists, architects, engineers and scholars. On any particular day, a visitor might find architecture students, faculty and a representative from a leading design manufacturer exploring new forms of learning and work environments; local school children enjoying a digital music ensemble performance; and scholars in a video conference room working on a project with their colleagues in Taipei.

MIT is perhaps the most internationally renowned university for its cutting edge research into new emerging technology and in using this state-of-the-art technology for research in numerous areas of study—from robotics to medical sciences, from art to linguistics. They have reached out beyond their Cambridge facilities with multiple projects such as "iLabs" which offer science and engineering students Internet access to real labs worldwide. OpenCourseWare, a Web-based publication, has made virtually all MIT lectures available to anyone across the globe.

A growing number of schools, both in the United States and abroad, are providing free content via the iTunes education portal offering limitless opportunities for sharing knowledge and experiences from research, lectures and supplemental videos, to sporting events and artistic performances.

Technology's impact outside of the classroom is evident in everyday scenes along the campus pathways and in the student centers, images that are a far cry from those a mere ten years ago. Students stroll the campus listening to iPods, texting and checking messages or chatting on their phones. They gather around flat screen monitors to check out the scrolling lists of the latest campus events. At Montclair State University, all incoming students receive a GPS-enabled phone which also offers resources to manage their academic and social lives. They can contact campus police for security emergencies, check the location of campus shuttle buses, check class assignment changes, find local merchant's specials and share their GPS location with friends.

With staggering speed, the changes in telecommunication have given us new ways of connecting as well as a whole new set of verbs. From texting and IMing to Facebooking or Skyping, students "chat" electronically with friends and family across campus, across the country or even across the world. Some love e-mailing parents on their own time, at three in the morning if that's when the spirit moves them. Many say they're likely to be more communicative online, when there are no interruptions or nuances of changing tone of voice—those subtle triggers that may lead to defensiveness or misunderstanding. Others reserve written modes of communication for quick exchanges of information, but prefer the phone for more intimate conversation. Some actually develop relationships online, and carry on electronic long-distance romances.

Technology has transformed the hidden administrative processes of universities as well. Frustrated students used to stand in long lines hoping to get the appropriate signature so they could register for a popular course. Today's students register online from their dorm rooms, many from their homes before arriving on campus. They take for granted easy access to course listings and requirements, their grades and grade point averages (GPAs), financial aid information and their financial statements, all available online. With the aid of their password or personal identification number, they can check on their status and carry on business with speed and confidentiality.

The access and convenience that technology brings are not without their problems and challenges. Educators are trying to deal with issues of privacy and plagiarism, and e-mail, text messaging and social networking add a whole new dimension to harassment. The Web provides endless distractions for procrastinators, and counseling services report increasing numbers of students who suffer from Internet addiction. Though chat rooms and social networking sites have the potential to form new kinds of communities, the computer can also isolate students, especially those who are introverted or depressed.

Distractions have entered the classroom as well. A Northwestern student complains:

> Everyone is plugged in during class. On one side of me a girl was sitting making a photo collage on her laptop. On the other side, a guy was reorganizing his address book on his iPhone. It was hard to focus on

the lecture. If I had my way, everyone would have a notebook and an inkwell!

Although some professors incorporate interactive technology into their classes and require students to bring their laptops with them, other faculty have banned laptops and all electronic devices from the lecture hall and seminar room. And though today's students are adept at multitasking, many comment that they find themselves on information overload. As one student put it, "We have access to more information and more communication than any generation before, but less time to reflect on what it all means."

In these early stages of this high-tech revolution, the sophistication of technology varies widely among America's thousands of campuses. All schools, however, are planning for an ever-increasing demand for technological equipment and services from each new entering class of students. Technology doesn't replace the need for physical and human interactions, but it has the potential to enhance learning and research and to enrich the connections among students and faculty alike.

Life Outside the Classroom: The Changing Landscape

College students of this generation are being well taken care of, from their culinary to their counseling needs. The amenities on college campuses today are far more extensive and elaborate than ever before. Consumer-minded students demand services that support their daily living, and colleges and universities have poured financial resources into out-of-the-classroom facilities—athletic complexes, student centers, and, in institutions such as the University of South Carolina, complete shopping malls.

Dazzling sports complexes cater to the health- and fitness-conscious student population with weight rooms, exercise equipment, and saunas adjacent to Olympic-size swimming pools. Even small colleges provide students with more sophisticated facilities than the simple gymnasiums that were standard in the largest universities a generation ago. Translucent bubbles housing indoor tennis courts and skating rinks dot campuses all over the country. Some schools, such as the University of Miami, have built multi-million-dollar wellness centers to provide a full array of integrated offerings. With a 10,000-square-foot weight room, Miami's center provides nutritional assessment, cooking classes, physical therapy—even massages. Students congregate at the juice bar and indoor and outdoor conversation pits. The University of Pennsylvania offers a golf simulator and Pilates studio. Evergreen State College in Washington is among the many institutions that include a rock climbing practice wall in its wellness complex.

Lavish student centers attest to the fact that today's students and their parents have high expectations of campus leisure facilities as well as classrooms and laboratories. The University of Texas Union houses more than 500 student-run activities. The Aztec Center at San Diego State sits on Mission Bay, a captivating waterfront wonder. Cal State Northridge's Sol Center was designed for sustainability and energy efficiency – incorporating natural light technology in a dramatic and attractive fashion. George Mason University's 320,000-square-foot George W. Johnson Center is an innovative experiment, integrating students' academic and social lives. A hub for both students and faculty, this streamlined facility houses an academic library, professors' offices and classrooms, along with a 310-seat movie theatre, dance studios, bistros and much more. Even small schools, such as Scripps College and Occidental in Southern California, boast artfully designed student centers with multipurpose gathering places and state-of-the-art dining facilities.

An entire community exists under one roof in many of these upscale centers—a bookstore, a bank, a travel agency, a post office, theaters and cabarets, video game rooms, art galleries, cappuccino bars and food courts catering to an assortment of palates—with everything from freshly made sushi to antipasto. Signs of the technological explosion are everywhere, from the reception desk which may have a touch-screen computer that displays a campus calendar to ATM machines, professional-quality video production suites and wireless networks which allow students to stay connected from all corners of campus.

MAKING CONNECTIONS: CAMPUS GROUPS

Activities fairs, a fall ritual on most campuses, provide a festival-like atmosphere with colorful banners, posters and students distributing leaflets and invitations to join the campus radio station, newspaper, literary magazines; a cappella singing groups and theater troupes, community service organizations and intramural sports teams, College Republicans and College Democrats. These kinds of organizations have been an important part of campus life for many generations.

The diversity of the current crop of college students is reflected in a mélange of new campus organizations, which might not look so familiar to visiting parents. There are more groups than ever before, representing a broad range of backgrounds and beliefs. These might include the Society of Women Engineers, College Libertarians, the Hispanic Business Students Association, the Muslim Student Association, Kyi-Yo Native American Student Association, the Pagan Students' Group, and Mixed, a group for multi-racial individuals. Additionally, a whole assortment of student groups such as the Alliance of Students Against Poverty, the Committee on Environmental Quality, Engineers Without Borders, and the Africa Technology Initiative challenge students to think more broadly about social and global issues. Most students thrive on the sense of connection that comes from affiliation with a small group united by a common bond, and these informal organizations are a vital part of colleges today. As students choose among this incredible range of campus groups, they are making a statement about who they are and who they want to be.

Students of Color: Ethnic and Cultural Groups

The racial and cultural mix on today's campuses brings new richness and intellectual energy as well as new tensions to the entire college experience. It influences the nature of the curriculum, the organization of the living units and the scope of the social life. Students, faculty and administrators engage in ongoing dialogue about what multiculturalism and diversity mean to the university and the daily lives of students.

Students of color on predominantly white campuses confront daily episodes of prejudice that take their toll. African-American and Latino students at the University of California at Irvine report that when they go to a local shopping center they are followed by security guards. Asian students from Maine to California complain that everyone assumes they are either premed or engineering majors, and they feel the thinly veiled hostility of their classmates who are worried about their raising the curve. Students from the Middle East sense the fear and mistrust of their peers whenever there is a widely publicized incident of terrorism. Chicano students describe the humiliation of arriving at a fraternity party where the Mexican theme includes Anglos affecting Latino accents.

African-American students face serious dilemmas and major struggles above and beyond the daily stresses of their white counterparts. Many have chosen to attend a school in which African-Americans are likely to represent less than five percent of the student body, to "brave it" in an environment that is at best tolerant and at worst hostile. There are subtle reminders daily that they are not welcomed by many of their classmates and professors—who don't recognize them or confuse them with other black students, suggest that they accept a mediocre performance rather than reach for higher academic goals, imply that they have been admitted as a result of preferential treatment.

For students who were used to very mixed social groups in high school, the separateness encountered on some campuses comes as a surprise and poses a dilemma.

An African-American freshman at a major research university addresses this:

> If I join a black sorority or hang out with my friends from BSA (the Black Student Association), the white kids say I'm segregating myself. If I go out with some of the white kids on the floor or a couple of them I knew from high school, then my black friends give me a hard time and say I'm turning my back on my own. I almost went to Howard, and I still think I might transfer. It seems like such a hassle a lot of the time.

Marjorie Nieuwenhuis, Director of College Counseling at the United Nations International School (UNIS) in Manhattan, says that many of her students are shocked by the divisiveness they encounter when they arrive on campus:

> Coming from an international school they are not predisposed to isolate themselves among others who look like they do. One of my students of Haitian background, at a very prestigious college, had a picture of her UNIS friends on her dresser, and—some of her friends were white—other students began taunting her with the epithet "Oreo."

And yet minority student groups, both organized and informal, serve a crucial need as a haven—a safe space where students of color can be themselves, where they don't have to represent all people of their race or culture, but can speak their own minds.

In *The Agony of Education: Black Students at White Colleges and Universities,* Joe R. Feagin, Hernan Vera, and Nikitah Imani write of their findings from interviews with parents and students:

> In contrast to certain critics of higher education like D'Souza and Bloom, many black parents see black students' sticking together in traditionally white places as necessary for their personal and academic survival, not as some type of organized anti-white activity. These peer group settings give many first-year college students a place to be themselves, and to find supportive friends, without the intrusion of racial barriers.[7]

In her book, *Why Are All the Black Kids Sitting Together in the Cafeteria?*, Beverly Tatum argues compellingly that separate centers and gathering places for students of color support their racial identity development. On predominantly white campuses, black students, struggling with questions of identity, have a need to immerse themselves in their history and culture among their same-race peers—something that their white student counterparts do on a daily basis. Tatum states:

> Having a place to be rejuvenated and to feel anchored in one's cultural community increases the possibility that one will have the energy to achieve academically as well as participate in the cross-group dialogue and interaction many colleges want to encourage.[8]

The following student comments echo these sentiments:

> When you're a minority on a big campus, even if you have friends from other groups, it's nice to know that there are other people like you. Walking into the black student lounge is so comforting just because it's like my place. It's just your area, your own private study room, and if other people are there, they look like you. It's really neat. There's a huge picture of Martin Luther King and art from black students on the walls—it's ours.

> At Oberlin, the black student house provides a social life. If you have all this comfort and support and have all the things on a college campus that white students get to enjoy just anyway because they're the majority—the idea is that you'll perform better, and you'll reach out because you'll be so happy with where you are and what you're doing—it will be natural for you to reach out. I really believe that's the case.

> It's important to me to be true to yourself. Joining ABS (Association of Black Students) was something I really wanted to do. Everybody fits into something. People look at you and decide where they are going to place you. Being light skinned and of mixed heritage—that causes more problems for you—cause it's less clear for people where they're going to stack you in their own minds in classifying you. Joining ABS was my way of establishing myself and telling people where I was. It's meant a lot to look at a group and say this is what I've invested myself in.

Many institutions have responded to today's diverse population of students by providing ethnic and multicultural centers. The Cross-Cultural Center at the University of California at Irvine houses student organizations for African-Americans, Native Americans, Asian-Americans, Chicanos and Latinos. The Swarthmore Black Cultural Center, a large stone house adjacent to campus, is guided by a director and committee of black faculty, administrators, and students, and provides comfortable places to study or just hang out. It also contains a library, art gallery and facilities for a wide range of social, cultural and educational programs for black students and others interested in black culture. These are just a few samples of an increasing number of gathering places for students of color on campuses across the country.

Universities also welcome international students with innovative programming. The University of Montana has over 500 students from 74 different countries. The administration works with the Missoula community to sponsor a variety of cultural and hospitality programs. UM Global Partners pairs first-semester international students with experienced students who help them adjust to life on campus, and offers support to ease the culture shock.

Some campuses, such as Berkeley, where there is no distinct majority, foreshadow the American pluralistic society of the not-too-distant future. But many students at Berkeley report feelings of isolation in the midst of diversity. They use words such as *balkanization* and *tribalism* to describe the break up of the student body into distinctly separate ethnic and racial groups at the expense of a common campus identity.

Other Berkeley students report that there is more mixing than meets the eye of the casual observer. Though students find support and social comfort by coming together with others of similar backgrounds, many also form bonds across racial and cultural boundaries, as they struggle together with difficult chemistry labs, enervating athletic practice or challenging community service projects. And as they celebrate their own culture, they often enrich the lives of their fellow students.

A student at Washington University in St. Louis spoke with intense emotion about her experience with a group whose mission was to cross the divide and embrace dialogue between different cultures:

> Black Women/Jewish Women was the most important experience I've had in college. The process of becoming close with a group of women from such diverse backgrounds and struggling as our discussions became more honest and at times painful was incredibly intense. We would plan on meeting for an hour and meet for three instead. I left every meeting with my head spinning.

■

For many students of mixed heritage, it's hard to sort out their identity and to find a niche on today's multicultural campus. One student who is of African-American and Korean descent spent his childhood and teen years in a small rural community where he was routinely ostracized. Even though he is now a student at a cosmopolitan university, he still feels on the fringe.

A young woman describes the complexity of her search:

> I'm Mexican-American and Jewish. My dad is Mexican. I was born in Mexico City and lived there for ten years. My mother is American and Jewish. Everyone here at school assumes like I'm American. It was comforting to know that there are lots of Jewish people here. I'm taking Hebrew and I'm surrounded by a lot of people on the Jewish holidays who understand where I'm coming from. As far as

> the Mexican part, unless people know me very well, they don't know that part of me. It's a part of me that I wish got more exposure.

Another student asserts her mixed heritage as central to her sense of herself:

> Both of my parents are of mixed heritage. It's very important that I get to be a woman of color of multi-ethnic heritage—that people don't put me in one box or another.

On some campuses, students have formed groups to celebrate and explore their mixed heritage, such as: Brown University's BOMBS (Brown Organization of Multiracial and Biracial Students), DePauw's HAPA (a Hawaiian word used in reference to biracial people), Bryn Mawr's Half & Half, and Grinnell's Mixed Plate. These organizations can strengthen and support their sense of identity at this crucial time of their lives.

One member, whose father is black and mother is white, reflects on this need for validation:

> It was interesting to hear other people's experience and the interesting thing about SHADES is—a lot of members are mixed Caucasian and black heritage, but then there are people who are black and Asian or Asian and Caucasian. So it's very much a multicultural group. Sometimes we talked about being a member of ABS, sometimes about the greater college community. We talked about what it meant to have one parent who was black and one who was white, and at the same time you were talking to people who are Indian, who had similar experiences. I think every group of color has issues of complexion. Our

> talks served a lot of personal needs, but it was also academic in that you were sort of broadening your horizons a lot on lots of different cultures.

Religion, Spirituality, and Cults

Many of today's students are looking for a sense of purpose and community in an environment that often seems fragmented; they are looking for answers, for rituals and traditions in an era of rapid change and rootlessness. Increasing numbers are turning to faith communities on campus.

The number of students affiliating with religious groups is rising. Across the country, participation at the Newman Centers and Hillels, traditional gathering places for Catholic and Jewish students, has increased markedly. Duke University has more than twenty campus chaplains serving the diverse faiths of their students, including a recently appointed imam, who teaches, counsels and provides religious leadership for Muslim students and interfaith programming for the university community. Georgetown, Wesleyan, NYU and Princeton are among the growing numbers of colleges meeting the needs of Muslim students and providing an Islamic voice to discussions of faith, spirituality and social justice.

The numbers of different religious and spiritual groups are mushrooming continually. MIT's thirty student religious groups include Asian Baptist Student Koinonia; Atheists, Agnostics, and Humanists; Black Christian Fellowship; Buddhist Community; Hillel; Hong Kong Student Bible Study Group; Lutheran Episcopal Ministry; Muslim Students' Association; Tech Catholic Community; and the United Christian Fellowship.

Young men and women attend traditional services, join Bible study groups, and some even live in small enclaves that carry on rituals or traditions of their faith. Students who join a group with a religious focus often find companionship as well. Many of these organizations sponsor parties, cultural programs or other social events. For some students, the identification with their own ethnic group is more important than the religious experience. Membership provides them with a longed-for niche on campus. For others, membership provides an oasis of calm in a stressful landscape.

Many students use the word "spiritual" rather than "religious" to describe themselves. These students seem to be searching for a personal and transcendent faith that they have been unable to find within organized religion.

■

Administrators on many campuses are concerned about students' susceptibility to destructive religious cults. A dean at the City University of New York explains that such groups usually have a "self-appointed, messianic leader claiming divine selection who focuses followers' attentions exclusively on him and exercises autocratic control of them." Cults manipulate, control, and isolate their members. They demand unquestioning loyalty and obedience.

College campuses are prime targets for cult recruiters. Using coercive and deceptive techniques, cult recruiters have been known to position themselves outside the counseling service or in the student center, looking for students who appear depressed or lonely. Cult leaders know that students who are on their own for the first time, though pleased with their freedom, are anxious about taking responsibility for their own lives. Young people are searching for answers, for an identity, for some stability in their lives; they are vulnerable to the offer of instant community, a set of clear expectations, and ready answers to complex questions. International students, lonely and eager to learn about American culture, have a particularly difficult time distinguishing between genuine overtures of friendship from religious congregations and the organized recruitment by cults.

For parents who are concerned about their own child, this is not the kind of problem to be tackled alone. This is a time to call the dean, the advisor or another appropriate university administrator. Parents may also turn to their own clergy, or to one of the organizations around the country that monitor the activities of cults. The International Cultic Studies Association (ICSA) does research, educates, and provides assistance to victims and their loved ones. ICSA also helps professionals in colleges and other institutions to educate themselves and their students about cults. Their website includes reviews of books that contain practical information for parents.

Gay, Lesbian, Bisexual, and Transgender Support Groups

Reflecting the growing acknowledgment and acceptance of the gay, lesbian, bisexual and transgender community nationally, university-sanctioned student organizations commonly include support groups for these students. Most of these groups offer social and educational programs and some serve as political action groups as well. They confront overtly discriminatory policies and incidents, and also attempt to sensitize the university community to the more subtle forms of harassment they experience.

The University of Pennsylvania is one of an increasing number of academic institutions that employ an administrator and a fully staffed center, to support lesbian, gay, bisexual and transgender students, staff and faculty. In addition to programs, support, and advocacy, the University of Pennsylvania Center maintains a 24-hour telephone listing of events of interest to their constituency. Their library of books and periodicals written for and about sexual minorities is a valuable resource for both students and faculty. Penn's Queer Student Alliance webpage provides links to specific groups on campus, such as: FLASH (Facilitating Learning About Sexual Health); the Christian Association, and Wharton Out for Business, as well as resources outside of the campus community. Dartmouth's Coalition for Gay, Lesbian, Bisexual and Transgender Concerns includes among its different subgroups the Gay Straight Alliance, whose mission is to bridge the college's gay and straight communities.

Campus recognition has changed the lives of many gay men and women, offering them a place to share their concerns with their peers—a far cry from the isolated, guilt-ridden secret lives of those in earlier times. While welcoming the safe haven of their own community, most are involved in all aspects of campus life. In spite of the improved climate, however, blatant anti-gay incidents still mar the lives of many gay, lesbian, bisexual and transgender students.

Greek Life Today

Although some colleges have disbanded their Greek system, fraternities and sororities are definitely back in vogue on many campuses. They have more than doubled their membership since the low point in 1971. New colonies arrive yearly on campuses that spurned them a generation ago.

The traditional Greek system has opened its ranks along with the rest of the university and no longer tolerates restricting membership based on race or religion. Though more diverse than they used to be, however, they still cater mainly to the affluent, and the students who are excluded still suffer the pain of rejection.

These fraternities and sororities are a study in contradictions. Many are notorious for their wild parties, excessive alcohol consumption, and drug use and may spend up to a third of their budgets to pay liability costs. Alcohol has played a major role in most of the claims. Many of the incidents have resulted in sexual assaults, serious accidents and some even in death. As a result, some nationals are adopting alcohol-free houses, and most are altering their policies. Hazing, with its sometimes tragic consequences, has come under scrutiny and almost all states have passed anti-hazing laws, yet hazing still exists behind closed doors on far too many campuses.

On the other hand, fraternities and sororities may offer affordable and intimate housing, monitored study spaces, and a focus on leadership development and community service. They provide students with a family of "brothers" and "sisters" and an instant identity advertised by the pins, jackets and sweatshirts they proudly wear.

Black fraternities and sororities have historically been noted for their commitment to lifelong community service and for the ongoing connections that they provide for their members. In the last several decades, reflecting the diversity of today's student body, a new generation of cultural interest fraternities and sororities have sprung up on campuses nationwide. Asian Americans, Latinos, Native Americans and other cultural groups that had previously been excluded from traditional sorority and fraternity life, have formed fellowships that celebrate their heritage along with the other benefits of Greek life.

All students today see "networking" as a plus in the stampede for professional success. Undergraduates have an opportunity while still on campus to interact with alumni and members of their advisory boards, providing the first stop on the "old boy" express and its "old girl" equivalent.

Fraternities and sororities vary dramatically from campus to campus and chapter to chapter. Students who are trying to decide whether or not to join a Greek organization might ask: Does the university provide an advisor? Is the chapter local or national? Have any chapters been closed recently; if so, why?

When is rush—first semester or second semester? Is there housing available? What is the culture of this chapter?

■

Today's colleges and universities have officially acknowledged the value of students' co-curricular involvements, whether through Greek life or social, religious, or political groups. Under the aegis of the dean of students, a cadre of student development professionals advises student groups and provides training in leadership skills. They coach and teach and act as confidants and mentors. Their mission is to help students gain confidence and competence in the world outside the classroom.

In their concern about their child's ability to meet academic demands and maintain a high GPA, many parents view student involvement in nonacademic activities as a frivolous pastime. Yet research by UCLA educator Alexander Astin highlights its positive influence on the way students grow and develop. Students who are active campus leaders bring that confidence into the classroom and tend to be active participants there as well. Charles Schroeder, Professor of Higher Education Administration at the University of Missouri, urges parents not to discount the impact that the co-curricular experience can have on their child:

> We try to encourage broad-based student involvement in a variety of settings. The intent is to promote character development and values, leadership skills, and the ability to communicate well. Much of this comes from involvement outside the classroom. Students spend approximately twelve to fifteen hours a week in class. Just think about how many hours kids spend together talking, playing sports, working together in a host of student activities. The intensity of their relationships is powerful. Part of what we do

in Student Development is help students make meaning out of the collegiate experience.

BEYOND THE IVY-COVERED WALLS: CHANGING NEEDS AND SERVICES

Beyond the venerable old edifices and dazzling new facilities that pervade the campus there are a legion of services for students that didn't exist a generation ago: sophisticated career centers, computer centers, learning, study skills and writing centers, disability resource centers, multicultural centers, gay, lesbian, bi-sexual, transgender centers, and centers for health and wellness.

Lively and energetic residence-hall staff join psychologists and specialists in addressing academic needs, student programming, and alcohol and drug abuse counseling in the daily pursuit of helping students to develop as well as to cope with the stresses and strains of college life. These are the adults who are on the front line and are likely to have the most interaction with students, particularly freshmen and sophomores. Their mission is to support students' learning, and to assist them in making the most of their college years.

In previous generations, house parents or proctors who lived in dormitories enforced codes of discipline and provided a haven for "tea and sympathy" as needed. There were clear-cut rules and expectations, and the concept of *in loco parentis*, a Latin phrase meaning "in the place of the parent," was a court-ordered fact of college life. The landmark decision in the 1911 *Gott v. Berea College* case stated that college authorities would stand in place of parents to watch out for the welfare of their children while they were under the college's care. Colleges and universities operated according to these guidelines until the late 1960s, when *in loco parentis* disappeared on most campuses, along with curfews, stringent rules, and young people's trust in adults over 30.

In the late '60s and early '70s, students assumed power in all areas of their lives. Along with civil rights and women's rights, students' rights became an issue in itself. In addition to their challenges to the national political status quo, students mobilized changes on campus from the dissolution of parietal rules to a more open and varied curriculum. They became responsible for monitoring their own behavior in all facets of their lives.

Edward B. Fiske, former Education Editor of the *New York Times*, recounts the impact of these sweeping changes on large numbers of students and on the colleges and universities themselves:

> The faculty gave away control of the curriculum, and the administration decided it was going to get out of *in loco parentis*. All this freedom worked for some kids, but for lots of others, it didn't. Colleges and universities realized this and began to pick up the pieces with expanded health centers and counseling services and career centers. A whole set of professionals stepped in to serve kids who couldn't handle the freedom. As Ernest Boyer (of the Carnegie Foundation) put it in his book *College: The Undergraduate Experience in America*, we moved from *in loco parentis* to *in loco clinician*.

Although there is little interest in returning to *in loco parentis* as it existed in the '50s or early '60s, today's colleges and universities are designing programs to involve faculty as active advisors and mentors and to increase their presence in the lives of students outside of the classroom. They are also re-evaluating, and in many cases redefining, their relationship with parents.

Students today are searching for more structure than students of thirty years ago. They actively seek out advice from adults and seem more willing to accept restraints. Almost all schools are reassessing the needs of their students and the role that the institution should play in their total development

Residential Life

Although residence halls on many campuses have been mixing the sexes since the early 1970s, first-time parents of college freshmen are often shocked by the sight of their own sons and daughters actually living side by side, brushing their teeth together, mingling in the halls in robes, pajamas and towels—casually sprawled on the beds in each other's rooms. The following tongue-in-cheek comments from the mother of a brand-new freshman at the University of Pennsylvania speak for the anxieties of many parents:

> Initially I was horrified by the fact that the small, squalid bathroom two doors away from Peggy's room was to be shared by students of both sexes. I had been prepared for the coed dorm and even for the coed floor, but the idea of sharing a bathroom with only a torn shower curtain between my naked Peggy and some unshaven lout was an ugly shock.

Residence halls range from the small, decrepit, and charming to the high-rise, impersonal, and air conditioned—from the convenient fall-out-of-bed-into-class variety to those located a bike ride or bus ride from the center of campus. It is not uncommon for today's residence halls to provide fitness studios and exercise rooms, computer labs, kitchens, and art studios for their residents. Many have seminar rooms for small classes or study groups, and mini-libraries stocked with DVDs as well as books. Some residence halls are single-sex; others are coed and separate the sexes by wing, floor, or room. Many offer choices of quiet floors or suites of students with common majors or interests. Recently an increasing number of schools are offering the option of gender-neutral housing—particularly for upper-class students, allowing students to select roommates regardless of gender identity.

Substance-free halls or floors have become a popular alternative for many students. These are particularly supportive environments for students who have struggled with addiction problems in high school. Some students choose this option because they want to stay free of temptation, but many simply want a quieter and more tranquil living environment.

Numerous colleges and universities provide living environments that encourage a sense of pride and commitment to a community. At Stanford, ethnic theme houses such as Ujamaa and Casa Zapata provide support and a home away from home as well as cultural programming and resources. The Program Houses at Cornell provide a haven for students who want to immerse themselves in a particular subject that they are curious or passionate about. These unique surroundings include such residences as Just About Music, the Multicultural Living Learning Unit and Ecology House.

The time-honored "houses" and "colleges" at Harvard and Yale, though now coed, have remained constant during periods of residential upheaval. With faculty-in-residence, they have their own libraries and dining facilities and support an active intellectual and cultural life.

A growing number of colleges are attempting to make the academic experience an integral part of residential life. For example, as part of the University of Pennsylvania's College Housing and Academic Services (CHAS), faculty members live in the residence halls, advising and interacting with students daily as members of the same community. At Duke University, East Campus is an all-freshman enclave that integrates residential living with academic and social programs. Duke's Faculty

Associates Program links professors with living units throughout the campus, hoping to bring the intellectual energy of the formal classroom into the informal settings of the dining halls and lounges. The Living-Learning Center at the University of Vermont is a home for students who study subjects around a common theme of their choice and offers the opportunity for faculty and students to connect outside of the classroom. Spelman's Stewart Living and Learning Center houses freshmen and upperclass students who are Presidenctial scholars and participants in honors programs. The University of Michigan, the University of the Pacific, Princeton, Bucknell, Indiana University and Colby are among schools that have innovative housing systems that bring the living and learning experience into closer harmony.

Without a multitude of rules and strict regulations, who fosters a sense of community? Who keeps the typical residence halls from deteriorating into anarchy? In many schools, the heroes and heroines in the trenches are graduate or upperclass students, often called resident advisors or assistants. The RAs, who frequently receive compensation such as room and board, act as the on-site supervisors and counselors responsible for the daily functioning of residence hall floors. On 24-hour call, an RA may be found rescuing a student who is locked out of a room, encouraging a stressed student to get a calculus tutor, admonishing a noisy resident, or counseling someone who is severely depressed.

RA training is often intense and extensive. The best is usually year-long, with supervision by graduate student residence directors and student services professional staff. RAs participate in workshops on everything from suicide prevention to time management; they discuss and learn about such issues as test anxiety, racism, homosexuality, substance abuse and eating disorders. They learn how to develop and plan programs that bring the students on their floor together—ranging from the tried-and-true ice cream socials and pizza parties, to sustainability competitions and community service projects in surrounding neighborhoods. They foster learning outside the classroom, challenging students to develop goals and explore opportunities. At the very minimum, RA training includes information and communication skills to help them be alert and reach out to students in need, listen attentively, and refer students to resources and professional help.

Career Centers

The Career Center is not high on the list of priorities for most freshmen in their first months on campus. As they revel in the many aspects of their new lives, thoughts about careers seem either irrelevant or something tedious and remote to be addressed in the distant four-years-from-now future. But on most campuses, the placement offices of yesteryear have expanded into multifaceted high-tech career centers, and those students who choose to avail themselves of these services early in their college stay have a jumpstart in designing their future, both during their undergraduate years and beyond. As freshmen and sophomores reflect on their talents, dreams, values, and aspirations, patterns begin to emerge and unfold and affect what courses they choose and what out-of-the-classroom experiences they have. Issues of identity are front and center, as students complement their passionate intellectual pursuits with courses that reflect a practical eye toward the future world of work

Students have a chance to meet with career counselors as early as their freshman year to begin the search for knowledge about themselves and the world of work. Many career centers have developed a four-year career plan, which guides students step by step from self exploration to job hunting skills. Through individualized counseling, workshops, computer guidance programs, and career resource libraries, students learn the process of career development—a process that will prove invaluable, since most of them will have many jobs and several career changes after they land their first position.

Contrary to what many students believe, there is no test that can tell them what their perfect career is or what they *should* be. But counseling and career interest testing can help students to begin to focus, become aware of their interests, skills, and values; and decide what fields they want to explore. Fortunately, most of today's colleges provide students with a lot of opportunity for exploration. In addition to the written materials housed in career libraries and information garnered from electronic databases, career panels of local graduates, networks of alumni career advisors, and mentoring programs all serve to bring students together with role models and information sources.

Innovative internship and cooperative education programs give students valuable work experience while still in school, helping to solve the age-old dilemma that most new graduates face—"only the experienced need apply." More and more career centers have reached out into the community to arrange on-the-job apprenticeships and internships. Many of today's upperclassmen, especially those who might have been tempted to desert the humanities, supplement their intellectual nourishment with these pragmatic steppingstones to the work world.

Career centers help with the nuts and bolts of job hunting too. Students learn how to write resumes and target job leads. In preparation for interviews, they attend etiquette dinners and workshops on professional attire. The best equipped of today's high-tech centers offer a sophisticated array of resources. Students can use a computer program to generate a resume. They can do practice interviews and critique themselves on video. They can search local and global databases for job leads, transmit their resumes electronically and interview with a potential employer thousands of miles away via videoconferencing. Most centers serve alumni as well as students, reflecting the contemporary view that career development is ongoing and career change is a common occurrence.

Health and Wellness

When students go away to college, they leave behind, not only family and friends, but also their physicians, dentists and others who have been involved in their care and well-being. Though most students are unlikely to give the health service a thought until they come down with a case of flu or a sprained ankle, parents often check out medical resources before they even bring their son or daughter to campus. Health Services range from the solo nurse practitioner in a rural setting to sophisticated multi-specialist services staffed by physicians and a variety of allied health professionals affiliated with an academic health center.

On many of today's campuses there is a new emphasis on the broad concept of health and wellness, and on a proactive approach that helps students learn lifelong habits of health and well-being. Students learn constructive ways to deal with stress, attend workshops on nutrition, sleep, and fitness—and other topics that foster a balanced lifestyle. There is a new recognition among college and university administrators that health and wellness are vital to academic performance and success.

Counseling Services

Counseling centers that were embryonic or nonexistent thirty years ago are now standard fare. Staffed by psychologists, social workers, and counselors, their primary mission is to support students so that they can make the most of the opportunities that college provides. This may include helping students surmount normal developmental hurdles, responding to crises, or directing them to resources for more extensive treatment when necessary. Increasingly, counseling centers report a shift from primarily seeing students who have benign developmental and adjustment concerns to treating students with major psychological illnesses. In a 2007 national survey of college counseling service directors, 91.5 percent reported a continuing increase in the numbers of students with serious mental health problems.

A twenty-five-year veteran of the counseling staff of a private southern university elaborates:

> My role is so varied depending on the student. There is no doubt that in recent years we see many more students with severe psychological disorders. However with some students, I am an educator, a teacher of a variety of coping skills to deal with the incredible academic and social stresses that are part of their daily lives. With others, I mainly provide support, letting a student know that what he is going through is normal and to be expected. And, as a psychologist, I help students correct distorted perceptions that may cause them to stumble.

"To stumble" often means to suffer from anxiety or depression, the most common problems students bring to counseling services. These can be brought on by anything from a disappointing grade, to a broken romance, to problems at home—the kinds of concerns that have always plagued college students. But the complications of contemporary family life, financial pressures, the uncertainty of the world, and the bewildering array of choices facing today's students have brought them in increasing numbers to university counseling centers. Counselors note the rise of disorders rarely seen before such as gambling or gaming addictions, and harassment and stalking via the

Internet. Although most of this extremely stressed generation of students exercise, do yoga or hang out with friends to relax; increasing numbers have dysfunctional coping methods, ranging from disappearing for hours into a fantasy virtual world on the Web to binge drinking, abuse of prescription medications or self-injury. In order to serve the broadest range of students, most colleges have increased the number of counselors on their staffs, but still have to place a limit on the number of visits a student can make. It is common for college counselors to give referrals to professionals in the community for more extensive counseling.

With improved medications for anxiety, depression, bipolar, and ADD, students who might not have been able to function in college in previous decades are now able to thrive. Many students arrive on campus having already been treated with medication. With the pressures of college life, many more students will have had medication prescribed before they graduate.

As more mental health professionals are hired to respond to the surge in numbers, they are also broadening their responsibilities—becoming more integrated into the university community, consulting with professors, advisors, and coaches, and offering training to RAs and peer counselors, who are available to respond to students at 24-hour drop-in centers or on hotlines. Drop-in spaces in residence halls or students centers offer opportunities for informal conversations with counselors to those students who might be intimidated by a scheduled session at the counseling center. At Cornell, for several hours a day, a counselor staffs a satellite space in the international dorm, serving a population whose culture might stigmatize formal psychotherapy.

In the aftermath of high-profile campus shootings, such as at Virginia Tech and Northern Illinois, many colleges and universities across the country have formed collaborative teams to stay informed about troubled students and intervene when necessary. These groups are constantly walking the fine line between protecting students' privacy and protecting them from harm to themselves or others. At RPI, for example, an intervention team that consists of members from the Dean's office, faculty, residential life, the counseling center and campus police meets regularly to assess potential problems. Faculty and staff can make note of academic or behavioral problems on a website monitored by the team. Many schools offer online educational programs to help faculty and staff recognize warning signs and learn how and where to refer students.

Students have access on the Web to instant information on a variety of psychological and developmental issues. For example, the University of Minnesota at Duluth offers information on issues ranging from procrastination to depression and sexual assault. At the University of Chicago, the Student Counseling Virtual Pamphlet Collection links students to counseling information websites at colleges all over the country, sharing their collective wisdom. For some students, this factual information may be enough; for others, this is a first step toward calling and making an appointment to talk directly to a counselor.

Although much of their work addresses developmental tasks and increasing clinical concerns of today's students, counselors also present educational outreach programs to deal with some of the critical concerns of contemporary college students such as stress reduction, sexual health, drugs and alcohol, and eating disorders. And with the growing emphasis on health and wellness, they are joining other professionals and peer educators in their mission towards a holistic approach to physical and mental health. Topics that may have been considered "ho hum" a decade ago, such as the importance of sleep, exercise and good nutrition, are seen as essential for a student's mental and physical health and are being given attention in new and creative ways.

CAMPUS PROBLEMS

Safety and Security

Campus safety is at the top of most parents' "worry list." In this era of crime consciousness, colleges have appropriated large sums of money for security measures to protect students. Gone are the days when bikes were left unlocked in campus bike racks and dormitories were left open until midnight. Today, computerized card systems have replaced keys; special lighting and emergency blue light phones have been installed on pathways to and from residence halls; security escorts provide nighttime transportation to libraries, labs, and studios. On most campuses, newly arrived freshmen find an orientation packet that includes information on security, rape prevention tips, emergency procedures and crisis hotline numbers. On city campuses, this comes as no surprise, but students who arrive at a halcyon collegiate setting outside of city limits are often skeptical about the message that they too are vulnerable.

Since the 1990s and the passage of the Jeanne Clery Disclosure of Campus Security Policy and Crime Statistics Act, colleges and universities have been required to publish their crime statistics and to make timely warnings about crimes that pose a threat to the campus community. Comparing one school's statistics with another's can be misleading, however. It's important to look at campus statistics in the context of the surrounding community, and to keep in mind that schools have different methods of collecting data.

It's possible that a school that aggressively encourages students to report crimes will look less safe than an institution at which students have little faith in the police and are unmotivated to report crimes. Parents can supplement statistical information about crime by asking what prevention strategies the school is using and what supports they have for students. For example, they might ask: Is there a shuttle service or security escort service? Is campus safety addressed in orientation? Are students taught what to do in case of weather emergencies or other natural disasters? When an incident occurs, are students informed and given safety tips? Does the institution send a clear message that hazing will not be tolerated? How does the university prepare for major crowd control during and after sporting events, concerts, or campus protests? Are crime alerts posted? Does the university have a text message notification system to alert students and keep them informed during emergencies? Parents might also ask current students about the visibility and responsiveness of the university police force.

Acquaintance Rape, Relationship Violence, and Sexual Harassment

From Stanford to Swarthmore, from Cornell to San Diego State, counselors and public safety officers actively address rape prevention with workshops and self-defense programs. But far more prevalent on college campuses, and more insidious than rape by a stranger, is the crime of date rape, sometimes known as acquaintance rape.

Data from a study done in 2000 by Bonnie Fisher and her colleagues at the National Institute of Justice estimated that nearly 5 percent of college women will be victims of rape or attempted rape in any academic year. Because they are unlikely to use the term *rape* to describe what happened to them, and they often feel guilty and ashamed, most women who are forced to have sex with an acquaintance do not report the incident officially. But the aftermath can be as devastating for them as the consequences of rape by a stranger.

In recent years, several drugs (GHB, Ketamine and Rohypnol, sometimes referred to as roofies) have become a growing problem on college campuses. Known as "date rape drugs," these medications have been misused to sedate young women involuntarily with the intention of having non-consensual sexual intercourse. Since these drugs have no odor or taste, and can induce blackouts with memory loss, women are at considerable risk. College administrators and peer educators are well aware of the potential dangers at college parties and local bars and advise students never to leave a drink unattended, to drink only from tamper-proof bottles or cans that they have opened themselves, to beware of mixed drinks, and not to leave a friend alone at a party or bar. Although alcohol is not usually listed among the "date rape drugs," Brown University's health education website includes it, pointing to the strong link between alcohol and sexual assault. In 90 percent of incidents of campus date rape, either the perpetrator, the victim or both had been drinking. Though it is never an excuse for or cause of sexual assault, alcohol can impair judgment. In any case, the person who forces sex on someone who physically resists, says "no" or is incapacitated by alcohol is always responsible for the act.

Colleges and universities are focusing attention on the sexual victimization of students, a widespread problem. Many campus organizations, such as Princeton's SHARE (Sexual Harassment/Assault, Advising Resources and Education) provide confidential counseling, emergency services, and legal and disciplinary options for students, faculty and staff who have experienced relationship violence, sexual assault or harassment.

On campuses across the country, many programs focus on the miscommunications and misconceptions that lead to sexual violence. They challenge the beliefs of many young men, rooted in existing sexual myths—"She provoked it," "Women say no, but mean yes," "I just lost control; you know how men are." Counselors and peer educators instruct students about sexual rights and responsibilities and teach women how to say no. They also emphasize that it is essential for both men and women to make active, responsible choices, and point out the role that alcohol plays in increasing the risk of miscommunication and poor judgment.

Since recent research indicates that freshmen are the group most at risk for sexual assault, many schools now include videos or student skits and peer-led discussions on the topic during orientation. And it's not unusual for fraternities, sororities, and residence hall staffs to follow up with related programs as the year progresses.

Colleges and universities have recognized that this is a community health issue. Increased awareness about the prevalence of acquaintance rape, relationship violence and harassment has produced student demands for more sophisticated campus support services, such as a specifically designated offices for prevention and response, survivors' support groups, more accessible campus reporting mechanisms, and more responsive judicial procedures that take into consideration the special psychological dimensions of sexual assault cases. Harvard's Office of Sexual Assault Prevention and Response was established in 2003 as a comprehensive attempt to provide resources, education, counseling and to promote social change within the Harvard community. With trained advisors in each house to be first responders to incidents, a 24-hour hotline and a drop-in center, among other services, the University has recognized that these serious problems exist even in the most prestigious of colleges and universities and made a commitment to address them.

Though women are most often the target of sexual violence, sexual assault is not just a women's issue, but a community issue. Organizations such as One in Four and Men Against Rape provide educational programs and training in rape prevention given by men, primarily for men, on college campuses.

Students can find information on sexual assault and relationship violence on university websites. If a student has been assaulted or raped, the computer is no substitute for personal counseling by a chaplain, psychologist or counselor. The Web can be helpful in providing resources and reassuring advice, however, for friends and family who want to give support.

Eating Disorders

A mixture of psychological, sociological, and environmental stresses make today's college women particularly vulnerable to eating disorders. An increasing number of young men, often driven by weight requirements in the sport of their choice, are also vulnerable to these disorders. Though some students have a history of anorexia and bulimia in high school, others turn early in their college career to the starvation diets and compulsive exercising that characterize anorexia, or the binge eating and purging through vomiting, laxatives, diet pills, or fasting of bulimia. The combination of leaving home, coping with the stresses of college life, and the societal obsession with thinness increase the tendency for some women to engage in these destructive, sometimes deadly, behaviors.

College counselors address these issues daily in individual and group counseling. They often act as consultants for worried roommates and groups of friends who may have found themselves embroiled in situations that are beyond their capabilities, seeing to it that troubled students get the professional help they need. And they also reach out to educate both students and staff about the pitfalls of excessive dieting and the physical and psychological implications of eating disorders. Websites abound on subjects relating to diet, nutrition, compulsive overeating and other eating disorders. Although there are many helpful resources, a dangerous phenomenon of pro-eating disorder websites exists proclaiming that these are "lifestyle choices, not illnesses."

In addition to individual counseling, resources on college campuses range from one-session workshops on body image to multi-dimensional approaches. The University of Georgia has developed a comprehensive, ongoing plan to address the problem of eating disorders on campus: distributing relevant literature; presenting films and discussions as well as educational programs that emphasize responsible nutrition and dieting. When a student is identified as having a problem, a multidisciplinary team of professionals, including psychotherapists, a registered dietician, a psychiatrist and a physician's assistant, do an evaluation, draw up a treatment plan and make referrals on or off campus. Boston College has an Eating Awareness Team linking students, faculty and administration to intervene on a variety of fronts to increase awareness and educate the campus community about eating disorders. The team includes students from women's groups, peer educators, faculty and administration from the Counseling and Health Services, Residential Life, Dining Services and the Communication and Psychology Departments.

Though the number of students with diagnosable eating disorders is estimated to be anywhere from 10 to 20 percent, a much larger number of college women have eating concerns. Sharing meals or living with others, young women often are hypervigilant when noting the habits of their peers and may "compete" by eating less or binging and purging. One student described a group of friends, who weren't anorexic or bulimic, but who had all kinds of rules about what they would eat. They even had a rule about keeping only non-caloric items in their refrigerator—just water and diet soda.

As one college physician put it: "Many of the students I see daily are on a slippery slope. They are obsessed with body image, and are comparing themselves with their friends, eating sparingly in their presence, competing for the smallest pants size, and contemplating behaviors that can and do lead to more serious problems."

Drugs and Alcohol: Use, Abuse, and Policies

Bathtub gin in the twenties, rum and cola in the fifties, keg stands in the nineties—alcohol is certainly not new to the college scene. But the extent of concern about alcohol abuse is. Tales of student deaths from alcohol poisoning, a fall from a balcony, or a car accident bring fear to the hearts of even the most sanguine parents of college students.

When students drink excessively or experiment with drugs, inhibitions fade and young men and women have to come to terms with questions of unplanned sex and irresponsible aggression and vandalism. On Monday mornings, deans and residence hall directors routinely review incident reports of the weekend's personal and property damage. The incidents run the gamut from lacerations and chipped teeth to wrecked cars and emergency trips to the hospital for alcohol poisoning. More private consequences, such as having sex and regretting it later or humiliating oneself in front of friends, rarely show up in official data or newspaper headlines, but may produce more permanent scars than the physical damage. Most of the reported cases of acquaintance rape involve substance abuse, and most university administrators agree that on a college campus, it is difficult to address the subjects of substance abuse and sex separately.

The widely publicized Harvard School of Public Health College Alcohol Study led by Dr. Henry Wechsler, conducted every few years between 1993 and 2001, focused on the prevalence and destructive consequences of excess drinking among college students. Wechsler's studies have stimulated a lot of debate about the definition of binge drinking (defined as five or more drinks in a row for men or four or more for women), and even the appropriateness of the term.[9] Almost everyone associated with higher education agrees, however, that binge drinking—or as some call it, high risk drinking—is a problem to be reckoned with. It can no longer be brushed off as a rite of passage, an inevitable stage of late adolescence.

In recognition of increasing concern about this persistent and pervasive problem, the Advisory Council of the National Institute of Alcohol Abuse and Alcoholism (NIAAA) created a special Federal Task Force on College Drinking. This blue ribbon panel of college presidents, scientists and students studied the consequences of alcohol consumption on college campuses and evaluated the effectiveness of interventions currently in use. In the spring of 2002, after three years of extensive analysis of research literature, they issued an unprecedented report titled, "A Call to Action: Changing the Culture of Drinking at U.S. Colleges."[10]

This was the first report to provide comprehensive research-based information about the nature and extent of dangerous drinking on American college and university campuses and its effect on both drinkers and nondrinkers. It offers recommendations to college and university presidents about the effectiveness of strategies currently employed on campuses to reverse the culture of drinking. The report also makes specific recommendations to the research community about the need for additional research in preventing hazardous student drinking.

A 2007 follow-up report, "What Colleges Need to Know Now: An Update on College Drinking Research," suggests that the results of these efforts have been mixed. Although there are promising indicators regarding the use of Web-based alcohol screening and brief intervention techniques, campuses are still grappling with significant alcohol related problems.

The authors of both reports emphasize that in order for a strategy to be effective, it must be multifaceted, and it must target three audiences: individuals, including students at risk; the student population as a whole; and the college and surrounding community. In addition, college policies and prevention programs must be based on scientific evidence. The most recent research emphasizes that "collaboration between colleges and the surrounding communities is key."

NIAAA encourages parents to educate themselves about alcohol abuse and alcohol on campus. In a special section, "What Parents Need to Know About College Drinking," there are facts, resources and suggestions for parents about what to look for when their child is choosing a college, and what to do if they suspect their child is having a problem with alcohol.

Colleges and universities have had to come to grips with the fact that for the majority of their undergraduates it is illegal to drink. Frustrated by the intransigence of alcohol abuse on campus and the difficulty of enforcing a 21-year-old drinking age, a group of about 100 college presidents has formed the Amethyst Initiative to stimulate national debate about lowering the legal drinking age from 21 to 18. From their perspective, the 21-year-old legal drinking age encourages underage students to drink off campus where colleges have little control, and contributes to the serious problems of binge drinking. Other college administrators, however, worry that lowering the legal drinking age to 18 would only exacerbate existing problems. The debate has strong proponents on both sides and illustrates the complexity of this controversial subject.

Although most schools have tightened their alcohol policies in recent years, many students find ways to get around the official rules. They load up on alcohol before they leave for the party or campus-sponsored social event. In the lingo of students, they "pre-game" or "pre-party," downing shots of hard alcohol, quickly drinking as much as they can out of the sight of college officials. When asked, students are likely to say that enforcement of alcohol policies seems arbitrary and the policies themselves are ambiguous and confusing: "I can drink at a party in a friend's room, and that's okay," said a freshman at a small liberal arts college. "I can get totally smashed upstairs and nobody cares. But if I walk downstairs to an official party in the lounge, it's no beer 'cause I'm underage. It doesn't make a hell of a lot of sense."

> We have a big concert on campus every spring and they make a huge deal about checking IDs and not letting us bring in any bottles. We all just booze it up off campus before we go to the arena. Half the people there are totally gone. It's ridiculous.

Though plenty of students never drink, most of them take it for granted that it's just part of what college students do—part of the culture—especially in their first year.[11] One senior recalled :

> Freshman year my friends and I had what we called "sober parties." We'd go out to dinner late, maybe go to a movie or play video games, then go back to the dorm around 1 a.m. We'd just sit in the hall and watch people stumble in from the parties, and we'd just laugh at how drunk they were.

Changing the drinking culture on college campuses is an ongoing challenge, but colleges and universities today are reviewing and revising their alcohol policies, tightening enforcement, and providing educational and support services on a number of related issues. Some of the policies and practices suggested in the NIAAA report that are being tested on numerous campuses include, eliminating keg parties, re-instating Friday classes where they had been eliminated, establishing alcohol–free residence halls, and eliminating alcohol and alcohol advertisements at sports events.

An increasing number of schools have instituted parental notification policies, calling parents about underage drinking and illegal drug use, often at the first violation. Many institutions require new students to take an online alcohol education course, such as AlcoholEdu, before arriving. The University of Minnesota has launched a Web-based program for parents about alcohol use and abuse. It includes information, topics for discussion and advice about talking with students about alcohol. Alcohol-free social events and alternative late night options are also popular strategies on many campuses. Ball State University's "Best Party on Campus" takes place every Saturday night at the Student Center. It's free entertainment and includes everything from bowling to billiards to DJs and dancing—and of course, free food.

On most campuses, there are any number of resources to support students' responsible use of alcohol—Adult Children of Alcoholics groups, AA chapters, and alcohol education programs. Health and counseling centers may employ alcohol specialists who provide interventions, assessments and referrals for students who have demonstrated problems. Alcohol and drug screening services are available on numerous college health websites. Student members of the national organization The BACCHUS Network offer programs to their fellow students about high risk drinking and health and safety issues. Information on alcohol and other drug use and exposure to intervention techniques are part of most RA training sessions and have even become part of the curriculum at some schools. Many schools offer the option of substance-free dorms or halls. Fraternities and sororities are turning to "dry rush" for all official events.

Though alcohol is the drug of choice for most students, and causes harm to more students than all other drugs combined, illegal drugs as well as the increasing misuse of prescription drugs, such as ADHD medications and painkillers, pose a danger to a significant percentage of today's college students.

In spite of a no tolerance drug policy on most campuses, marijuana and other illegal substances are readily available. However, approximately 64 percent of students indicate that they have never used marijuana—a statistic that belies most students' perception of marijuana usage as the norm on college campuses.

Sex: Private Issues and Public Problems

The wide range of behavior that is acceptable to today's college students stands in contrast to the unwritten codes of earlier generations. Perhaps nowhere is this more dramatic than in the area of sex.

The sexual standards on college campuses before the late 1960s were for the most part clear-cut. The double standard operated; nice boys did, nice girls didn't. Women were supposed to ignore sexual longings. For them, the underlying message was, "Sex is dirty; save it for the one you love." There were accepted stages of courtship and dating, and although many deviated from the norm, the public stance of most college students was to follow the rules. And many rules there were.

Women's dorms above the first floor were off limits to the opposite sex. "Man on the floor" meant a father carrying a heavy suitcase to his daughter's room. In men's dorms, women might be allowed to visit, but there were parietal hours and rules. The door to the room was to be left open no less than 6 inches. At midnight, droves of couples hid behind bushes in front of women's dormitories or dashed from parked cars as housemothers flashed porch lights to signal the midnight curfew. And there were notorious rules on many campuses, though hardly anyone can actually remember seeing them written down, that when men and women were together alone in a room, each of them had to keep at least one foot firmly on the floor at all times.

The social upheaval of the late '60s and early '70s, along with the ready availability of birth control pills, brought about a sexual revolution, which exploded on college campuses. The changes were radical: new freedoms, new notions of right and wrong, and the disappearance of rules, both institutional and personal, that had guided the generations before. Experimentation, spontaneity, and openness became the buzzwords of this new era—the celebrated Age of Aquarius. In the '50s, "nice girls didn't." By the '70s, women who "didn't" felt the pressure to join the sexually active mainstream.

The whole subject of sexual practices among young people changed when the threat of AIDS reached the ivory tower in the '80s. College administrators and students debated the format of educational campaigns: Should we dispense condoms? Should we educate about "safe sex" or should we promote abstinence as the only responsible solution to this frightening problem? Ethical, moral, and legal questions relating to university policy brought into the public domain questions usually re-served for private and intimate relationships. And students responded with varying degrees of anxiety. Some heterosexual students tossed AIDS off as a problem for gay students, wearing a cloak of invincibility typical of their age and denying the reality of the threat to the heterosexual community. Others made significant changes in their sexual behavior and reevaluated this whole arena of their lives.

As a result of the widespread media coverage, students became increasingly aware of the dangers of other sexually transmitted diseases, such as chlamydia, herpes and HPV, and these STDs continue to be treated with regularity in college and university health services. Many students and parents are unaware that Hepatitis B is a serious STD that can be prevented by a vaccination. And a vaccine is now available to prevent HPV, the leading cause of cervical cancer. "Safe sex" no longer alludes simply to protection from pregnancy, but protection from disease as well.

Educated about the dangers of STDs, date rape and date-rape drugs, some students are understandably vigilant about sexual encounters. A young woman at a midwestern university remarks, "People are cautious about who they meet and what they do. There's a lot to be nervous about. This isn't the '60s." On the other hand, 18- to 22-year-olds often throw caution to the winds. The 2007 survey by the American College Health Association indicated that approximately 50 percent of sexually active students had not used a condom the last time they had vaginal intercourse.

Today premarital sex is more the rule than the exception, but clearly there is no *one* standard of sexual conduct. Many believe that the sexual activity of their peers is greater than the statistics show. The ACHA report noted that approximately 23 percent of the college students surveyed had never engaged in intercourse, and the numbers were almost equal for women and men.

When asked to describe the sexual practices of today's college students, a young woman on a popular online message board wrote:

> On my college campus, I see long-term relationships, long-distance relationships, dating with an aim toward a future relationship, friends with benefits, random hook-ups (anything from making out to sex), people who want a relationship, people who want to hook-up, and people who don't really care about any of it. It all seems pretty normal to me. Maybe casual sex is more socially acceptable now and/or more talked about, but I'm pretty sure it's always existed. Relationships still happen today, too, but keep in mind that not everybody wants the responsibility, intimacy or commitment of a relationship.

Another wrote:

> I see college turning into a place for friendship and networking (and the occasional hook-up if that's what you prefer) and dating has become what you do after you get settled in "the real world."

An engineering student described his social scene:

> There's no real dating here. It's either random hook-ups or a committed relationship. Mostly we just hang out in groups and party together.

And there are some students who strongly believe in abstinence, based on religion, family or personal values. One lively junior, an African-American campus leader, tells of a family ritual.

> When we all turned thirteen, my dad gave each of us a chastity ring—and I still wear it. It's a rite of passage thing. It has Christ and the year you turned 13 inscribed on the inside. My parents didn't have to say anything when I went to college about premarital sex; it was so engrained in me. Sex is not an issue for me—I'm cool.

In spite of generally available sex education courses, students remain surprisingly ignorant and cavalier about the relative safety and risks of various protective methods. Traditional dating gave way to group partying in the '70s, which may have ended in a pairing up for a sexual encounter, but the '80s was the first decade that the term "hooking up" became a part of the campus vernacular. Today the "hooking-up culture" is pervasive. While many students do "hook up" and alcohol is usually involved, others are in intense "joined-at-the-hip" committed relationships. At the majority of campuses, students define hooking up as a sexual interaction with no commitment. Exactly what they mean by sexual behavior is, however, purposely ambiguous—ranging from kissing to intercourse. Today's technology with instant accessibility encourages spontaneous connections. Whereas traditional dating requires planning, students can now IM or text message a "friend with benefits" or make a "booty call" for a spur-of-the-moment sexual encounter.

Although the hooking-up culture is accepted on most campuses, there still exists a not-so-subtle double standard. Women who hook up a lot, even though there seems to be no definition for what that means, are labeled "sluts." Men who do the same are called "players" or "studs." Those who have studied this phenomenon all seem to agree that the majority of women have ambivalent feelings about the contact. They describe feeling confused, hurt or awkward the morning after.

Most campuses provide workshops and seminars on sexuality . . . from the "When I Say No, I Mean It" variety to popular programs featuring celebrities like media personality Dr. Drew. When peer educators run workshops for their fellow students, frank discussions usually follow—discussions that would not take place in the presence of an administrator or faculty member.

Parents might be surprised to see posters and banners promoting Sex Week, a health education series that's become popular at many schools. On one idyllic-looking campus, a laminated banner hanging between two giant oak trees announced "SEX WEEK: IT'S ORGASMIC," and the campus radio station publicized their show called "Missionary Positions," featuring a rabbi and a priest. Right after Sex Week one young woman called to warn her parents, who were coming to visit,

"Don't freak when you come to my room. My roommate was handing out condoms during Sex Week. She used the leftovers to spell out SAFE SEX on our wall. It's just a decoration!"

■

It is clear that in spite of the timeless image they often project, the colleges and universities our children attend are not the same institutions they were twenty-five or thirty years ago. Reports and studies about today's students and campuses give us insight into the changes that have taken place. They confront the assumptions we tend to make based on our own experience and views, but they are by their very nature limited when it comes to understanding what our children are going through. College students have much to tell us about themselves and their generation. The challenge for parents is to listen to what they have to say; to encourage and advise; and without resorting to stereotyping and labels, to try to understand them within the context of today's college experience.

Part II

A PARENT'S GUIDE: FROM START TO FINISH

4

GREAT EXPECTATIONS

"THANK GOD THE BEST YEARS OF MY LIFE ARE almost over!" a college senior yelled into the phone, leaving her parents stunned at the other end of the line. That all too common phrase, "These are the best years of your life" had been uttered once too often and at just the wrong moment. She clicked off the phone and stormed back to her room in frustration.

This phrase is familiar to most of us. We probably have heard it or said it, often with an added phrase, "so make the best of them" or "enjoy them while you can." As parents, we transmit to our children countless images and expectations of college life. Whether or not we are explicit in our comments, we are likely to herald the college years as a golden time.

THE BIG BUILDUP

Although we are all well aware that no one is continually happy in any period of life, we and our children tend to develop great expectations about the next four years as we get caught in the big buildup that precedes entrance to college. The buildup culminates during the senior year of high school, but for many families, expectations about college begin when our children are infants, that wonderful time when they seem perfect and filled with infinite possibilities.

College admissions officers tell tales of parents of newborns calling for advice about preschools. Horror stories abound about Manhattan 3-year-olds being prepped for preschool interviews and parents even hiring stretch limos so the family can arrive in impressive style.

Applications to private primary and secondary schools are increasing each year. Prep schools throughout the country report that cheating is widespread and that many students seek counseling and medical care for stress-induced symptoms. One psychiatrist has coined the phrase "the valedictorian syndrome" to describe the condition of his steady stream of anxious, highly capable high school patients. It is not unusual for parents of college preparatory students to hire tutors when grades slip from A's to B's, as the jockeying takes place for top class ranks. Hoping to help their child stand out in the applicant pool, some parents hire college consultants or plan high-impact summer experiences, such as a community service project in a third world country or an internship on Capitol Hill. Most parents of high school seniors, however, are already tightening their financial belts and are worried about the next four years of tuition bills.

The stress of it all catches many parents by surprise, as this mother of an only child recounts:

> I never realized how much work, time and energy the process of applying to schools would require. Looking back it was a year filled with anxiety. Not only about my son being accepted at a school that he wanted to attend, but wondering if he would make all the dead-

> lines, meet with each college rep who visited, do well on campus interviews, etc. At the same time, school and his final year of high school soccer were in full swing. His team won Districts and it was an important time for him. So it was like too much was going on at once. My foreign-born husband was happily oblivious to it all. He had studied for a national exam at the end of high school that determined everything about his admission to college. After that exam, the rest was relatively easy for him. He let me handle the parenting of our son throughout this process, which was fine by me. No additional emotional players were needed. It was stressful enough.

A Seattle parent of a college junior dreads having to go through the admissions process again with a second child:

> I detest the current admissions process. It's far too competitive and demoralizing. It's absolute madness! I understand that these are middle-class blues—many around the world can't even get a minimal education—but there simply must be a better way.

Though many families enter the admissions process in a low-key manner, they may find themselves caught up in the whirlwind as classmates of their sons and daughters take prep courses for the SATs, go to private college counselors, and build their resumes with carefully chosen co-curricular activities. Are we letting our children down? we ask ourselves. Will they be left behind if we don't join the race, even if we do find the race distasteful? And so we get caught up in the intensity of the pursuit, and in doing so promote the unspoken expectation that college is the be-all and end-all, the magical answer to all these years of preparation, as well as the ticket to continued success.

We convey to our children that these will be four wonderful years, but that it's also important to keep the motor running, to keep up, to stay on track.

In high schools all over the country and in international schools abroad, there is more interest than ever in the so-called hot colleges, a designation that shifts somewhat from year to year along with *U.S. News and World Report*'s rankings and high-profile athletic championships. The number of applications to selective colleges has increased dramatically in the last two decades, and the whole admissions scene is very different from what it was a generation ago. Some schools that were highly selective when parents were college age no longer are, and others have gone from regional obscurity to national popularity.

In the midst of all this frenzy, however, national statistics about college admissions can serve as a reality check. The popular press inundates us with stories about the rejection rate at the relatively small number of highly selective colleges. But according to the 2007 CIRP Freshman Survey, 80 percent of current first-year students were admitted to their top-choice school.

The most competitive schools claim that they could more than fill their freshman class with valedictorians and students with perfect SATs. The lower the percentage of applicants a college accepts, the more desirable it appears, perpetuating the cycle of anxiety and rejection of highly qualified applicants.

In spite of the increased competition for admission to a small number of selective schools, competition among colleges for the best and the brightest students is fierce. Many colleges compete for academic superstars by offering them attractive, merit-based financial packages. Some schools lure top applicants by promising research stipends, guaranteed internships, reduced tuition, or even employment upon graduation. Some have replaced loans with need-based full-tuition scholarships. High-achieving underrepresented minorities are actively sought after and receive invitations to multicultural recruiting weekends on campus. Scouts and coaches pursue talented athletes with extravagant treatment and lucrative offers.

A record-setting high school track star recalled the excitement and the pressure of the recruitment process:

> I felt a lot of pressure during the season. I knew people were looking at me. But most of the pressure came from myself. It was pretty exciting though. The coaches called me at home and wrote me letters. They'd fly me out to Princeton, Penn. . . . They'd put me up with a campus athlete and show me a good time.

A mother describes the special treatment her athlete daughter got when she decided to apply early decision:

> The hockey coach said, send the application to me. He took the application to Admissions himself. What treatment! He e-mailed her two weeks before the official acceptance letter to tell her she had been accepted. And all because he was excited that she had a left-handed shot. Such are the vagaries of the admissions process!

Most colleges have never been more focused on attracting the optimum freshman class, and students have never been more anxious about being admitted to the school of their choice. The atmosphere is highly charged on both sides.

College admissions staffs play their part in heightening expectations as they vie for position in the competitive scramble to keep their schools alive and well in financially shaky times. Twenty-five years ago a student inquiry to a college admissions office produced simply a catalogue and an application form. Today, slick view books, DVDs and sophisticated webpages with virtual tours and videos are designed to entice prospective freshmen. Even the most selective schools employ large staffs who monitor their admissions techniques and formulate strategies to increase their yield of accepted students. College admissions departments do sophisticated marketing studies, and phrases such as "prospect lists" and "overlap schools" are part of the jargon spoken by admissions officers in every school in the country.

We are in collusion—parents and high schools and college admissions staffs—in setting up unrealistic images of the college experience. We are not doing this intentionally. Most of us believe that a good college experience is important—a once-in-a-lifetime opportunity. The unspoken message that often permeates the frantic years leading up to admission, however, is that college is also a haven of constant intellectual stimulation, wonderful friendships, camaraderie, and young love.

In actuality the college experience *is* rich with stimulation, wondrous new experiences, and relationships, a unique and special time that is never repeated in quite the same way. It is also a time of enormous stresses—a time of confusion, loneliness, and uncertainty; and this too has its own uniqueness, never to be experienced again from the vantage point of a young adult whose perspective is clouded by inexperience, insecurity, and the struggles of discovering a separate identity.

■

Where do parents get their idealized views of college? For some who have never been to college themselves, this may be a dream of what they never had, a fantasy of something special they missed. They form images from television and the movies, pictures of ivy-covered paradises, filled with endless opportunities and a guaranteed passport to a life of professional success. Rarely do the media images include the relentless everyday stresses of the classroom or residence hall living, and many of our frozen images are outdated.

Parents learn of college life from friends. Dinner party conversation is often sprinkled with happy news about their successful offspring: "Alice is premed, getting straight A's and immersed in her tutoring work in the inner city"; "Jack's a finance major and is already being sought after by companies at phenomenal starting salaries." Occasionally we hear the war stories: "My daughter has spent the whole first semester miserable, trying to figure out how to get her roommate's boyfriend to move out. He's been living there since the semester began." But often when we hear about some of the more difficult times, they are mentioned with humor, after the fact, with the sleepless nights of parental worry omitted.

Many parents know about college because they went there. They often look back with rose-colored glasses and selective memories of the good times: the football games, first loves, an inspiring professor, immersion in fascinating studies. They tend to forget the all-nighters with No-Doz and countless cups of coffee, the periods of loneliness, the anxiety before midterms or dates, the boring lectures and tedious assignments, the times when first loves were no more. They also forget that today's college experience is very different from the experience of twenty-five or thirty years ago. Although parents know things have changed, they don't really believe it—or, they don't want to believe it. It is difficult to separate the fantasies, memories, and myths from the reality, and it takes a conscious effort for us and our children to develop realistic expectations about college, especially when we have become so caught up in the race for admission.

THE ADMISSIONS MARATHON

The admissions marathon usually begins in earnest during the spring of junior year in high school with college visits and fairs and the inevitable onslaught of unsolicited view books. A veritable courtship between college and students has begun. SAT scores become a new identification tag, and the question "To coach or not to coach?" is the topic of discussion among parents and counselors alike. Today's students take practice tests online hoping to raise their SAT or ACT scores. Students and parents surf the Web for college home pages and financial aid information. They browse through online course catalogues, take virtual tours of campuses, and check out the social life on campus calendars. They read uncensored student blogs on the college admissions website. They go on message boards and chat rooms to "talk" to current students and get the personal, frank views of "insiders." Parents, too, seek out other parents on sites such as College Confidential or College Parents of America. The sheer quantity of opinions and advice can quickly lead to information overload—confusion rather than clarity.

Most bookstores have a whole section devoted to college admissions. The shelves are lined, not only with SAT and ACT preparation books and college guides, but also with dozens of handbooks of the "how-to-get-in" genre. The diversity of today's campus is reflected in books targeted to a range of special populations, such as: women, athletes, gays and lesbians, and for students who are Jewish, Latino, disabled, first generation to go to college, international, or searching for a school that emphasizes community service. Beyond the comprehensive directories filled with statistics, most students and parents also turn to a few of the college guides written by students or educators that offer a more colorful and subjective view.

Many parents and high school juniors start the college exploration process with a sense of excitement. It is a time of possibilities and dreams and an incredible number of options. Parents may enjoy looking at the college view books and websites more than the students do. They often find themselves reminiscing about their own college years, or simply about the days when they were 18. Although students are quick to acknowledge their desire to get out of high school, many of them seem overwhelmed by the choices now facing them. After showing initial enthusiasm about college materials, they may start to withdraw from the whole process.

Conflict about deadlines, plans for college visits, and filling out applications seems to be de rigueur between seniors in high school and their parents. Most tend to look back on the year with a sense of relief after it is over. Tension about whose decision this really is lies behind much of the conflict. Many parents believe that they know what's best for their children, and that it's their responsibility to select the schools to which their child will apply. Other parents bend over backwards not to interfere and to stay totally uninvolved. Most parents try for a middle course, sometimes rushing erratically from one extreme to the other.

Parents can often be helpful by providing some structure to this emotionally laden and complex process. They can help students decide what's important to them and develop a list of priorities that might include: location, level of competition, curriculum, social climate, availability of financial aid, diversity of student body, and support for special needs and interests. Of course, sometimes students come up with criteria of their own, as this parent from Wyoming recounts:

> Kyle's idea of working on college applications was to make 45 piles in alphabetical order that sat on the floor of our computer room. A friend suggested he try the career room at the high school, where he found software that allowed him to enter things like area of study, part of the country, size, sports, special features. When he brought the computer printouts home, I noticed that he had requested "mountain biking" as a special feature. "What the ______ is this?" I asked.

"Well, I had to narrow it down somehow, and this really worked. I found some great schools." Guess what? This kid made a great choice, has had a terrific education and plans to graduate in four years!

Helping a student who is living at home is likely to be quite different from providing support to a child who is away at boarding school. A mother who had both experiences notes:

> With Mason I had to be the time-keeper and gate-keeper and calendar-keeper. Boarding school did all of that for Clint—my second child. They kept him on deadline, reviewed his essays, and told him what schools were realistic for him. There wasn't nearly as much emotional angst. Clint asked for our involvement when he wanted it. Mason had no choice. We were right there all the time. A lot of the time it was too much for him—and for us too.

Some students manage the whole process very well with little or no intervention from their parents:

> Both my parents were born and educated in the Philippines. They knew nothing about the American college application process. They left it up to me. I got all the stuff I needed ready to go. It was just me in the basement.

Other students need some help to manage the logistics. One parent describes the approach she took to get her daughter started:

> Tiffany's very social and easily distracted. She got excited with each new school, but soon the novelty

> wore off and what was left was a pile of papers and view books on her bedroom floor. One night, we sat down with her and talked about size, location and what her academic criteria were. We got rid of the extraneous stuff and helped her set up a filing system in a big box. She made fun of us, but after that she began to get things more in hand.

In helping his son to narrow down his choices, an African-American father stressed:

> We spent a lot of time researching how welcoming and supportive the school was to people of color, both in the classroom and out. We spoke to students and their families; we looked at programs and visited campuses. We asked a lot of questions.

There is, however, a difference between being helpful and stepping over the line. An admissions director at a highly selective university explains:

> I've had a bunch of parents call this year and pretend to be the student. It is always obvious to me. Forty-five-year-old voices just don't sound like eighteen-year-old voices. I just say to them—"Oh you must mean that you are helping your son." . . . Then I give them the information they want. It's OK with me if parents call sometimes in the middle of the day while their kids are in school if it's just to conduct some routine business. I do worry about these students though. If students don't engage in the application process, they aren't likely to engage in the transition process. It's not a good sign if the student abdicates all responsibility to the parents. It's not a good way to start out.

At some time during the course of the year almost all families find themselves talking about college admissions more than any of them find palatable. A freshman in high school complains:

> We spent this whole year talking about college, because my brother was applying. I got so sick of it I felt like screaming almost every night. I don't think my brother liked it any more than I did, but my parents never seemed to want to talk about anything else. No one seemed bothered by my problems. I guess they seemed unimportant by comparison. It really bugged me.

Most college-bound students are inundated with college literature. National Merit Semi-Finalists may get as many as three or four hundred pieces of mail. Underrepresented minority students with high SATs, musicians, and athletes may receive even more. Students often misconstrue these marketing efforts as a signal that the school wants them and has picked them out of the crowd.

Overwhelming is a word used repeatedly by parents and students when they describe the marketing blitz and the whole college admissions process. There is, first of all, the sheer quantity of the choices. And there is the intensity of the rhetoric. After a while one of the few things that most students and parents agree on is that all of the view books sound as though they were written by the same person. "Have you ever found a school that doesn't claim to have an outstanding and accessible faculty, a diverse student body, and a commitment to excellence?" asked a bemused high school senior.

Choosing a college is the biggest decision the majority of 17- and 18-year-old applicants have ever had to make. And because most of them still think in terms of absolutes, they are likely to feel very anxious about making the right choice. A lot of students respond to this anxiety by procrastinating every step of the way. They may wait until the last minute before they narrow down their list to a manageable number of schools. Their overriding fear is that the school they cross off may be "the perfect one." They wait as long as possible before writing their essays, believing somehow that the right essay may be just the key that will make the difference between admission and rejection. It is not unusual for these students to carry their procrastination right down to the wire, exemplified by the enormous number of applications that arrive at admissions offices all over the country on deadline day.

A student whose parents worried about her procrastination recalls:

> For me it's hard enough to decide what clothes to put on in the morning. It took me forever to decide where I wanted to go to college. My mom was getting quite concerned as each month passed and deadlines approached. In all reality, you think about your college choice 24/7. It may not appear that way on the outside, but it's always internal, always in your head, rolling around.

And a Loyola freshman recalls:

> I was going to apply to Pepperdine and they had six essays, and I just didn't feel like doing it, so I didn't apply. And the U. of Washington—ten pages and filling in bubbles and I thought this is going to go on and on forever. I did two online applications and the rest on paper. I thought—I am doing my college applications. I should be doing this on paper. It

seemed more formal. When I did it online, I would think—Oh my gosh, I just did that online and sent it in. It's done now. It was kind of scary!

It is important for parents to realize that young people have diverse ways of dealing with their ambivalence about college applications. They also have different styles of making decisions. Some students want as much help as possible from their parents and actually would prefer it if their parents assumed all the responsibility for them. Others want no help whatsoever; for them it may seem too threatening to take any kind of advice from someone they still see as an authority figure without feeling as though they have to follow what they have been told. Students need their parents to respect their individual styles, and to help them stretch as they assume increasing responsibility for their own decisions. This is a delicate balance that is rarely achieved without turmoil on both sides, as parents and their children negotiate this aspect of separation.

Many students have a clear sense of what kind of college they want to attend. They make an informed choice, apply early decision and if they are accepted, there is a familial sigh of relief: "I knew I wanted to go to Kenyon after I spent a weekend there last fall," said a freshman. "I sat in on three classes and slept in the dorm. I think I got a good feel for the place in three days. I was sure it was for me, and I still am."

Other students make their choice early, based on little knowledge about themselves or the college. They avoid information about other schools and refuse to consider alternative choices. If they visit the school, they look only for confirmation of the decision they have already made. The negative aspects of the school are avoided or unnoticed. They, too, apply early decision in an attempt to put the whole issue out of their minds. This method of coping probably causes less tension in the family than the more common one of procrastination, but it can lead to a poor match. Both responses may be methods of coping with the anxiety inherent in the belief that there is a perfect answer rather than a number of options for each student.

In recent years, many colleges have been accepting a higher percentage of their class early decision, provoking uneasy questions from anxious applicants: If almost half the class has already been accepted early decision, will it be impossible for me to get in later? Am I more likely to get in if I apply early? Will applying early decision affect my chances for a good financial aid package?

It's not easy to answer these questions, but almost any college admissions officer would say that early decision students have an advantage. And statistics confirm that the percentage of early decision applicants who are accepted is higher than the percentage of those who apply in the regular pool. Even if early decision applicants are deferred, their interest is noted, and this may tip the balance in their favor when decisions are made in the spring. Admissions counselors caution, however, that only students who are certain about their choice should use this option. Once they are accepted, they have made a binding commitment, unless the limited financial aid package makes it impossible for them to attend. Early decision works only for those who are not concerned about getting the highest financial offer possible, since the opportunity to compare and contrast financial aid packages is lost.

The issue of early decision has received high-profile attention in the media in recent years. Although it can be beneficial to many students, there is no doubt that early decision favors the colleges. An increasing number of schools such as the University of North Carolina, Harvard and Beloit have eliminated the early decision option, breaking with this controversial but popular trend.

The college admissions process forces students to assess themselves, to face their limitations and to define their values. As they go through the ordeal of writing essays and preparing for interviews, they come face-to-face with basic questions about their emerging identity. And for many, competition with classmates, even with dear friends, becomes a reality to be reckoned with.

A high school senior wrote the following as part of her application for admission to Dartmouth:

> Senior year has definitely been a time of self-reflection and appraisal. When I went to my first interview, I was petrified. I could think of no reason why anyone would care to talk for a half-hour about me and my interests. I am basically a shy person, opposed to being phony or fake, so I was shocked to find myself talking to a stranger about such a variety of topics. I became flushed and animated. It was almost as if I were in a play, only I wasn't acting and there was no script. The whole time I had this terrible feeling that I was there to be judged, and heaven help me if I was not adequate.
>
> I think this is what has worried most of my classmates this year. We have had to look at ourselves and think, "Am I good enough? Am I an acceptable candidate?" That fear has changed some of us. People who have always been self-assured and poised refused to reveal their SAT scores, and blushed at the memory of their results. Everyone has become excessively competitive, and our school, though an excellent one, does not promote cutthroat competition. When preliminary class ranks came out, they were the topic of conversation for days. I criticized a friend who was complaining because she was number seven and not

> in the top five. However, I then found myself plotting murder to raise my class rank from number eleven to ten. I realized I was even gossiping over who deserved their class rank, and who didn't. This from a person who had always worked for her own satisfaction and pride, not to outdo anyone else!
>
> The feeling of inadequacy and competition came to a head when I actually began to write my application. Academically, I have never felt inferior to anyone. Yet, when I looked at the questions and tried to answer them so they would reveal an appealing picture of me to the reader, they were not appealing, they were appalling! First I was afraid of being conceited; then I worried I was not being revealing enough; then I was too sappy; then, affected. On paper, I could not truly show who I was.

As students struggle with who they are, a conflict may arise between their parents' hopes and dreams for them and their own emerging sense of themselves. Many parents notice that their children withdraw during the months when college decisions are being considered. Closed doors, blaring music, and silent shrugs are familiar teenage strategies for shutting parents out. Communicative young people who formerly have been very close to their parents may retreat for a while. Conversations turn into parental interrogations or nagging sessions, equally unpleasant to parent and offspring alike.

On top of this, *senioritis* sets in. Students may stop doing their work, may even stop going to class. Formerly highly energetic and motivated students lose their focus. High school teachers and administrators complain about this phenomenon, but parents have to live with it.

A Philadelphia woman whose daughter recently completed her freshman year at Northwestern recalled:

> My daughter spent her senior year separating and rebelling. It was as though she had to make things really miserable here, so she could eventually leave. We fought a lot, and there were a lot of frozen silences. It escalated as the year went on. Nicole was always the kind of kid who spoke her mind, but this was a whole new ball game. She refused to go to family functions. She spent more and more time in her room with the door closed. She even withdrew somewhat from her high school friends, and talked on the phone a lot to friends from out of town whom she had met at a college summer school.
>
> One thing that helped me to figure out what was going on with Nicole was that there were still times, usually at 12:30 a.m., when she was ready to talk. And when that happens you have to be ready to drop everything and talk. Those precious conversations can help to distinguish the kid who is in trouble from the one who isn't.

The college admissions process can be particularly difficult for students who are not academically successful, but are surrounded by friends who are. And even the most supportive of parents are likely to have unsettling feelings of their own, as this mother of a high school senior describes:

> The other night I ran into one of those friends you make when your children are young and in nursery school together, when SAT and ACT scores are distant concerns. I asked her how her daughter, Becky, was doing. It was a frivolous question, one made to be social. She said Becky was in the midst of applications to Stanford, Princeton, and schools of that ilk. I

> knew the answer to my question before I asked it. While it was fairly clear that her child would be able to get into her college of choice, we were holding our breath to see if Elisa would just get out of high school.
>
> So as my friend asked where Elisa was applying, I could hear the concern in her voice . . . or at least I imagine I heard concern when I mentioned a school that few have heard of. I felt a degree of embarrassment, a bit of bitterness, and a drop of jealousy . . . hard to admit . . . but true.

It's also a challenge to help a child with special needs find a school where he or she will thrive. One parent of a child with a learning disability advises:

> We did a lot of research to find which colleges had the best services. They all say they have them because they must by law, but some are very good and some are terrible. You need to go to the department on campus and speak to the professionals. Ask a lot of questions. Do they offer tutors? Who are the tutors? What kind of training do the tutors have? What special arrangements can be made? You have to advocate for your kid. . .and teach your kid to advocate for himself.

Many college students remember their senior year in high school as a time of tremendous ambivalence. They want to be told what to do—to be given clear-cut advice about the choices facing them—and they also desperately want to break away, to be independent. They are worried about letting down the people who believe in them. And through it all they are struggling with who they are and how they will manage to separate from home and friends. A sophomore at Johns Hopkins recalls the pain of her senior year in high school:

> The application process was a real self-analysis for me. Who is Lauren Gibbons? What are her interests? Why is she applying here and not there? Why is she getting in here and rejected there? And on and on. What are your strengths? What are your weaknesses? What word best describes you? It was an unpleasant process for me.
>
> From October to March of my senior year we were all consumed with the college application process. There was lots of pressure. I had lots of self-pity. I remember thinking I don't do *this* well; I don't do *that* well. I disappoint my parents in *this* respect; my friends in *that* respect; myself in *another* respect. It was a time of very low self-esteem. I was very insecure about academics and SATs and all that.
>
> The worst part was those few months when everyone in the world was asking: where are you going to college next year? I remember thinking over and over, what if I just said I'm not going to college? Then I would think, what would I do if I didn't go to college? What could I do? What would I be good at doing? Nothing. What do I want to do? Nothing, nothing, nothing! I felt really lost. I had no idea what I would study in college. I had no idea what I would really do in college. I began to worry, what would I do when I started missing Mom and Dad? What happens when my dog dies? What's going to happen to my friends from high school? Wait a minute, do I have any friends from high school? I started a total evaluation process of the people I'd been hanging out with for the past twelve years. Through the whole

> thing, I didn't talk to anybody about what I was going through. I just couldn't. I guess it must have been hard on my parents too.

Parental ambivalence about sending a child off to college, particularly a first-born or only child, is common. The sense that family life will never be the same again, a sense of loss, even envy—all are likely to be mixed with the anticipated satisfaction of launching one's offspring. For many parents in the midst of all the hustle and bustle of daily life, this is a period of reflection—of poignant memories about times past. For many there is a coming to terms with one's own limitations, while exploring the ever-expanding horizons of the next generation. A father wrote the following description of his recent tour of colleges with his 17-year-old son:

> As we worked our way through several campuses in New England, the visits started to fall into a routine. Always starting with registration at the subdued admissions office, we gathered up a multitude of materials, took the student-guided tour of the campus, and attempted to observe and catalogue our thoughts. Ever mindful of the role of overbearing parent, I tried valiantly to hold back on questions, deferring to Andrew, but each time finding it impossible not to keep probing, attempting to unlock the subtle differences among the schools.
>
> What was Andrew thinking about the people and places we were seeing? Despite my urging him beforehand to actively probe his hosts, he was virtually silent on the student-led tours. However, he reassured me, "Don't worry, Dad, I'm taking it all in." And I'm sure he was, just as he always had. Rehashing at the end of each day we seemed to be very much in

sync in our views of what we had observed. While I sat happily conversing with this suddenly grown person in the same Cambridge restaurant and Maine lobster shack where I had carried him in my arms fifteen years earlier, my mind shuttled back and forth across time.

As the week wore on, it was clear that my excited anticipation of the trip was being realized. The sheer freedom of moving about a favorite part of the country, the energy of college campuses, and the increasingly precious time alone with my 17-year-old son, exhilarated me. How idyllic it all looked, too, even in the bareness of late winter, with the feel of old brick, patterns of walkways crisscrossing the campus, venerable old buildings with venerable names, and overburdened bulletin boards.

For a middle-aged adult, time spent on a college campus can bring some pangs of jealousy. In a period of life when career, family, and financial demands sometimes seem overwhelming, the prospect of spending four years in a peaceful environment, with almost total devotion to matters of intellect and one's own development, seems to be an incredible luxury.

The mother of a Williams College student explained that she felt jealous when she took her daughter to the campus for the first time. She found that she couldn't help making comparisons between her daughter's opportunities and her own:

> My sense of envy surprised me. There is a certain irony to children budding into beautiful young women, when most of us are becoming more aware of aging. I've spent the last twelve years juggling career and family, and it's just beginning to get easier. When I took Carla to Williams for her interview, I kept

> thinking how wonderful it would be to be in that kind environment with so much support and only oneself to take care of. I also started to anticipate the loss of Carla. I knew I was going to miss her, and I kept mulling over the question—where has the time gone?

In this era of single parenthood and blended families, separation and family dynamics have become increasingly complicated. For single parents the anticipated departure of a child may be particularly difficult, especially when that child is a treasured companion. Students from single-parent families often worry about leaving their mother or father alone. Children of divorced or widowed parents have had to deal with separation at an earlier age, and this leave-taking may echo the painful feelings of earlier loss.

The financial pressure of supporting a child through college is an issue for almost all families. Parents often find themselves sending a double message to their children. On the one hand they are saying that education is invaluable, and they'll pay a premium for the best. On the other, they may imply that it is costing them a fortune, and the child had better take advantage of it. Taking advantage of it means different things to different families. For some, the message is clear: get good grades and go premed. For others, the implication is simply that it is OK to pay all that money for a so-called name school, but not for a lesser known private institution with a high tuition rate.

One Director of Admissions at a southern university emphasizes that today's parents are concerned about cost. They see themselves as consumers. They are asking as they look at schools: Am I going to get my money's worth?

> If families are from a state that has a strong public system such as Virginia, Michigan, or California, they

> are going to look very carefully at private college price tags. Parents not only want to know about the quality of the university, they want to know how strong a specific program is. They ask questions about rankings and about the success of graduates.
>
> More students today have parents who have been to college themselves. They have a lot of hopes and dreams for their children. They are hoping the student will be happy, the roommate will be compatible, the courses will be stimulating, and the grades will be good. If at the end of the semester the student's grades come home and they are barely a two point, and the tuition bill arrives the next week, those parental hopes and dreams may turn into expectations—which will in turn feel like demands to the student. It is not unusual for money to be a source of conflict between parents and their children during the admissions process and throughout the college years.

The popularity of books and articles about "great schools at great prices" or "best values in college education" is a telling indicator of the role that money plays in college selection. There is a broad spectrum of tuition costs in both public and private colleges and universities. A handful of colleges, such as Berea, Cooper Union, and Curtis Institute of Music are tuition free for all who are admitted. For families concerned about the high pricetags of private colleges, there are many state universities that have a small honors college within the larger institution that may be just the right answer to a family's financial dilemma. For example, the University of Montana's Davidson Honors College or Barrett, the Honors College at Arizona State University, offer many of the advantages of a small private college at a potentially more affordable cost. Indiana University's LAMP program provides a unique opportunity for students to combine a high quality liberal arts education with management skills and focused career development opportunities.

Though the financial aid literature is confusing, filled as it is with its own arcane language and acronyms, it is well worth taking the time to become informed about it. Some parents narrow their child's options unnecessarily by eliminating all high-priced institutions from the outset. It is important to remember that it's not so much the college price tag as how much the parents will have to pay. There is a wide range of financial aid options, including combinations of grants, scholarships, loans, and work-study positions. Though there are no guarantees that aid will be forthcoming, many colleges and universities are increasingly seeking ways to expand access and reduce loan obligations across the economic spectrum.

The number of websites for financial aid can be daunting. A good "first stop" is the award-winning, comprehensive FinAid (www.finaid.org). It includes information, advice, links to reliable resources, and a calculator parents can use to show them what they might be expected to pay. Every college has a financial aid office that can help parents and students navigate this overload of information. The financial aid information pages at some college websites are a useful resource. In addition, parents and students turn to books, to the federal government's financial aid hot line, and to financial consultants to find the best possible package. College counselors warn parents to avoid organizations that offer scholarship information for a fee; this information is usually readily available through any of the above resources.

Discussion about finances and financial aid packages often provides the first occasion for parents to share such adult family matters with their children. Honest conversations about what the family can afford, and what the plans and expectations are, can prevent tension and resentment on both sides later. Parents need to be clear about their guidelines. They should tell a child from the outset the extent of the financial aid package they will need in order for him or her to attend a particular school.

"Most parents find the financial aid forms intimidating," says Linda Jacobs, independent college counselor and former Director of College Counseling at the Northwest School in Seattle. "This is a time to be honest, not a time for great pride. Filling out the financial aid forms is the one place where the responsibility belongs to the parents, not the student."

Finances are often a factor in determining how far away students will go or whether they will go away at all. In addition, family tradition and unfamiliarity with other parts of the country, concerns about travel and safety in our post-September 11th world, as well as the psychological impact of distance, all play a part in setting geographical boundaries. A sophomore at Harvard who grew up in the Bronx, said laughingly, "My mother told me I could go as far as the West Coast to school—only to her the West Coast meant Philadelphia."

And a senior at Carleton stated that her parents, both college professors, were emphatic about the locale that they thought was appropriate for her:

> My mother wanted me in the Midwest. She wouldn't let me apply to Stanford. She talked as though California was going to fall off the continent and slip into the ocean. Her objections had nothing to do with distance, but according to my mother, there are weirdos in California, and she didn't want me there in my formative years. I think she was afraid I'd wander off into a cult.

The headmistress of a private school in New Orleans explained that parents of her students feel very tied to the place where they live. For the most part they want their children to be within a day's drive of home:

This has a lot to do with Southern tradition and a sense of place. It's also about identity and the comfort that comes from being a family everybody knows. Decisions about college are very much influenced by these family values. Sometimes the students' real needs get lost.

ACCEPTANCE AND REJECTION

After all the applications are finally in, there is usually a respite from the oppressively frequent discussions about college. But most students and their parents are still thinking about college admission even if they have stopped talking about it. Though applicants to many colleges can now access acceptance or rejection information online or by telephone, notification via mail is still common. As notification dates approach, it is the rare family that isn't checking the computer or mailbox at the first opportunity.

When the acceptances and rejections start coming in, students and sometimes parents, too, rush home to see if the letter is fat or thin. When the acceptances to first-choice schools arrive, the dream seems to be in hand. All those years of preparation, the mountains of college literature, the essays and recommendations culminate—or so it may seem at the time—in one appropriately fat letter that starts with the word, *Congratulations*. Surely this is a time to celebrate with our children. But in their enthusiasm, parents can unwittingly convey the message that acceptance to Yale is the essence of their child's value. In their relief and excitement, they may also perpetuate the expectation of four years of bliss and happiness in New Haven. We are not doing our children any favor if we convey the message that acceptance by a particular college means they've "got it made"—or that a letter of admission is a ticket to success.

Inevitably, many students face rejection during the spring of their senior year. And for a lot of them, this is the first major rejection of their lives. The word slips through high school corridors instantaneously about who was accepted and rejected where. Unseen scores are tabulated, and friendships sometimes buckle under the strain. Parents may find themselves standing by, wishing they could comfort their inconsolable child. Sometimes, however, parents feel more devastated by the rejection than their children do.

Both parent and child may suffer a perceived loss of status and feel embarrassed to tell family and friends. Parents as well as students talk about feeling inadequate at this time. Admissions officers talk candidly about being deluged by phone calls from parents of rejected applicants, demanding an explanation or pleading for reconsideration. One admissions director recalls his first year in admissions work at Princeton. As rookie of the staff, he was assigned the task of signing thousands of rejection letters. After they were mailed, his phone rang constantly for three weeks:

> Congressmen called. Alumni called. Mothers, fathers, counselors called—crying, yelling, venting their anger on me. It was a horrible experience, especially since so many of the students we turned down were highly capable.

The way a student and his or her parents handle rejection is likely to have a major influence on the student's eventual college experience. Parents can play an important role at this time by empathizing with their child and then trying to be encouraging about the remaining options. If the parent has become overly invested in the first-choice college, this will not be an easy task. Too often students report that their parents were terribly disappointed about their rejection and sent them off begrudgingly to choice number two or three.

Unfortunately, this kind of parental disapproval and shortsightedness colors students' attitudes toward the school right from the beginning. They often seem depressed and unmotivated from the time they arrive on campus. It may take a lot of work on their part and assistance from deans and counselors to help them separate their personal desires and aspirations from those of their parents, or to relinquish their own lost dreams and embrace current reality. Only then are they likely to make a commitment to their college and their success within it. A parent who helps a child to enlarge his or her perspective and to understand that there is no such thing as a perfect college is bestowing a valuable graduation gift.

Edward B. Fiske, former Education Editor of the *New York Times* and author of *The Fiske Guide to Colleges*, urges parents and prospective students not to limit their horizons to the few dozen most competitive schools:

> The fact that you don't have a designer label on your diploma doesn't matter. There are hundreds of good schools. We have in this country a system of higher education that is the envy of the world. There aren't just ten places that are excellent. There are probably about three-hundred. It's important to keep some perspective.

Once a student has been accepted by at least one college and is actively considering options, the pain of rejection often fades into the background. Some high school students have instituted a ritual of rejection parties, requiring that guests bring at least one rejection letter to gain entrance to the celebration. Paradoxically, of course, the rare student who received no rejections will finally be rejected—from the party. The students build a bonfire and burn the rejection letters along with their collection of college view books, a mock exorcism of the whole stressful year.

MAKING THE CHOICE

For many students the stress continues throughout April, as they struggle with the decision about which of their acceptances to choose. This is a time of weighing definite offers against indefinite waiting list status. Is it worth staying on the wait list, or is it better to just get the whole thing over with? What about acceptance as a January student—an offer of admission that doesn't go into effect until the spring semester? What about a gap year?

Questions about financial aid and comparative expenses add to the confusion. A Princeton admissions counselor suggests:

> At this point the best thing a parent can do is step back and help the child look at the pros and cons of each school. The key is to ask meaningful questions rather than give answers.

The father of a student who was trying to decide between the University of Pennsylvania and Dartmouth asked his son to make the proverbial list of the pros and cons for each school, then to make his decision and keep it to himself for two weeks. His son made the list and struggled with it for a long time. And after he finally made his decision, he didn't tell a soul. He lived with his choice for two weeks and then announced that he had picked Penn. His sense of assurance surprised even his father, who had suggested the process in the first place. The young man explained that although he still saw lots of pros and cons for both schools, when it came right down to it, "Penn just felt right."

Part of the decision is based on what a particular school's image means to the prospective student. What will it mean if I become an Aggie? Will I be a different person if I go to a small rural college or a big city university? What kind of person do I want to become? Is it foolish to turn down a prestigious school for one that I think I'd feel more comfortable at? Is it worth taking out loans to go to Vanderbilt when I can go to the University of Tennessee and graduate debt-free? Will I be able to get into the courses I need so I can graduate in four years?

For most families, financing a college education includes a combination of scholarship money, parental contributions, work study and student loans. Financial aid offers are not always set in stone, and students have nothing to lose by appealing what seems to be an inadequate offer. Parents and students may need to do this together. One university dean of admissions notes:

> We appreciate applicants who don't merely ask us to match the funds another school has offered. It helps if the parents explain their financial situation, while the student tells us why they would prefer to come here. The most compelling cases are the ones in which students describe what they hope to do—what they want to study or be involved in—and demonstrate their enthusiasm for our school.

And a director of financial aid adds:

> The financial aid form is a template . . . one size fits all. People in my office actually want the family to call if the size of the award will make it impossible for the student to attend. It's our job to create an award that looks at the whole family picture. Perhaps one of the parents has lost a job; they may be immigrants

> who have financial responsibilities to family members overseas; there may be unexpected medical expenses. A lot of families feel that the financial aid office is trying to keep them out of the university. In reality we are trying to help them come.

At a time when their personal identity is fluid and stereotypes about colleges abound, students often have a very difficult time making that final decision. The fear of closing off options can be paralyzing. Students may feel as though their whole future is at stake. It is not unusual for the decision to be made and remade several times before it is final, as this college freshman describes:

> When I first started thinking about college I wanted to go to Carleton or Macalester. Later it became Bryn Mawr or Brown. After I was accepted at both, it was an arduous decision. It was really an awful time. I had lots of wonderful reasons I wanted to go to Bryn Mawr, and I had lots of wonderful reasons I wanted to go to Brown, but the reasons were the opposite. Brown has a lot of freedom and opportunities. I kept thinking Brown is like the real world that has both men and women. But Brown doesn't offer particular encouragement to women. Even if I wouldn't be as encouraged there, I told myself that's what it's like in real life. So it's good to be in a real world environment. But the other part of me wanted to be at Bryn Mawr where I could develop, where I thought there would be more support for me as a woman.
>
> One day I decided—I'm going to Bryn Mawr. I told everyone I saw all day—my teachers, people who wrote my recommendations, my friends. I think I did

> that so I could hear it out loud. I wrote it all over my notebook. It made it more real. But the next day I changed my mind, and I had to tell everyone I'd changed.
>
> For the first few months I was at Brown, I couldn't even talk about Bryn Mawr. All I could think of was all the good reasons to go there and I hadn't, and I wasn't very happy at Brown. But now I'm used to being at Brown, and I see that it's not perfect. Now I like it. Part of it is I'm settled in and have gotten used to it and see its good parts. Part of it is I've changed my expectations.

Lori Tenser, Dean of First Year Students at Wellesley College, emphasizes that finding the right fit is at the heart of the admissions decision—and what seems like a perfect fit for one student may feel just the opposite for another:

> A place that has a firm first year curriculum, for instance, may feel really important and be great for some students who like structure and think having that path will help them crystallize their interests. For other students that structure might feel really restrictive. First year residence halls might feel great for some students, others might prefer a hall with students from all classes. Finding out how well the school can meet the individual student's most pressing needs—whether they be financial, or support for health or learning issues or other disabilities—is an essential part of the equation.

A springtime campus visit with time to sit in on classes, stay in the residence hall, and talk to current students often tips the balance, and the decision suddenly becomes clear. If students can't travel to the school, they may be able to attend a college-sponsored gathering of accepted students in their own city. Sometimes, an online chat between accepted and current students provides the personal touch that can't be found in traditional admissions literature. These dialogues are a chance to address unanswered questions: Is it easy to get into the classes you want? What do most kids do on weekends? Where do Korean students hang out? What's the party scene really like? How's the food for vegans? How hard is it to get internships? Can freshmen get into any small classes?

This is a time for students with particular talents to ask questions and compare the opportunities each school has to offer them: What chance does a competent violinist who is not a music major have to play in the college orchestra? How much competition is there to get a beat on the campus paper? What is the athletic profile of the players already on the football team, and what chance will I have to play? What do I have to do to keep an athletic scholarship from year to year?

Rarely does the student make the college choice in a vacuum. A call from a coach, a faculty member or an upper-class student can turn the tide. The pressure to go to a certain school comes from parents, peers and the secondary school itself. Students often buy the image of a college and the lure of the success it will supposedly bestow on them. Sometimes the most prestigious school or the toughest one to get in to isn't the best choice for a particular student.

Stephen Spahn, Headmaster of the Dwight School in New York, cites an example:

> One of my students who had been accepted at several Ivy League schools really wants a career in theatre. I think she'd be best off at NYU, but it's hard for her to turn down the more prestigious offers.

Spahn sees the role of parents as path-clearers, who know their children and can honestly assess their strengths and talents as well as their weaknesses.

> In choosing a college, parents should help their kids look at appropriate options, at paths that will use their assets. Then once the decision is made, they should give as much support and expression of confidence as they can muster.
>
> And parents should put the college decision into proper perspective. Choosing a college is just one step in a process that begins when children are small. Parents start acting as path-clearers for their kids when they encourage them to play soccer, or take violin lessons, or volunteer in a hospital. Each choice is another step along a particular path, each commitment a limiting of alternative choices, so to speak.

For some students the decision brings them face-to-face with the question of who they are separate from their parents. Family traditions and cultural values may seem to be on the line. Families that have always sent their children off to the University of Virginia may find it hard to understand when their child rejects the school they had always assumed was the best and chooses Vanderbilt instead.

A Washington University African-American sophomore rejected her parents' preference for her to attend an historically black college. Her father, an attorney and an alumnus of Morehouse, felt strongly that the black college experience would be an important phase of the education he wanted for his daughter. She found it difficult to make a choice that was in direct conflict with her father's firmly held belief:

> I went to a private school where we started talking about college in eighth grade. By the time I was a senior I was

> sick of the topic. I applied to five schools. Only one of them was a black college, and the only reason I applied there was because my Dad wanted me to. I was accepted by three of the five, including Spelman. My Dad really pushed Spelman; it's the sister school to Morehouse. For a while I just couldn't talk to my Dad at all. It was so confusing. If I decided to go to Spelman, I didn't know if I'd be going for him or for me. My Dad and I are very close. We have that special father-daughter relationship; I'm his baby and all that. It was so hard for me to decide what to do. I finally decided to come here, and now I'm glad I did. I know my Dad was real disappointed though. He still holds out hope for my sister and Spelman. I respect him and want him to respect me.

A young woman who did choose to go to Spelman did so because she had grown up in an almost exclusively white suburban community. Although her parents had gone to historically black colleges, she made her decision for reasons of her own. She had had a generally positive experience in high school, but she had always felt like the "odd one out."

> I wanted to be with people of a like mind . . . people who would look like me. I liked that I didn't have to worry about trying to make a decision about who to hang out with based on race. Freshman year, there was an adjustment, having grown up in such a different world, but I am very glad I made the choice and would do it again.

Students want their parents' respect for the choice they have made. Though they don't always tell their parents directly, they want to know that their parents support them. Even students who choose the college that was also their parents' first choice want to know that their parents see the choice as the student's own, not as an extension of the family or its traditions.

Increasingly, colleges are offering a limited number of students the possibility of January admissions. One student described a process that started with disappointment and ended with resolve and even enthusiasm.

> I was very upset for about a week. I was afraid I would be left behind by my peers. But ultimately I asked myself, do I want to spend three and a half years at my dream school or go somewhere just so I can start now? I decided it was an opportunity to do something challenging and went and studied art history and photography in Florence in the fall.

In weighing the pros and cons of accepting January admission, students might ask such questions as: How will I catch up if I don't enroll until the spring? Does the school offer fall term options or counseling about how to spend the gap semester? Can I still be on a sports team, join a fraternity or sorority, study abroad? What kind of housing will I have when I enter? Will I be able to get a job on campus? Will I be able to make some extra money to help my family with expenses? Corresponding with previous January students will often provide ideas of creative and challenging ways to spend the interim time and tips on how to integrate into the freshman class when they arrive.

For students who feel burned out from the whole admissions marathon or who want a break before immersing themselves in college life, a gap year may be just the thing. A long-time popular choice for students from Great Britain and Australia, a gap year between high school and college, has recently caught on in the U.S. Books and websites abound, filled with information about adventure programs, community service opportunities in the U.S. and abroad, as well as work/study options and language immersion programs.

Most college counselors advise students to go through the college admissions process during their senior year in high school even if they are considering a gap year. And students should check to see how each college handles deferred admissions. Most colleges will hold a place for an admitted student, but some will not. And even if their acceptance is held, students may have to reapply for financial aid.

Students usually return from a gap year more mature, more world savvy, more independent—and more focused and prepared to engage in college life. "Though it's certainly not for everybody, I've never seen a student who hasn't benefited from it," said one college admissions director, whose sentiments are echoed again and again whenever the subject of a gap year comes up.

THE PRESSURE IS OFF

Just at the time when students, parents, teachers, and counselors are sure that they cannot bear to hear another word about college, the race grinds to a halt. Students send in their reply cards to the colleges and then don't want to think or talk about it anymore. Thoughts turn to high school graduation and to fun and relaxation. Many parents stand by and watch their 17- and 18-year-old offspring regress to childlike behavior.

One mother described with incredulity the scene she found in the family room of her house a few days after her son's last high school class:

> I couldn't believe it when I walked in the door. There were my son and two of his friends lying on the floor playing with their old hot wheels cars! It was quite a

> sight. Three huge 18-year-old boys who are going off to Amherst and Grinnell and Macalester next fall, whizzing those cars around a yellow plastic track. They had Bob Dylan blaring from the stereo and a candle burning in the middle of the floor.

At last the pressure is off. Students brag about the crazy things they are doing and flaunt their irresponsibility. They watch TV more than they have for years, or go to the beach, or as they put it, "just veg out." There is a reprieve—some well-earned time before they turn their thoughts to the next phase. Many of them, even if they weren't particularly happy in high school, feel temporarily on top of the world.

Even as they are enjoying the freedom they haven't felt since the college marathon began, students and their parents are aware that their time together is going by fast. One young woman from New York said that from the time she decided to attend a mid-western college, she knew that she had made a decision that might permanently lead her away from her family, at least geographically. She knew that her mother realized it too.

> I was home alone with my mother for four years after my sisters were out of the house. After I graduated from high school, there were many times that my mother and I would be cooking dinner and my mother would say, "I can't believe you're not going to be here next year." And I'd say, "I can't believe it either." But we always said it lightheartedly, because we knew we were close and that I would come back for holidays and special times no matter what. We felt kind of solid about the connection. But once I had decided to go a thousand miles away to school, I knew that meant I might never go back to New York to live.

ANTICIPATION: EXCITEMENT AND ANXIETY

It is a long time from the fall of senior year in high school to the summer before the first year of college. Throughout that time, the anticipation mounts, a mixture of excitement and anxiety.

In interviews with prospective freshmen, we asked them to tell us what they were excited about and what their concerns were. Their answers to both questions were variations on the same theme. They told us they were excited about meeting new people from different backgrounds, but were concerned about getting to know different kinds of people, being lonely, and getting along with their roommates. They were excited about living in a more independent atmosphere and having freedom; at the same time, they were worried about handling responsibility, making decisions for themselves, and managing their time. They were excited about having fun and "wild times," and they were worried about handling parties, drugs, and alcohol. They were looking forward to intellectual challenges, and were anxious about doing well academically. And most of all they were excited *and* concerned about leaving home and family.

Just as students feel a combination of excitement and anxiety, so for the most part do parents. At the crux of this duality is the pull toward the new—toward risk taking and fresh starts—as opposed to the tug toward familiarity, safety, and family ties. And intertwined through all of this is the ambivalence about separation and letting go.

Parents and children express their enthusiasm about starting over. For many parents there is a reawakening of the feelings they had when their children were babies, feelings of the new possibilities that come with a clean slate. Perhaps John will finally get organized, or Carol will become more responsible or more social or more successful academically. There is always the hope that the so-called late-bloomer will finally blossom.

Students, too, may look forward to shedding uncomfortable labels. Those who were unhappy or unsuccessful in high school may expect to create "a whole new me." And those who were high school superstars may have the equally strong expectation that they will repeat their high school experience in the broader arena of college. Either expectation can be a trap.

When freshmen leave for college, they take themselves along. They take their strengths, their weaknesses, and their capacity to grow and change. Even if college can't possibly live up to the idyllic scenes in the view books, or the idealized images in their parents' memories, it can provide students with special experiences that will help them to make the most of their natural capacity to grow and change as they discover who they are becoming. And that is the vital expectation with which we and our children can approach the college years.

5

READY, SET, GO

The Departure

MIDSUMMER—AND THE "LIVIN' IS EASY"—OR IS IT? Sometime during the steamy days of late July or early August—after the roommates have been assigned and the dorms designated—the countdown begins.

TEN . . . A sudden catch in the throat as a parent realizes this may be the last summer that this particular twosome, buddies since kindergarten, still unselfconsciously meander through neighborhood streets with such carefree abandon.

NINE . . . Should we pack her winter clothes now or wait 'til it gets cold?

EIGHT . . . A seemingly spontaneous—but carefully orchestrated—attempt to recapture frozen moments of family good times with a nostalgic trip to a favorite ice cream stand, beach, bike path.

SEVEN . . . Will he stand still long enough to figure out what clothes he needs to take to college so that I, he, or we can get them?

SIX . . . Standing over her while she cleans out her room: Am I really so concerned about cleaning out seventeen years of debris, or is this a good excuse to reminisce together, assuring ourselves that our memories will retain what is being carted off in boxes? How does one weigh whether a note written in class, a playbill, a beloved pair of jeans is worthy of the keep and store pile, the Goodwill pile, or the trash pile? How do we reduce the past to plastic bags neatly tied with wire twists?

FIVE . . . Lists of things to get: extension cords, masking tape, hangers.

FOUR . . . A flash of anger—or is it fear—at finding crumpled dollar bills falling out of jeans pockets in the washing machine, the front door left open once again, reappearances in the early morning after sleepless nights wondering where he's been, full of worry—how can this kid make it on his own?

THREE . . . Is it cheaper to ship via UPS or the college student trucking service?

TWO . . . Nightly rituals of good-byes as gangs of friends move from one house to another, exchanging e-mail addresses, philosophical viewpoints, and emotions ranging from casual disinterest to sheer terror.

ONE . . . Blast off—the day of departure, the launch.

THE LAST FEW MONTHS

The prelude to the actual countdown starts with a familiar invasion of the mailbox—no longer overstuffed with shiny view books as it had been last year, but now carrying a steady stream of letters about housing options, campus organizations, and course selections, all with the same increasingly familiar college logo—a relentless reminder of the fall to come.

Parents often discover these letters unopened days or weeks after delivery, scattered all over the dining room buffet or discarded among the piles of dirty socks and magazines on the floor of their child's room. Noted writer Gail Sheehy describes an official looking form stuck under her daughter's journal:

> "What's this?" A small alarm goes off. "It looks like the forms for your meal contract at college."
>
> "Mmm, yeah." She starts humming.
>
> "You haven't sent in your contract yet?"
>
> Here it comes. She knows it.
>
> "Where is your head, Maura? Why can't you ever follow through?"
>
> "Thank you," not allowing a nick to show in her expression. "Now would you mind leaving me alone?"[1]

Words like *ever* and *never* are pro forma in these exchanges between parents and children—exchanges that know no geographical boundaries, but are familiar refrains repeated coast to coast. The underlying theme from the child's point of view: Leave me alone. Stop reminding me that I'm growing up and leaving. And from the parent's point of view: I'm not so sure you're ready to leave. I'm not so sure you can make it without me.

One mother describes her son's avoidance with an expression halfway between exasperation and amusement:

> The letter sat on his dresser for weeks unopened. My curiosity turned to concern, and when I finally couldn't restrain myself another minute, I suggested that there might be something important in the letter with a deadline that needed to be met.

When her son grudgingly opened it, he found an announcement for a tempting array of freshman seminars—special offerings of the kind that had attracted him to this small college in the first place. The announcement went on to say that if he was interested in participating, he was to choose one, and that each seminar was limited to twelve people and would be filled on a first-come, first-served basis. The young man barked at his mother, "Why didn't you tell me to open it?" She decided not to respond or attempt to discern the logic in this query from her tall, strapping, bright son who ordinarily bristled at intrusions into his life.

The summer between high school and college seems like a giant exhale—a release of tension, a respite from responsibility, perhaps perceived as a last gasp of childhood. To interrupt it with a series of new choices about meal plans, seminars, housing, and roommates seems an affront: *Somebody else attend to the nitty-gritty details for me. Let me be to wander with my friends, have a summer romance, do some mindless work that keeps my head free and my pockets full.*

A Harvard student recalls receiving a form to help with the selection of roommates—a form that seemed a "silly piece of bureaucracy"—a nuisance that he dashed off on the day it was due. When asked what kind of person he'd like to live with, he jotted down, "I don't care. I can live with anyone." He regretted it later when he found himself living with two extreme eccentrics. There were indeed people he couldn't live with, and he spent much of his first semester sleeping on the floor of a friend's room.

Almost all schools want to know students' preferences about quiet halls, coed, single-sex or gender-neutral living, substance-free environments, and other basic conditions. Although residence hall staffs may not be able to provide ideal matches, students are more likely to find themselves in a compatible situation if they take the time to fill out the questionnaires thoughtfully and return them on time.

Parents may choose to offer advice about completing forms and meeting deadlines, but ultimately the responsibility lies with the student. Students who don't take the time to complete or send in forms learn to live with, and adapt to, the consequences. The young man from Harvard who found the roommate selection forms silly had a bit more discomfort his freshman year than he needed to have, but now he looks back with amusement and a new respect for and understanding of bureaucracy. The freshman who missed getting into the courses she wanted because she registered late often becomes the sophomore who plans ahead to make sure she doesn't make the same mistake twice.

Still, in their eagerness to see their child get off to a good start, parents may make a last attempt to take the reins. Even minor decisions can produce out-of-proportion hassles. A young woman from the Southwest describes her last summer at home.

> All through high school, my parents gave me a tremendous amount of freedom. I never had curfews. I had a car much of the time. I was treated as a pretty mature person. So for them to suddenly act very pro-

> tective, and a lot more parental, was a shock. My mother was very nervous; she had always been so rational, and now she was absurd. She thought it was crucial that I do everything correctly. I lectured them and reminded them that I was 18 years old and could take care of myself and everything would work out. and I wouldn't be rejected and I would have a social life despite the fact that my mother said that no one would ever call me if I wasn't in Facebook!

Although it is helpful if parents back off as their children assume the responsibility for their own decisions, there are certain circumstances in which it is important for parents to be involved. If, for instance, a child has special problems or needs, parents should make sure that they establish a partnership with the appropriate university professionals. The health service should be told about chronic illnesses; the dean, or appropriate office, about learning disabilities; and the dean or residence hall director about family problems that may affect the student's adjustment—a recent death, an impending divorce, a severe illness in the family.

Donna Shalala, President of the University of Miami, acknowledges the importance of the role that parents continue to play in supporting the well-being of their children. She writes in a letter to parents of new students, "If you are concerned about your child's health as he or she comes to campus, please take a few moments now and call us so that we can develop a plan for continuous care and support."

Whenever a parent informs the college about special needs or problems, the child should know about it. A dean at Franklin and Marshall who receives numerous phone calls from parents about everything from course selection to health or learning disabilities, explains:

> I like to be informed, but, whenever possible, I prefer that the student make the call—or if this is particularly difficult, that the student and parent contact me together. This can be an important step in the student's assuming responsibility for dealing with his or her problems.

Some parents worry that their child may start off on the wrong foot if it is known that he or she has been in therapy or is on psychotropic medication. On the contrary, college administrators and mental health professionals strongly advise parents to prepare for continuity of care when their children enter this new environment. Often freshmen want a "fresh start" and go off their meds or stop therapy when they arrive on campus—the very time that they most need the support. Coordination and encouragement can make all the difference in a student's college experience.

A student with Attention Deficit Disorder (ADD) may need understanding from the residential life staff or support from the learning and disability resource centers as well as the health service. Even with access to all these services, a mother whose son has ADD tells of the ongoing challenge:

> The most difficult aspect of the transition is not being around to help with his ADD. This is a major issue for our son. Learning to take his meds, challenging the need for meds, not having a consistent adult voice around to ask the important questions, to channel the energy and curb the impulsivity. We still play this role, but it is very hard from afar.

Some of the summer mail is addressed directly to parents, with information about parent orientation, tuition payment, and health insurance options. These call for careful assessment.

In many schools, there are a variety of payment options that may be advantageous, and university health insurance may turn out to be a necessity even for students covered by their parents' policy. Some schools require health insurance and build it into the tuition charges.

One health service director at a university, which does not have mandatory health insurance, urges parents to seriously consider buying university health insurance even if they think their own policy will cover their child in college. She recounts an incident that is becoming more common in this era of managed care. A student broke his hand during finals. His parents' East Coast HMO would not approve payment to the local hospital and insisted that he fly home to Boston to have it taken care of, making a difficult situation even more disruptive.

The residence hall and roommate assignments that arrive in the midsummer mail begin to make concrete what up to this point has been a rather distant, vague, and idealized image of college living. Often students convince themselves that they have to get into a particular residence hall in order to be happy, or that all will be lost if their roommate isn't a potential best friend. They may agonize over what kind of computer to bring or whether to take a bicycle. They may pore over course catalogues, trying to pick the perfect schedule, or spend hours trying to decide what color blankets to buy. Instead of facing their general anxiety about leaving home, they may focus on something that seems totally out of proportion to perplexed parents. Tension in the household begins to build again.

Finding oneself assigned to a triple or to the less popular off-campus housing brings disappointment and even tears to some, as if anything short of perfection is a harbinger of a ruined freshman year. Because many prospective freshmen still see the world in terms of polar opposites, right and wrong, they truly believe that if they don't make perfect course choices or get the perfect room assignment, the implications will be disastrous.

Some parental reassurance may help students to see the subtleties and shades of gray. But logic and information and even the best intentions of parents are not sufficient to change the mind of an adamant 18-year-old. It usually just takes some time. Some of the things that loom so large during the summer fade into the background as freshmen settle into the day-to-day flow of college life.

One young woman's comments reflect her change in perception over the course of her freshman year at Haverford:

> I didn't dwell on it, but I was upset last summer when I was assigned to the "apartments." When I had visited and stayed in a dorm, the woman I stayed with said "anything but the apartments." I had always imagined myself in the dorm when I thought of myself living there, and now I had to reorient myself. Actually there are some real positive trade-offs living in the apartments. I guess I discovered that anything is the best or the worst depending on your vantage point.

How does one know if the housing or roommate is "good"? There is no way to know ahead of time, of course; stereotypes are often all one has to hang one's hat on—so coed dorms are "good" and single sex dorms are "bad." If your roommate's name is Brooke, "she's probably a snob"; if he's from Nebraska, "he's probably a hick." "Is Edina a rural town in Minnesota?" Google it to find out. "No, it's a suburb of Minneapolis." "Is Essex Junction, Vermont, even on the map?" Students—and sometimes parents, too—surf online profiles, which may or may not reflect reality. At the click of a name, an entering student's spirits may soar at the mention of a favorite band or sports team or may plunge at seeing a preference for video games or a fascination with entomology.

Parents can be helpful at these times by simply acknowledging their children's anxiety or disappointment, and by helping them put information in perspective, dispelling myths and sweeping generalities as well as encouraging them to find out more information, if they can, from upperclassmen at their school.

Unfortunately, some parents are more intolerant and anxious than their children. Residence hall personnel rarely hear requests from students for roommate changes during the summer. It is the parents who are more likely to intervene because of a Facebook profile. Increasingly, residence hall directors have to fend off unhappy parents who see the party behavior of a designated roommate or are upset about his or her nationality, race, religion, or sexual orientation.

One residential life staff member told of a mother calling him more than ten times during the summer wanting her son's room changed because his roommate was from Puerto Rico. It was clear from their conversations that she had all sorts of assumptions about this young man's background and social status—all of which turned out to be completely false. In most cases, residence hall staffs will not make changes unless it seems as though the situation will be truly problematic for all involved. Usually, the student is not the one who perceives the situation as a problem, and often he or she is embarrassed by a parent's intrusion. Indeed, parental intervention of this sort may impede a student's growth. The university's diverse student body is a rich resource. To live with, understand, and appreciate people whose values, habits, and cultures are substantially different is a large part of the learning that can take place in college.

Most students seem to take housing and roommate assignments in stride and suspend judgment until school is underway. They are likely to connect with their roommates online or by phone in an effort to begin to know one another. Finding that a roommate listens to country music, or likes to go to sleep at 1 a.m. may be a future freshman's first encounter with the inevitable compromises of dorm living. A woman from a middle-class family in Iowa recounted her shock when her future roommate from Virginia called and said she was bringing her horse to school with her. And a Latina woman from New Mexico, on a full scholarship, recalled the awkwardness she felt when her roommate from the north shore of Chicago asked if she was bringing a flat-screen TV with her to Wellesley. The diversity of the college campus had expanded these students' limited horizons, reminding them in personal ways that life was going to be different from now on.

A young man from Pittsburgh, who was entering Colgate, was reassured after talking to his roommate:

> I called my roommate. We talked and found out some interests in common, who would bring what to school, and when we were going to arrive. As soon as I talked to him, I felt like I knew one person there. When I saw him at school, I just picked up from where we had left off. I asked him how his job at the pool that summer had gone. It really made a difference talking to him ahead of time.

Some students prefer to contact their future roommates electronically. Searching for words of introduction can be awkward, however. A vivacious young woman of many talents tried to think of ways to introduce herself to her future Berkeley roommate: "If I tell her I was a cheerleader, she'll think I'm just a boppy airhead. I can't describe myself in two paragraphs," she wailed. Music seems to provide a shorthand that helps youngsters to place themselves in a context. "He listens to Radiohead and the Dave Matthews band; he can't be half bad," one young man from Portland exclaimed after an introductory exchange from his roommate-to-be at the University of Maine. "She's into Snoop Dogg; she wasn't too thrilled when I mentioned Tom Petty," was the essence of a quick conversation with a Tulane student's assigned roommate. An entering freshman at Brown reported the good news—"She likes jazz, does sports, and goes to bed early"—and the bad, "It all sounded good until I mentioned the word 'feminist' in a sentence, and there was this silence—she just said, 'Oh.'"

Based on numerous interviews with college students, there seems to be little or no correlation between roommates' initial contacts and their ultimate compatibility. Too often, brief notes or abbreviated phone calls encourage fantasies of becoming best friends and soul mates—only to discover later that an affinity for pink comforters and Brad Pitt doesn't guarantee friendship or similar lifestyles.

■

Some universities have tried to reduce the hectic atmosphere of fall orientation and registration by scheduling smaller group programs staggered through the summer weekends. Students meet with an advisor and register for classes, and get to know their way around campus. At some schools, parents are invited for a parallel track. Though summer orientation may give students a head start on the transition process, it can also burst the bubble of idealized college life. The dorm rooms probably look small and bare, and the food isn't like home. Preregistration and the frustration of dealing with prerequisites and closed course sections introduce students to the realities of institutional bureaucracy.

This slice of college life may seem out of sync with the summer's steady pace—a frenzied few days of the new and unknown interrupting the security of familiar friends, family, and surroundings. Some students panic, usually just for a brief period of time, and wonder what they are getting into.

One midwesterner, despite the additional expenses of travel and time away from her summer job, flew to Burlington for the University of Vermont's summer orientation. The program included pre-registration, and she was afraid she wouldn't get into the classes she wanted if she didn't attend. Although she had fallen in love with the school on an earlier trip by herself in the spring, she called home daily during the few days of summer orientation, teary and miserable. Most of the students who showed up drove with parents or friends from nearby cities and neighboring states. Many seemed to know each other from high school, and she felt lonely and worried that she might have made the wrong choice of schools. After several late-night phone calls, her parents prepared themselves for the fact that she might withdraw and go instead to Indiana University, closer to home. As she stepped off the plane wearing a University of Vermont sweatshirt and beaming smile, they knew they had been premature in their assumptions.

THE LAST FEW WEEKS

> That's the summer that feels like it's not going to end. You're out of school; you know you're done with high school and you're spending every single moment of your time with your friends because somewhere in the back of your mind you realize you're not going to see these people very much in the next couple of years, and it never really hits you until you're at that famous last part, the last get-together. For me the summer was all about trying to hang on to those friendships.

There's no denying it now. The long days of summer aren't as long as they were a month ago. The students who are procrastinators continue to put off shopping or packing, but the tempo of their social lives may increase as time with friends begins to run out. Couples linger together, planning ways to stay connected during their next nine months in different locations. All members of the family are acutely aware that a big change is about to take place, that life won't be quite the same again. One day their child is exclaiming, "Leave me alone; I'm eighteen years old; I'm independent." The next thing they know he's complaining, "You're so busy. You're never around when I need you." The seesaw of snapping tempers and unusually tender exchanges between youngsters and their parents are reminders of their ambivalence toward separation—and its proximity:

> The few weeks before she left for school, Julie and I would truly scream at each other about stupid things. There was a time when we were on the parking lot of a drugstore just yelling at each other in the front seat of our car. She was screaming and I was screaming, and I'd like to think it's not reflective of our relationship, but it really was then. It was very painful.

With a sense of dwindling time, some families make an effort to formally mark the fast approaching departure in creative ways that connect past, present and future. Some have special family dinners or celebrations. One woman describes the ritual she and her sister planned to mark their children's leave-taking:

> I have been reflecting for some time on the need for tradition and ritual in my life. I read about a "leaving home" ritual, and since my sister's daughter and my son were leaving for college at the same time, we decided to plan one together. We picked poems and music and decided to have the ceremony in my parents' garden. We invited each member of our

extended family to write something to honor Sarah and David and to bring a gift that symbolized their sentiment about them.

It was a powerful and moving experience for all of us, as we each summed up in our own unique ways what David and Sarah mean to us. I was so glad that the kids were able to witness the love and honoring of their individuality from their parents, grandparents and cousins—three generations of our family. It is something I hope they can carry with them to each new adventure and renew continuously.

Wanting these last weeks at home to be quality time, parents try to restrain themselves from commenting as their children sleep away mornings or party away nights. Time becomes the most precious of commodities—moments together to be begged, borrowed, or stolen. Some of this is spent on the practical aspects of the move, the question of getting to school; who's going, when, and how; the shopping, packing, and sending of clothes and equipment. Many colleges send suggestions, even lists, of what to bring. Most include specific information about computing facilities on campus and advice about purchasing computers. Hometown upperclassmen at the college, as well as their parents, can help prospective freshmen. Much, if not all, of this can be handled by the student alone, but more often than not, parents are actively involved.

Sometime during this period, the decision is usually made about how the student will actually get to school, whether alone or accompanied by a parent. In some families this isn't even discussed, especially when there are family traditions or norms. In other families the child makes his or her wishes known directly, or economics and distance dictate a particular decision. But many families find themselves approaching this topic delicately. It seems laden with everyone's feelings about the impending physical separation and the simultaneous desire to establish independence.

Some students are very clear about their preference—wanting a family member to take them either for reasons of practicality, to stuff the car with the last-minute accumulation of belongings—or for emotional support. One dean of freshmen explains:

> Freshmen may not spend much time with parents once they finally arrive on campus, but they take comfort in looking over their shoulders and seeing that Mom and Dad are there. If students express an interest in having their parents accompany them, it's probably a good idea to try to do it. It may boost the student's confidence just at the time he or she needs it most.

Just the opposite is true for some students, who find making the trip on their own a great confidence booster. Those who want to go by themselves may feel more secure and better about themselves if they are allowed to do so.

But, as is true with so many of the decisions facing parents and students at this time, the impact one way or another isn't likely to be a major one. If parents don't accompany their child to school in the fall, they may find it even more satisfying to come later for Parents' Weekend when the turf truly belongs to their child. Those who do go, however, will have the chance to begin to put some names together with faces and places right from the beginning—laying a foundation for sharing experiences as the year wears on.

■

As they concentrate on organizing and checking off on last-minute "to do" lists, parents and children often neglect attending to the central long-range issues that will involve their continuous interaction throughout the college years. Families might save themselves unnecessary friction and misunderstanding if they think about and discuss four key areas: academics, finances, health and safety, and communication.

Most parents approach their children's college years with expectations and assumptions, although they may not express them explicitly. As a matter of fact, they may not even be conscious that they have assumptions at all. But all too often, college students and their parents find themselves locked in frustrating battles about money, grades, a live-in boyfriend, or a dearth of phone calls home because they were each operating on a different set of assumptions. Just talking about these issues ahead of time obviously doesn't mean that you will agree about everything, but being aware and thoughtful now will lessen the likelihood for misunderstandings later.

How does a family come to this understanding? Lectures by pontificating parents are definitely not the way, in spite of the fact that it can be tempting for even the most well-meaning parents to take that last chance to express a disdain for drugs, or expound on the financial sacrifices they are making and what they expect in return.

It's not easy to capture the attention of teenagers on the run, especially at this time of escalating emotions. Periods of intimacy and long discussions are interspersed with weeks of hellos and good-byes and grunts and groans from teenagers who are always in motion. Some students keep their parents at arm's length, making it difficult to talk to them about anything. The father of an entering Reed College freshman recounts:

> She was nasty. The summer was brutish and long. She was mean to everyone, dismissive; everything we

> said was stupid. She was ready to go and we were ready for her to leave.

Often in the closest of families, students seem to need to assert their separateness. A single mother describes the summer before her daughter left for the University of Illinois in Chicago:

> My daughter completely changed personality. We were always very close. She had always confided in me. But now she didn't talk to me. She wasn't unkind. But in high school she worked at a theatre, and when she got home late at night, she would come in and lie on my bed and talk to me while she was winding down. During this summer, I had to make her wave at me when she passed my bedroom. Maybe subconsciously, she was preparing to not have me around.

From the parent's point of view, there are so many last-minute matters to cover:

> She seemed very mature in a lot of ways and incredibly poorly prepared in others, and every time I wanted to talk about it, she didn't want to talk about what I wanted to talk about. I wanted to talk about bank accounts, and she kept spending all her money, and I wanted to talk about what kind of winter clothes she would need, and she'd say, but mom, it's 90 degrees outside. . .so we were out of sync for a while. I was trying to get her ready to go, because ***I*** needed to know she was ready, and she was doing something completely different on her own time.

Meanwhile, students are dealing with their own stresses:

> There are so many people to have those last moments with, everyone from your boyfriend to your grandparents who live in town, to your parents. Do you spend your last night at home with your family, or do you go out with your friends, who you're not going to see for three or four months. I remember feeling like . . . OK, I've got seven days left, so I should have four days with family and three with friends . . . or no, no, no, I should spend the daytime with my Dad so I can go out at night with my friends. It's such a balancing act. It's a matter of guilt. Your parents don't try to make you feel guilty, but they want their last moments with you, too. I would say that was the most difficult part of the summer . . . the last two weeks.

As families prepare for their child's departure, the most effective means of talking with each other will probably be the one that is most familiar. This isn't the time to adopt a new style of family communication no matter how well it works for someone else. Whether you carve out time to sit down for a heart-to-heart or talk in spurts on the run, these conversations will be setting the groundwork for the inevitable changes and challenges that parents and their children will confront as time goes on.

ACADEMIC EXPECTATIONS

"Just do the best you can." These are the standard parental words of advice to offspring when the conversation turns to the academic side of college. But, if "the best you can" has meant A's and B's until now, most parents simply expect that to continue. Many students complain of the double messages they receive from parents. "I don't care about your grades as long as you try" may have as its hidden message, "I know if you try, you can get an A." Students are acutely tuned in to their parents' expectations regarding academics and they feel enormous pressure to "pay them back for their financial sacrifice" with A's and B's.

A lot of students place pressure on themselves to get good grades. Actually, most of them want the same academic success for themselves that their parents want for them. They want to be excited about their courses, stimulated by their professors, and they want to do well. Many have glided or plugged their way through high school without a C or a D, and as they begin their college careers, they want, and perhaps expect, to keep up their stellar record.

Some of the superstars will find themselves in academic situations that are totally different from high school. In the most selective colleges that fill their freshman classes with the upper 10 percent of high school students, 90 percent of the students will be in an unfamiliar position—no longer at the top of the academic heap. And half of them will be at the bottom half of their college class. Obvious as that may sound, it can come as a shock to students and their parents when they have become accustomed to the accolades that accompany acceptance to the most prestigious colleges and universities.

Parents of high academic achievers probably haven't spent much time worrying about their child's academic performance. They may have come to take it for granted and focus their concern on other aspects of development. With the marathon for the select college sticker behind them, some even hope their youngsters will relax more in college and take more time for friends and extracurricular activities. They may not realize that they have high expectations and assumptions about academic performance until their child hits an unexpected academic snag.

A Massachusetts mother gained a new perspective:

> We finally accept the idea that our children won't be all-American or Yo-Yo Ma—but we still expect them

> to excel academically in all their courses. My son was a bacteriology major, took philosophy and got a D. We were shocked. We expected him to be good at all subjects. That may be as unrealistic as the mentality that says we should all weigh 110 pounds. If we can accept the fact that a kid that is 5'7" won't play college basketball, then we should be able to accept academic liability.

Parents whose children did not do well in high school may have thought a great deal about what they expect from them in college. Their expectations are often mixed with anxiety that the high school pattern will be repeated, and the eternal hope that the student will turn over a new leaf at last. These are the parents who are prone to giving late summer lectures to their children about study habits, discipline and buckling down. The more they lecture, the more their children turn a deaf ear. But the temptation to "tell her one more time" is difficult to resist, in spite of the rational knowledge that it's out of their hands, and now it's up to her.

A lawyer from Cincinnati whose son was about to leave for Oberlin said:

> Ted didn't really work in high school. He managed to do okay, but not great, with very little effort. I don't think he was ever turned on to a course. He just didn't get much out of school at all. He'll have to work harder at Oberlin, and I expect him to make a reasonable effort to hit the books and stretch his mind. He doesn't have to get all A's and B's, but we're paying too much for him to just jerk around. I'm not concerned just about grades; what I really want is for him to open up intellectually. I want him to be interested in what he's doing. He's so narrow now; he's not

> curious or adventurous intellectually. I'm hoping Oberlin will be broadening for him. He's going to a place that fosters caring about the world and other people. I'd rather he become really excited about a European history course and get a C than take yet another math course that he hates and get an A. But it's hard to get away from the subject of grades. They are the inevitable barometer; they are some reflection of what is going on.

For most parents, even if grades aren't paramount, there is a grade threshold—some number below which a grade-point average becomes unacceptable. That number will vary not only from parent to parent but from one child to another in the same family, and for the same child at different periods of his or her career. Likewise, the messages that parents transmit may mean different things to different students. Telling some students not to worry about grades may be a license not to go to class. To a young person who has always been a plugger, the message "Do the best you can" may simply increase self-imposed pressure and the tendency to be a workaholic. The same message to a more easygoing sibling may not be clear enough; she'll be likely to benefit from more specific guidelines—perhaps even a mutually agreed upon grade-point average to aim for during the freshman year.

There are some parents who not only expect a certain grade-point average from their children but also assume that they'll select a certain major—usually one leading to a high-status or well-paying career. It is not uncommon for parents to introduce their children who are barely out of high school as: "Janna's our premed; Jim's our prelaw." Some parents even threaten to withdraw financial support unless their child follows a prescribed course of study. Students who are embarking on their college years are just beginning to explore their own interests and capacities. Parental expectations and assumptions about what they should study act as barriers to the student's development. The underlying communication to the student is, "I know what's good for you better than you do."

Every college counseling staff in the country can tell war stories about students who have been pressured to study business or biology or engineering against their will. And though consciously trying to appease their parents, these students may be fighting for their own identity. Some finally come to a turning point during their later years of school and choose the course of study that they really want, but only after having paid a painful price.

James E. McLeod, Washington University's Vice Chancellor for Students and Dean of the College of Arts and Sciences, advises:

> This need for freshmen to have a certain future, to know what they will be in 2030 or 2040, runs counter to their growth and development. It leads to low or no risk whatsoever. They need to pursue interests—to reach and stretch. They do need to know the implications of their choices. They need to have conversations with faculty and advisors, people who know about the institution and about life. But a certain future is not the thing to seek in their freshman year.

Eventually, if they are to separate and become independent, students must take responsibility for their own academic goals and the consequences of their performance. They have to decide whether they are willing to work hard enough to get the grades it takes to be accepted to medical school, to keep a scholarship, or to graduate with honors. They have to discover what they are capable of and what sacrifices they are willing to make.

Students grades are only part of the equation. A rich academic experience and academic success can not be measured by a GPA *alone*. Academic success is about learning and discovery—about passion and engagement in intellectual community. Pretty heady topics for a parent-offspring dialogue on an August evening. But there are some specific questions parents might ask to stimulate thinking and discussion: What do you hope to accomplish your first semester? How do you think the academic challenges in college will be different from high school? What are you most excited about learning?

Parents may also want to read, and make available to their child, Richard Light's book, *Making the Most of College: College Students Speak Their Minds*. Based on more than ten years of research, it's filled with lively stories and voices of college students, and includes practical tips about time management, course selection, relationships with advisors and mentors, and the value of involvement in out-of-the-classroom activities.

Many students feel more secure when they know what their parents expect from them at the outset. And perhaps parents feel more secure too, when they know they have made themselves clear. But as time goes on it will be up to the student to decide to what extent parental goals really fit with his or her own aspirations. And the challenge to parents will be to remain supportive and to be flexible and open to change.

Dean Mcleod believes that it's important for parents to acknowledge this shift in the relationship:

> I'd like parents to let their child know "I am an interested party. I remain engaged in who you are and who you are becoming." But the baton needs to be passed to the child. The student needs to have license to take the baton—to take charge of his or her own life.

> Parents and students are in the race together, but it's the student's chance to carry the baton.

FINANCES

Money may not be the root of all evil, but it can become the rope that binds children to their parents with stifling knots. A clear discussion of expectations can help to prevent this. In fact, sound financial planning can foster a student's growing independence. If parents can be straightforward with their children about financial realities, their children often will surprise them with their resourcefulness and willingness to assume responsibility. Indeed, an increasing percentage of today's college students are taking financial responsibility for a portion of their education. So money is very much on the mind of today's college students and their parents.

Filling out college financial aid forms may have brought out into the open a subject that has typically been taboo in many families—How much money do we have? What is the accurate picture of our financial worth? For many families, however, this is still an off-limits subject, and some students leave for college with only a vague notion of their family's finances. Some simply know that they are comfortable and that their parents will support them financially and are not concerned about money. Many students are confused by mixed messages:

> My parents never talk about money, but I can see them trying to cut corners all the time now. And I know it's 'cause of the big tuition bills.

> My parents say they are strung out by college expenses, but they just redecorated our house.

> My mother and father are divorced. My tuition is due and it's gone up substantially from last year. My mother says, "Ask your father." My father says he can't afford any more, but he just took his girlfriend on a cruise. Sometimes I feel guilty, and other times, I'm just plain mad.

It is important for parents to be straightforward with their children about what their limits are, what they will be contributing to, and what the student's responsibility will be. Before a student leaves for college there may still be some unanswered questions regarding money. Though costs for tuition, room and board are usually clear and precise, estimates for living expenses, books and supplies are more fluid and difficult to assess. Colleges and universities' calculations for personal expenses vary widely, ranging from $1000 to over $2000 a year. A good place to begin a discussion may be with information from the financial aid or admissions pages of the school's website or directly from the financial aid office. It's a good idea to talk to sophomores and juniors at the college to get an idea of how much money to set aside for extras, such as snacks and Sunday dinners, lab fees and art supplies, laundry, entertainment, and cell phone plans. But only time will tell exactly how much will actually be needed for expenses, or how many hours a week a student can work and still handle academics. Some basic guidelines and open discussion while the student is still at home can set the tone for later negotiations.

Some parents feel comfortable with depositing an allowance for the semester's expenses. Some make it clear that they can contribute to tuition, room, and board, but that the student will be responsible for any added expenses. Other parents agree to pay for travel home or for books, but not incidentals. One mother of a Yale sophomore took this approach:

> We said we'd pay for books. We didn't want him to pick his courses by the price of the books. But clothes and all other expenses came out of his summer savings.

The decision about who will pay for what is made on the basis of available resources, priorities, and values. Parents who are sensitive to the issue of developing autonomy will set up a system that allows their child room for financial choices and responsibility:

> My Dad asked me to keep track of my daily expenses for two months. From that we arrived at an amount for a monthly allowance. It was a good exercise for me because it made me realize what I spend money on. I decided to get a job second semester though, because I liked having a little extra in case I wanted to be extravagant or travel to see a friend.

> My parents used to send me money as I needed it my freshman year, but I really hated it. I always felt guilty when I asked for more, or like I had to justify where I had spent the money. Now I get one lump sum at the beginning of the semester and that's it. I like it a lot better. I know what I have, and I can budget accordingly. If I want to blow it on a ski trip or a couple of six-packs, it's my business—and I'll scrimp for a while to make up for it.

> My parents told me they would supplement my financial aid package and would take care of the remaining tuition and board. All the other expenses are up to me. I thought I had earned enough last summer, but I ran out by March. Luckily I picked up a part-time job to keep me solvent.

One entrepreneurial junior, sensitive to the economic impact of her private college education on her family, tells of her financial college journey:

> I have three younger siblings, and I thought, Am I going to cause too much strain on my brothers and sisters? I have work-study, but after freshman year, we had to readjust. I told my parents, Every year I stay here, I'm going to find a way to make it cheaper for you guys. If that means I have to take out more loans, whatever. So, sophomore year, I moved off campus, and that was significantly cheaper, and junior year, I moved back on campus and was an RA, and so I got a stipend for that. And I had reallocated some of my resources and got a fellowship. And so I tell them every year, Don't worry about it; I've got it covered.

Most colleges and universities have banks and ATM machines on or adjacent to their campuses, making it convenient to have an account locally. Opening and maintaining a checking account helps a young person to feel more competent about handling his or her own affairs. For the student who has never done this before, it is one more step on the road to independence.

Credit card companies are courting college students, with great success for the companies and devastating results for many students. Although credit cards can be useful to establish credit, for plane tickets, course textbooks or emergencies, statistics show that dangers abound for naïve customers. From the day a new student walks onto the campus until graduation, he or she will regularly encounter tempting "deals" from aggressive credit card vendors offering everything from a free T-shirt to extremely low interest rates for a limited time period. Some students get three or four cards and juggle the payments from month to month. This generation was brought up on credit and debit cards, and the "spend now, worry later" mentality often leads to delinquent loan payments, ruined credit ratings, and even personal bankruptcy.

One savvy dean of an engineering school spoke from experience as her son prepared to leave for his freshman year:

> Credit card offers started flooding the mailbox close to high school graduation. We cautioned our son not to accept or enroll for a credit card. We warned him that in college vendors come onto campus and offer freebies to sign up for a card. Lots of students sign up for the gift and plan to cancel the card, but instead they soon realize how easy it is to charge things and get themselves in a bind.

The introduction on many campuses of all-purpose identification cards, sometimes called "smart cards," is both a convenience and a potential hazard for freshmen who haven't learned to manage their money. A smart card not only provides access to campus buildings, but can also be used to make cash-free purchases at the campus bookstore, copy shop, campus cafés and food markets, dining facilities, and vending machines. Students can even use it for the washers and dryers in the laundry room. At some universities, vendors in the local community also accept university smart cards, making it all too tempting for students to drain their balance on pizza and beer.

One parent who cautioned his son to check his debit card balance online regularly, explains how his son's method is still a work in progress:

> We got our son a debit card. He's on my account so we can deposit or move money quickly while he's away at school. Luckily we have a national bank that

has a branch across the country in his school's town. He's done pretty well—has not yet been overdrawn. Close but not quite. Ideally he would have set up his own online password so he could check his balance from his computer. That seems like a lot of work to him, so he walks over to the ATM every few days so he can check his balance instead.

Parents who are resolute about educating their children about the dangers of alcohol abuse or safety issues need to counsel their children about financial risks as well. Though lectures may appear to fall on deaf ears, conversations about the judicious use of credit cards to establish credit and develop financial skills as opposed to the long-term pitfalls that could lie ahead can have an impact.

Parents can support their child's emerging financial independence by advising them about setting up e-mail alerts for their checking or debit accounts or automatic minimum monthly payments for their credit cards. Creating a system now can ward off problems later, such as charges for overdrawn accounts or late payments.

The major expense of college tuition may bring to the surface once again a financial tug-of-war between separated and divorced parents. Counseling services in colleges and universities regularly see students caught in the continuing crossfire of bitter ex-husbands and wives who seem to lose sight of the fact that their child is the loser in this battle. Obviously, it is in the child's best interest for the financial arrangements to be clearly spelled out and understood before he or she leaves for school, even if it takes, as one divorced woman put it, "mini-summit meetings" to do it.

The child also loses when parents use money as an unspoken bargain, the "after-all-I've-done-for-you" syndrome. Bribing students to get good grades or to study a subject of the parent's choosing will usually boomerang and lead to resentment.

As students move through their college years and struggle to become increasingly independent, money and financial ties to parents inevitably cause concern. For many students, the struggles for separation and independence are complicated by their prolonged years of financial dependence. Parents can help loosen the financial ties by educating and encouraging their children to assume responsibility for the management of their financial affairs, by being honest with them about family finances, and by being clear about their expectations right from the beginning of their children's college career.

SOCIAL LIFE: CHOICES AND RESPONSIBILITIES

> I drank a lot those first few weeks. I found myself in situations that were really hard for me to handle, and I didn't handle them the way I would have sober. I finally woke up well into the first semester and realized I didn't have to be a "party girl" to have friends and a social life, but it was hard to get people to take me seriously.

> I smoked a lot of pot in high school. When I got here I decided to hang out with a different kind of crowd. They're into drinking, and sometimes it gets out of hand.

It is the rare high school graduate who hasn't had to grapple with personal decisions about alcohol, drugs, and sex: Should I or shouldn't I? How much? What kind? Where?

By the time students arrive on campus, they are well on the way to formulating their own value system, usually based on many years of observing and listening to parents and peers.

Their actual degree of experimentation varies widely, but almost all of them will find that college life brings them face-to-face with more choices than they have ever had before. More choices, more pressures—and now perhaps for the first time, no familiar parental boundaries to keep them in line.

Throughout their teenage years, young people have been used to a certain amount of structure and limit setting by their parents. "I have to be home by midnight." "My parents wouldn't let me walk out of the house wearing that." "I better not have another drink 'cause I have to check in with my mom when I get home." "We always go to eleven o'clock Mass as a family Sunday morning." Phrases like these have saved many teenagers from having to take a stand—making it easier to say no when under intense pressure from peers, or to refuse to try out a new behavior before feeling ready. Students may find parental rules arbitrary and aggravating, but often they depend on those rules to keep their behavior within safe limits.

Sometimes college students don't realize that this parental backing is missing until they are in the midst of a problematic situation. No one in college will be checking to see when they come home, or even *if* they come home. Roommates and friends won't be checking for red eyes or alcohol breath. Students have to put themselves on the line; they are responsible for setting their own limits.

A letter from the Dean of the College and the Dean of Student Life at Brown University asked parents and guardians of freshmen to do their share in preparing students to live in a campus community:

> The freedom of our atmosphere has on occasion, unfortunately, led some to lose sight of their corresponding responsibilities to themselves and to the community. We therefore ask your help in reminding your children that boundaries do exist at Brown and

> that serious penalties are imposed on those found guilty of overstepping them.

The letter expressed concern about the misuse of alcohol and other drugs, and made a particular plea to parents to join the university as partners in dealing with this problem.

> It is our hope that parents will take time to review issues of chemical use with their children, including their expectations for behavior at Brown. In a country where rules and customs vary so greatly from region to region, students can easily be confused as they make choices of their own. Parental direction can be of great value to children and provide enormous service to those at Brown who wrestle with this vast national problem.

Parents are confronted with an infinite number of "teachable moments," and the challenge, of course, is to recognize some of them when they occur. The father of a Bucknell freshman described how he almost blew his chance to talk to his son in a meaningful way about marijuana use:

> Two weeks before Tim left for school, I was driving home from work and reached into the glove compartment to get out a map. A packet of cigarette rolling paper fell out with the map. I could feel my blood start to boil. "Now he's smoking pot in the car!" was all I could think.
>
> I barged into the house and was about to start in on a tirade but something inside me stopped me and I calmed down and just presented him with the packet and said, "Come on in and talk. I'm worried about this."

At first Tim just looked at me sheepishly, and then he said angrily, "What do you want me to do? Tell you every time I smoke a joint?"

I said, "You're leaving the evidence that you're smoking, you know how I feel about that." He kind of relaxed and started talking—reassuring me, giving me space to ask more questions. I probed a bit, but mainly listened. He told me about a lot of stuff he'd been exposed to in high school and let me know he'd done lots of thinking about his own limits and how to deal with pressure from other kids. One thing led to another and before I knew it, almost an hour had gone by and our conversation had run the gamut from cocaine and a messed up friend who was in jail for dealing, to spirituality in nature and organized religion.

Students fortunate enough to have older siblings who will counsel them often turn to them rather than parents for advice. A freshman at James Madison University recounted his precollege conversation with his older brother: "He basically told me to wait until I was sure of what I was doing—to use my best judgment and not to do anything for someone else."

Another experienced upperclassman advised his younger sister, "Just make sure you always leave yourself a safety net. If you're going to drink a lot, don't go back to a guy's room with him. If you're going to go to his room, don't drink."

Counselors often see the casualties from the first month or two of college—students who have jumped into new lifestyles too quickly without taking into account consequences or personal values. One counselor regularly advises freshmen not to make any major lifestyle changes during the first month of school: "It's better not to jump into dramatic experimentation—whether the experimentation is with sex, alcohol, or a new religious commitment." Many students regret starting off by creating an image that doesn't reflect their own sense of themselves, and find backtracking an awkward and stressful process.

Parents whose children have made responsible decisions in high school, may find this topic irrelevant, but students tell us otherwise. A student who had been a non-drinker in high school, reflects on the conversations about drinking and drugs that he had with his parents before he left for college:

> I think my parents helped me prepare pretty well. We'd go over various sorts of situations and encounters that might happen and think about what my attitude towards them would be, but I feel like there were always certain assumptions made on my parents' part about who I'd be or what my participation would be, and there wasn't perhaps a very realistic perception of what *actually* goes on and what the pressures and expectations are like.

And a sophomore at the University of Maryland, who spent her first few months at college in turmoil after experimenting with drugs and alcohol, looks back:

> The only thing I wish is that my parents had prepared me better for what I might face in college. There was never a real discussion about sex, drugs, or even money management. They just trusted that I would be me and do my best. Trusting that your child will do what they know is "right" is important, but also . . . it's college. College is a chance to taste every temptation you could imagine. I'm not sure how you can prepare a person for this other than talking about it. Just talk.

When Jennifer Burden, Director of Health Promotion at Skidmore College, surveyed freshmen about ways their parents could have helped them prepare for the social scene in college, they overwhelmingly responded, "Back off, let go, leave me alone." Yet when she asked sophomores, just one year older, they had a very different take on this: "Have conversations." "The freshmen really need you." "Those of us who cannot share with our parents typically wish we could."

Parents may think that being honest and direct about their own values and concerns seems fruitless and redundant at times, when confronted with, "Yeah, yeah, Dad," or eyes that roll back in disgust, or tolerant amusement when talking about such provocative topics. But, though loath to admit it, students do care about what their parents think, and often these discussions at home can serve as a grounding to refer back to when the students are faced with difficult choices at school.

COMMUNICATION: HOW WILL WE KEEP IN TOUCH?

In previous decades, students returned to their dormitories to make a call or to write a letter home when they needed something from their parents, whether it was a piece of clothing, a bit of advice or a long-distance "hug." For today's students there is the ever-present possibility of an available parent at the end of a cordless tether.

By the same token, parents are afforded an opportunity at virtually any time of day or night to satisfy their urge to connect. A cell phone can be an irresistible "invitation" to parental intrusions into a student's day.

Today's families have become used to a world of constant availability, instant answers to questions and immediate problem solving. Global positioning devices have allowed parents to know where their school-age children are at any time of the day or night. From middle school on, students are seldom far away from their cell phones and therefore, from access to their parents. And this has been a handy convenience. Parents could arrange the logistics for last-minute plans while still at work or just touch base after school to see how a teenager's day was; children could contact parents in emergencies; parents could monitor curfews with "time to come home" text messages.

So why talk about communication now that a son or daughter is ready to leave for college? Why not just continue this oh-so-familiar routine?

It helps to take a step back and reflect on the changing nature of the relationship. How are college students' needs different from high schoolers'? How will our role as parents change? How do we support and foster our children's growing independence? How can we best help them make this transition? With today's fast pace and easy access, it is so tempting for parents to keep in constant touch—to check in the way we did when our children were in high school—to try to protect them from all disappointment, hurt or failure. It is difficult for a loving parent to slow down the process and encourage this emerging adult to take charge of solving his or her own dilemmas. However, not to do so is to deprive our children of the sense of satisfaction, mastery and self-confidence that we all want them to experience.

When parents are faced with those inevitable phone calls, Lori Tenser, Dean of First-Year Students at Wellesley, suggests that parents say things such as: "Wow, that sounds like a challenging problem; what will you do about it? Or who on campus is there to help you with that? How can I be supportive while you figure out what to do?"

Sorting out the best methods to keep in touch can be confusing. From IM to Skype, from webcams to text messages, from e-mails to cell phones—we need to figure out which will work best for our family. And then the question remains . . . how often? The potential number of contacts is unlimited . . . every day? five times a day? once a week? when the spirit calls?

There are no rules, not even one common answer or right way. It is not the quantity of phone calls in a day, week or month that is at issue. When a parent makes the call, he or she might ask, Am I doing this for me or for my child? Is it because I feel lonely and need to hear her voice to perk up *my* day? Is it because I am worried about his inability to be responsible, and I need to be sure he is getting up to go to class or taking his medication? And what about the student's calls: What does it mean when she calls daily, having a meltdown about what to do about a grade, or a problem with a roommate or a coach? Is he calling from his advisor's office wanting me to help him decide what courses to take? Does he expect me to intervene on his behalf whenever things don't go his way?

Cell phones are, of course, useful to get instant information: to check on a son's schedule in order to grab a low airfare while it is still available or to text a message of support just before a daughter's swim meet or a son's final. Calls with exuberant "I aced the test!" or a "Thinking of you; just wanted to say hi" can be welcome interruptions in a parent's day. An Ohio mother of a Yale freshman delights in these calls:

> She communicates more frequently since she left and I love it! She'll call and say, "I'm waiting for the bus," or, "I'm on my way to class," and I feel like I can keep up with her life. It's way better than back in the days of waiting for Sunday night.

Some students love to call home to celebrate a success or vent about a poor grade or a messy roommate. Often all they want is a good listener who will share their joy or empathize with their disappointment.

How often and with what method to keep in touch will vary from family to family, even from one sibling to another. A group of Minnesota parents discussed their very different experiences:

We're still experimenting. I started out calling her, but she was always busy or having four other conversations, so I found that unsatisfying. Then I would wait for her to call, which was erratic. Now I find I will send an e-mail or text message and she'll call me back. . .so I think we're still trying to figure it out.

I struggle with lack of communication so much so that I called the dean of freshmen to see if she was still alive. The dean was sympathetic and said, "It is hard to drive from Minnesota to New York to see if your child is still alive." So my husband and I instigated a routine that she had to call us on Sunday. I finally gave up on that because we'd get the call *(in a grumpy voice)*, "It's Sunday, so I'm calling." Now I find that IMing is much freer. She chit-chats more.

I deliberately signed up for fantasy football this year. He's been doing that for a few years. I asked him if it would be all right if I joined his fantasy football team and he said it would be fine, so there is this e-mail chatter back and forth about that and you can be talking about that and slip in something else. My wife doesn't get as much information as I do. That worked. It was a good strategy.

We decided to do Facebook as a way of augmenting the weekly phone calls. It was our daughter's idea for us to join to see all the fun pictures, but last week I decided it wasn't fun anymore. It felt intrusive; it felt creepy. She goes to McGill where drinking is legal at 18, but it made me uncomfortable, so I "unfriended" her.

One thing students all seem to agree about is that they love to reach into their campus mailbox and find mail or a care package from home instead of the usual flyers or bills. Hearing about the mundane daily comings and goings of brothers and sisters, neighbors, and friends lends a sense of permanence and familiarity to a tenuous time. It is no coincidence that we use a word that suggests a safe harbor, rootedness, and stability to describe the nightly television newscaster—anchor—steady and familiar. Parents, too, serve as anchors to disperse the news from home as reliably as NBC or CNN.

A freshman at the University of Tulsa speaks with affection of the regular mail she received from her mother:

> My mom would write about how the street looked in front of our house—or about our cats. She'd tell me that our neighbor painted his door red, or that my old school won its first football game all season. Football isn't really important to me, but home is, and she made it come alive for me in her letters.

Reassuring correspondence from family members can be read and reread, giving a boost to a wounded ego and reminding students that they are not forgotten. Some parents send clippings from the local paper; some just send the Sunday sports pages with a brief note attached. Students rave about care packages and holiday cards and surprise gifts, no matter how small. There are innumerable ways to stay in touch—to let your child know he or she is on your mind.

A Colorado College sophomore from Long Island speaks fondly of his mother's regular correspondence:

> My mother often sends me a quick note saying, "I'm at the office writing a report and was thinking of

> you." Or she'll send me a silly card. It's great just to be remembered and get something in my mailbox.

A student from Hong Kong talks delightedly about a special care package:

> My mother ordered a carton of my favorite foods from a Chinese grocery store here in St. Louis. It came to my room. It meant a lot because my parents are so far away. It was such a nice gesture to get that package.

For some families e-mail and instant messaging are the favored options for regular communication:

> My husband is not a letter-writer, nor does he talk much on the phone before turning it over to me. However, he does e-mail our daughter when he wants to find out something or make arrangements with her. I am no longer the "middle man" for them.

> My son seems to tell us so much more in e-mail than he ever does on the phone. It's on *his* time. He usually writes us at about 3 a.m.

> My daughter tells me she likes to e-mail her father because he doesn't interrupt her.

One divorced parent finds e-mail a bonus in communicating with his son and his ex-wife:

> The e-mail traffic between Jim and me often includes his mother as well. We share more information than we would have otherwise. Jim often writes to one of

> us and sends a copy to the other. Especially concerning travel plans and money issues, we routinely share the e-mail among the three of us.

Texting is a great way to dash off a quick message to ask Mom about a financial aid question or when you've just found out you made the volleyball team and you're bursting with excitement. Tap away while the excitement is still fresh! While text messaging may be the preferred mode for quick bits of information in the middle of the day, e-mail may be used for late-night musings or for more touchy subjects.

For some students who feel the pushes and pulls of being on their own, e-mail may still be the favored way to contact parents. It offers the possibility for connection in a casual, leisurely and unthreatening way. Need time to write about a dicey subject? Two in the morning may be your time of choice.

Many students e-mail to transact business or communicate with professors. They laughingly say "E-mail is for old people. I Facebook or IM my friends." Parents often complain:

> I can't tell if he's reading my messages or not. It seems like such a great way to keep in touch, but I get frustrated after three or four messages in a row without a reply. When I ask him about it he says casually, "Yeah, I read it."

Many parents and students say they use e-mail, texting, or IMing for day-to-day messages, but prefer the phone for more in-depth conversations. Some families still keep in touch weekly by phone, and the Sunday phone call is a predictable ritual.

A senior at Stanford, who refers to the cell phone as "the electronic leash," prefers e-mail or texting:

> It keeps my parents from calling as often as they might. And it significantly lowers my annoyance level, which in turn leads to better conversation when we do talk. We are not living down the hall from our parents anymore, and it shouldn't feel like we are.

Of course, many students regularly screen their calls or turn off cell phones, leaving one parent to remark, "Sometimes when I want to hear my son's voice, I just listen to his voice mail greeting."

Students usually prefer to initiate the calls, rather than receive them at awkward or busy times—another indication of a need to take charge of their lives. For example, one student commented:

> I think it's important that I do the calling, because then I don't resent them. If they call, and I'm grumpy, the whole conversation goes downhill from there.

Parents should remember, however, that freshmen often reach for the phone at "down" times, and that parents often receive a skewed view of their son's or daughter's psychological well-being. The "ups" are reserved for friends and the "downs" for them.

For many international students and their families, Skype, webcams, and e-mail provide welcome means of bridging the great physical distance between them. A young woman from Thailand explains that being able to talk to her mother when she gets back to the dorm each night—as her mother is getting up in the morning—allows them to stay close and not "get extra lonely."

A junior from Taiwan uses Skype with a webcam.

> I Skype my mom a lot. My Jewish roommate is taking Chinese, and he loves to try to chat with my mom. It's really fun for him—and for my mom. Sometimes it's hilarious to watch.

An engineering student from Argentina says, "My parents call twice a week. I especially like it when they call on Sunday. I talk to everyone in the family because they all come together at my parents' house every Sunday for lunch." She balked, however, at her father's plea that she keep her cell phone on all day so that he can reach her at any time.

Reading about the experiences of parents who have "been there" can lead to some thoughtful discussions about the changes which are about to take place and how they may affect the way the household has been used to communicating. When it comes to keeping in touch, each family will need to find its own way, being sensitive to the issues of control and independence that are at the heart of all the logistics.

THE LAST FEW DAYS

There does come a time finally when the suitcases are brought down from the attic or the trunk up from the basement. The very act of packing may be another reflection of the way a student handles leaving home.

Parents speak of their children's underpacking:

> The night before she left, she threw some things into a backpack and some duffels. I was horrified, but she kept reminding me that they sold tissue and toothpaste in Ann Arbor, so not to worry.

And overpacking:

> She seemed to be moving her entire room to Penn—her bulletin board, high school yearbooks, stuffed animals, wall hanging. We packed five or six large boxes to send UPS the week before, plus the suitcases she took on the plane. I tried to explain that she would have trouble fitting all that into a small room with another person and her things, but it seemed so important to her, I guess. At the time I thought I was being too indulgent, but it really seemed to help. She kind of "nested" when she got there and seemed to relax when she replicated a corner of her room at home in her new surroundings.

In these last hours of packing, the most ordinary actions can take on a special magnitude. Cleaning out a closet becomes a night-before-departure ritual, and the gesture of taping the last box is done with emphatic finality. All the while, nostalgia permeates the scene.

Some parents add a special gift to the already overflowing duffels and suitcases—a gift that provides a sense of continuity, inspiration or reassurance for the coming years—a scrapbook of family pictures or mementos; a letter which includes family reminiscences; a journal for their son or daughter to keep while away; a good-luck charm or special care package. A publishing executive packed her daughter off to Vassar with a toolbox adorned with quotes from Dr. Seuss—a beloved childhood favorite—and filled it with rubber bands, duct tape, a stapler, microwave popcorn and Life Savers.

A divorced father slipped what he refers to as his "letting go" letter into his daughter's suitcase:

> I told her, "I'm not going to talk to you about alcohol and safe sex. I've already talked to you about all that." I simply told her, "I trust you and love you and want

> this to be a wonderful experience for you." She called after she opened it and we shared some tears.

A New Jersey mother of two writes wistfully of her own departure for Skidmore a generation ago, as the images from that time mingle with the present reality of her daughter's leave-taking:

> I believe that part of the mixed pain and joy I felt as we packed the college-bound boxes and bags were the memories of my departure for college more than thirty years ago. My own remembered clothes kept getting tangled up in my daughter's very different clothes as we filled the suitcases.
>
> Just as she, opening the doors to her new life, believes everything is possible, so did I. Her small cartons of books reminded me of the Emerson, Byron, and Camus I took with me, certain in the knowledge that I, too, would one day write a book. I smiled at the favorite stuffed animals my usually pragmatic, practical daughter gentled into her trunk, particularly the small, green kangaroo—given to me so long ago by the boy I was so certain I would one day marry.

Each leave-taking is unique and has the stamp of that child's own personality printed on its style and pace. A mother of two college-aged children recognized the characteristic patterns of their approaches to new adventures. Her sensitivity to their individuality helped her to support them in different and appropriate ways:

> When our daughter was young, she always rushed into things and then got scared. She would race to the top of the slide and then get scared at the top,

> and I would come and help her down. Our son, on the other hand, would stand next to me and watch for a long time until he'd figured it out and then he would attempt it without looking back. They left for college the same way. Steven went first to the University of Michigan. He researched it and spent time during the summer talking about it and planning. We talked over details endlessly. He was miserable for the first twenty-four hours, but never after. Stephanie didn't seem to want to talk or think about it ahead at all. She went to Michigan also, packed the night before and went off fearlessly, or so it seemed, but then she got scared and had a hard time. We did a lot of long-distance handholding.

And so the journey begins . . .

6

ORIENTATION AND DISORIENTATION

IMAGINE YOURSELF STANDING AT YOUR FRONT DOOR with your bags packed, ready to leave on a long-awaited journey. This is a special trip, different from the family vacations or business travels you are accustomed to.

- You are leaving behind everyone you know and moving to a new place where you have made a commitment to spend the next four years of your life.

- When you arrive in this strange place, you look around and see a landscape of unfamiliar faces. A lot of these people talk differently from you; they have strange accents and use expressions you've never heard before. Some of them wear clothes that are different too. They all look smart, confident, and outgoing.

- No one here knows anything about the status you had in your previous position—or about any of your past accomplishments.

- You have left behind your family, friends, colleagues—all the people who are important in your life.

- You're not too sure where anything is or who might be able to help you.

- You have to share a small room with a perfect stranger. There are no set guidelines about bedtime, playing music, or entertaining guests. You have to negotiate everything.

- You have more work to do than ever before, but you're not too sure how you will be evaluated or what people will want from you. You may not get your first evaluations for many weeks.

- You have a lot of unscheduled time and there are plenty of distractions: sports centers, concerts, movies, parties, clubs—and lots of attractive potential partners.

- You need to keep track of a little plastic card so you can unlock your door, check out library books, buy your meals or get into the gym. And you have to handle financial and housekeeping matters that used to be done for you or, at least, you shared.

- You're not too sure where your work and new relationships are heading and you don't know where

> or how you will ever fit into this new place. But everyone has told you that your whole future depends on your doing well during these four years—preferably better than those other bright, confident-looking people who live here with you.

This is the freshman's journey. The student who arrives at college is confronted with a totally new world, as alien as a foreign land. And when seen from this perspective, we may wonder how anyone survives freshman year. Of course, most will survive—even thrive. Yet in many families, college has been a topic of family conversation for so long, especially during the senior year of high school, that parents may lose sight of the magnitude of the transition that freshmen encounter.

ORIENTATION

Most colleges and universities plan carefully orchestrated orientation programs to help freshmen get their bearings. Though many schools hold orientation during the summer, in most colleges, orientation—or welcome week—is a three- or four-day affair that kicks off the fall semester. More schools than ever before begin with an intense small-group experience, from Colby's C.O.O.T. (Colby's Outdoor Orientation Trips) exploring the surrounding hills and coastline of Maine, to Wake Forest University's S.P.A.R.C. program (Students Promoting Action and Responsibility in the Community), a four-day "urban plunge" offering a variety of volunteer service opportunities in the city of Wake Forest. Students who participate in these pre-orientation programs usually rave about them and feel that they have a head start.

The official orientation period, no matter how it begins and when it takes place, is designed to take advantage of new students' eager attentiveness, imparting vast amounts of information and immersing them in morning-til-midnight social activities that encourage friendship and aim to keep homesickness at bay. Seminars and speeches, parties, tours, and excursions, a seemingly endless series of meetings and greetings fill the first days. And, through it all, upperclassmen, administrators, and faculty attempt to introduce freshmen to the resources, philosophy, rituals, and culture of their new home. In retrospect, students are often both grateful for and disparaging of the bombardment of back-to-back programming. Some can't wait for all the frenzy to stop and the semester to begin. But most of them emerge with tentative feelings of belonging to a new culture and a new place, using campus acronyms and nicknames as though they had always known them, talking about "my friends" or "my advisor" with a possessiveness that bespeaks a long-standing acquaintance.

Parents who come to campus with their children are kept busy too. Many attend orientation programs that are offered especially for them in an increasing number of schools, introducing them to the resources of the college, telling them what to expect, and encouraging the process of letting go. Most of the programming is planned so that parents and students are separated from each other for a significant portion of the day. Parents have an opportunity to ask questions without fear of embarrassing their children, and to gain a first-hand exposure to their children's new world.

Parent orientation is, to some extent, an exercise in reassurance and letting go. All parents want to know, of course, that they are leaving their children in good hands. Knowing what the campus security system is, or how the advising system works, or what the Learning Center and Counseling Service offer, is not only reassuring, it is also information that may help parents to foster their child's independence. Later on, when a child calls home with a problem, a parent who knows what kind of assistance is available is more likely to suggest using the appropriate service on campus rather than trying to take over the problem and solve it.

Parents who understand something about the rigor of the academic program will find it easier to give much-needed support to a discouraged and tired freshman rather than offer unsolicited advice about studying harder. College orientation directors and other administrators urge parents to take advantage of the sessions planned for them and learn how they can help their children find help for themselves.

Parents can also learn what the college or university's established relationship is with parents. They might want to ask, "Will my child's grades be sent to me?" "Will I know if he's on academic probation?" "What about if she gets into trouble with alcohol?" "Who should I call if I think my child is depressed or in trouble?"

Whether or not parents actually attend the orientation sessions on campus, they all have access to information about campus services and academic programs through handbooks, which can be tucked away in a readily accessible place. In addition, many schools offer ongoing information throughout the year on special parent Web pages and via electronic newsletters. These might come in handy when least expected. Even if they are never used, most parents feel more secure just knowing where to turn if help is needed.

■

On the day fall orientation begins, the campus starts to bustle early in the morning with a steady stream of new arrivals. Some students arrive in airport vans with only a backpack and small duffel; others, in their parents' cars, loaded with suitcases and cartons and racks of clothes. Though some have traveled across the world, and others have commuted from across town, the air is thick with anxiety, tension, and excitement for all.

The scene reflects the multicultural climate of today's campuses. Walkways, dazzling with newly planted colorful flowers set off an array of family constellations: a family from the Middle East, the mother dressed in a head scarf and an ankle length loosely fitting dress, moving with grace alongside her traditionally garbed husband; a single dad, looking slightly bewildered and ill-at-ease a step ahead of his son; a jeans-clad freshman, her mother, and her mother's female partner joining her father, stepmother, and baby brother for lunch outside the campus deli. Parents and their children can be heard snapping at each other in spite of the fact that they all want this to be a perfect day. The new students walk uneasily, often with heads down, looking up as they pass each other and exchanging awkward glances. Many wear T-shirts with advertisements for the status they used to have—Oakland Soccer, Ypsilanti Basketball—or where they spent the summer—Yellowstone, Oak Bluffs, Vancouver Island. Others sport the names of their high schools or favorite icons—from Harry Potter to the Beatles, all in an attempt to hold on to and present to others who they are.

During those first hours on campus, it is easy to distinguish the freshmen from the upperclassmen who serve as resident advisors and orientation assistants. The RAs and OAs, as they are called at many schools, typically move with the grace and ease of those who are at home in their environment. They greet each other enthusiastically, share breathless tales of summer adventures and unselfconscious hugs. They all seem to look fit and relaxed. It is not unusual for a freshman to look at them and wonder, Will I ever be like that? Will this place ever feel like home?

The very first moments of collegiate life are filled with the ubiquitous pastime of waiting in line. There are lines of cars in front of the residence halls, waiting for their turn to unload. There are lines to pick up orientation packets, lines for luggage carts and elevators—all before the students even get into their rooms. Then there are lines at the bookstore, drugstore and bank. And more lines to pick up student ID cards. The larger the school, the more numerous and longer the lines. After all the preparation and anticipation and emotions of departure, college begins with a series of tedious waits.

Parents, too, feel the disorientation of arrival on someone else's turf, where customs and logistics are unfamiliar. Suddenly their child is just one of many, and the family unit joins the ranks of outsiders. Their son or daughter who had been eager for their presence may now walk self-consciously five or six feet ahead of them—already placing distance between them, reminding them that the time to part is near. One mother, when asked how the first day was going for her, answered bemusedly:

> As well as can be expected, considering I drove 500 miles yesterday and now my son is telling me I can sit in his suite, but should stay out of his room—that it's OK if I talk to other parents, but not to students. He literally jogs ahead of me. He's keeping his distance. And he and his "friends"—he met them this morning—are going out for pizza tonight.

Many parents are surprised by the subtle and sometimes not-so-subtle cues from their son or daughter that their presence is a mixed blessing. As one faculty member said to an assembled group of parents at the opening orientation session of a small liberal arts college: "This person you brought with you, who was clinging to you two hours ago, won't even know who you are three hours from now."

An exaggeration to be sure, but the pull toward separation and the desire to make the break are coupled with the wish for parental reassurance—or just a bit of help with the mundane tasks of moving in and getting settled.

A freshman at Colorado College, who had asked his parents to drive him to school, described with a wry smile:

> Having my parents at school with me when I got here was nice. I cannot say that we had anything to do, but it was nice not having to walk in completely alone. Once they had taken me to get Wal-Mart stuff, I was ready for them to leave. I felt like it was time for me to deal with making friends and they could do nothing to help me. So, I wanted them to leave a little earlier than they did. After they left, I called them every day for a month.

A student who emphatically tells his parents he wants to be alone and unpack by himself urges them a moment later to be back in time to meet him for lunch. Another, who had handled the packing and departure from home with utmost bravado, tells her mother she wants to spend the first night with her in her hotel. This desire to surge forward and then to check back with parents is a familiar echo of the separation behavior of the 2-year-old, who careens off into new worlds, only to run back anxiously to make sure that Mother is still there. The beginning college student is also plunging into new worlds, and the lure of adventure and separation from parents, as well as the need for security, may produce behavior during these opening days that is as inconsistent as it was those years long ago when he or she was a toddler.

Parents who bring their children to college with preconceived expectations of sharing the orientation experience in a particular way may miss the very rich experience that is actually available to them. Dreams of a last family dinner together at the best restaurant in town are often dashed by a student's scheduled orientation event or spontaneous first meal with a new friend or floor mate. Images of an idyllic shopping spree to buy plants and posters together may never materialize. Not only that, but the weather may not cooperate. Instead of the anticipated crisp, cool fall day, students and parents often find themselves moving in on the hottest day of Indian summer or in the midst of a downpour.

Parents may feel like awkward bystanders in a world that is quickly enveloping their child. Relishing the opportunity to provide tangible assistance one more time, they assume the roles of porters, gofers, and personal shoppers. The mother and father of a University of Minnesota student laugh as they describe a frenetic thirty minutes at a Minneapolis discount store while their son was getting settled in his room:

> We madly ran from aisle to aisle filling our cart with essentials and nonessentials, everything from double-stick tape to plastic drinking cups; from a popcorn maker complete with a jar of popcorn to a big shiny red wastebasket. We even threw in a tie. We must have looked like those prizewinners in a supermarket contest. "Fill your basket with all you can in thirty minutes!" The truth of the matter is, we did it as much for us as we did it for Ted. We knew he wanted to stay in the dorm and unpack by himself, and we had all this nervous energy and this was something concrete we could do. When we brought the stuff back to the dorm, it was clear that it was a hit. The popcorn maker was our best bet. We got a kick out of seeing Ted and his roommate leave for their first floor meeting, carrying the wastebasket filled with freshly made popcorn.

It isn't always easy to refrain from last-minute hints about study habits and course selection and discipline and making friends. It may even be difficult to stand back and leave the bed unmade and the suitcases half full. A Bowdoin senior recounts:

> My mother hadn't set foot in my room since I was 13. When we arrived at college, she wouldn't leave until she had made my bed; it freaked me out. She got upset because I brought my favorite bedspread, which had holes in it. She was acting as if my college career was doomed because I had three holes in my bedspread.

It is not uncommon to hear students and parents fighting in the campus store about mundane decisions, such as what color sweatshirt to buy, or which type of desk lamp is best. Some parents even try to have dorm rooms switched, or show up at meetings for students and advisors, or make special requests to the RAs to look out for their children. All of these actions, no matter how well intentioned, make it more difficult for the new freshmen to separate and assert their independence.

Though many schools invite parents to accompany their children to school, they also gently encourage them to leave campus after the parent programs are over. Phrases such as, "now that parents have departed" and "dinner with your classmates while your parents enjoy the restaurants in town" appear in most orientation schedules, pointed hints that it is time for parents to go. It is apparent to college faculty and administrators that even the most self-confident freshmen feel uneasy when their families linger on beyond the activities intended for them.

Recently some parents have complained about the "welcomes" they have received from seemingly judgmental administrators, lecturing them about their "helicopter parenting." Though the term "helicopter parents"—parents who hover—is a media-driven stereotype, most college administrators can reel off a few extreme anecdotes which usually leave listeners aghast. In their zeal to ward off some of the more intrusive and misguided behaviors that they have witnessed, some administrators have used their captive audience of new college parents to give heavy-handed lectures

One proud father of a son entering a prestigious small East Coast school was outraged:

> The first afternoon we were there, we were scheduled to meet the president and I thought that would be cool, that he would tell us about his philosophy of education or what goes on at school. I was looking forward to it. Instead it was an awful lecture, the worst. I'd never heard the term "helicopter parent," but I know what it means now. He talked as if we were all hovering, and I wasn't feeling that way at all. Here's my one shot. I made the effort to drive across the country. We're going to be paying for four years. Tell me something about the college and what's going on here. Instead we got this lecture. It was small-minded and really negative. That was the only part of the visit that was bad.

And a single mother whose very independent son went to a small college in the Northwest close to home had a similar experience:

> I brought my four daughters with me. All these lecturers were saying: YOU PARENTS HAVE GOT TO LET GO NOW!! People were sobbing; it was horrible. I felt like this is hard enough. I don't need to sit here and listen to this, so I just went for a walk.

Parents often interpret what they hear as a mixed message: "Let your children solve their problems without your intervening; we are here to help so be sure to call us when there is a problem." Professors, deans and college presidents walk a fine line between counseling parents to let their children struggle with problem solving and decision making on their own and encouraging parents to feel free to contact the school if their children seem to be in trouble or incapable of accessing resources on their own.

Patricia Whitely, Vice President for Student Affairs at the University of Miami, is aware of the complexity of the college transition for this generation of parents who have been so involved in the lives of their children:

> I think there has to be a balance in the way universities relate to parents. We all have to figure out what that balance looks like. What I like to say to parents is, you've created this foundation for your children, and our goal is to build on it.

Most parents who go to family orientations come away, albeit full of emotion, also full of information about everything from campus resources to a new understanding of the family transition that is about to begin. A Dennison parent describes a positive experience:

> There was an appropriate gathering for students and parents with a lot of information and then there were peer groups for the kids to help them select courses; no cell phones were allowed. Maybe this was a way for the school to encourage them to make their own decisions. The small groups for parents allowed us to ask those questions which might have embarrassed our kids.

The mother of a University of Minnesota freshman recalled:

> The parent orientation was one of the best things I've ever been to. I don't know how many of them

> they had, because the campus has fifty-five thousand students. After a tour together, the parents and students separated. They had all these people talk to us who would be there to support her—even someone from the campus police. I thought it was fabulous. It is such a huge place, and I found it so reassuring.

As the moment of parting draws near, many students seem anxious to say good-bye to their parents; others have last-minute jitters and become tearful and panicky. The long imagined final good-bye may be, in fact, a self-conscious and hurried affair in the student-filled lobby. One father said wistfully of the last minutes at Kenyon with his son:

> Like most symbolic moments, we have a picture in mind of what it will be like, but it's not finished off like a Kodak commercial. I can't even remember the actual moment of parting, because he was surrounded by his RAs and friends.

The orientation experience isn't picture-perfect for students or their parents. But parents who approach this experience with open minds, who are flexible and willing to take their cues from their children rather than attempt to direct them, are likely to feel the deep satisfaction of having shared an important passage even as they are parting.

DISORIENTATION: THE FIRST FEW DAYS ON CAMPUS

"A whirlwind," "a blur," "a fog"—these are the words students use in retrospect to describe their earliest days on campus. Overwhelmed by new places and people and rituals, they have a sense of unreality and a world turned topsy-turvy. The first glimpse inside an ivy-covered, brick residence hall is often a shock. And the room itself, bare and colorless, shows little promise of the home it will eventually become. A University of Oregon student recalls:

> When I got to my room, my roommates' stuff was there, but they weren't. I started putting sheets on the bed, and I broke down. It didn't look good. Anything that unfamiliar that I know I'm committed to for the next ten months couldn't possibly have looked good—to sleep at night with total strangers—and wake up the next morning in this strange place.

And a Vassar student remembers:

> I had a single and I was really glad about that. But when I saw it, I just couldn't imagine how I could ever think of it as my place.

For a University of Vermont freshman, the first problem was finding her room. It certainly didn't seem funny at the time, but now she chuckles as she tells the story:

> I asked my Dad to drop me off at the dorm, and made plans to meet him later. I knew I didn't want him to be there as I met my roommate. I grabbed two of my suitcases and took the elevator to my floor. When I got to the room, there were two girls already in there. It was then that I found out I was in the wrong dorm. I was too embarrassed to go back down in the elevator. I was afraid someone would see me and know what happened, so I took the stairs. Later that day I was supposed to go to a freshman barbecue, and I couldn't find it. Everything seemed to be going

> wrong. I was really in a daze. It was sort of like floating around in a sea of people. I felt very vulnerable.

Indeed, many college students talk about how vulnerable they felt during their first days on campus; they acknowledge with hindsight that the road to becoming a suave sophomore is paved with a series of minor embarrassments. They remember desperately wanting to make a good first impression, while trying to decipher the codes of their fellow students' behavior. Some work hard to stand out and be noticed. Others want nothing more than to blend into the crowd. Many try to be whoever it is they think others want them to be.

As they meet their roommates and floormates with whom they will spend the next year, they are confronted with people whose lives thus far inevitably have been different from their own.

A Franklin and Marshall dean observes:

> When students come to college, they bring a whole series of cultures with them: their individual family, their high school, their town, their part of the country. An only child may find herself rooming with someone from a family of ten. Even if the two students are from similar racial, religious, and class cultures, their personal family cultures are foreign to each other in many ways. One has most likely never shared a room with anyone; the other has never had a room alone. One student may be appalled by the other's casual borrowing of clothes and other possessions; the other may think that the roommate is selfish.

And in this era of diversity on college campuses, a lot of students will also find themselves living with classmates who *do* come from different religious, racial, and class backgrounds. They may use different slang, or even speak a different language. Soon after their arrival, students are confronted with a mélange of styles, values, and attitudes—a coming together of many worlds:

> My roommate went to boarding school. That wasn't part of my world. She had her friends from St. Paul's.

> I wasn't prepared for the racism I encountered here. It's sometimes subtle and sometimes not so subtle—like if I play my music at the same decibel level as a white student, I'm the one the RA tells to lower the volume.

> I never realized how skewed my perception of the peoples in the American population was. I'm from Miami and most of my classmates, including myself, were Hispanic or had strong ties to Latin America. It's really different here. There is A LOT to learn.

> I felt so alone. Even though I spent time in the U.S. before, it was hard to connect with Americans. Everyone connected with childhood ideas—childhood experiences—the same TV shows, the same movies. No one knew my world in Penang.

> I was very conscious of the eighteenth-generation Harvard people because my father was so into the fact that his daughter, the daughter of an immigrant, was going to Harvard, the quintessentially American university.

> I came here—to this Ivy League bastion—with a chip on my shoulder about prep schools, because I went to

> a big public, urban high school where half the class dropped out by senior year, and most of my friends don't have much and a lot of them went to community colleges. I was surprised by how much people mix here.

Although many students find the discovery of this diversity exciting, parents sometimes intrude in an attempt to assure that their child won't stray far from the fold. A young woman from Cleveland recalls a series of phone calls from her parents the first week of school:

> My parents had talked to other parents when they dropped me off here. There happened to be a few other people whose last names ended in *ski* in the dorm, and Mom and Dad asked them if they were Polish Catholics. They wanted me to meet all the people on the floor who were Catholics. It happened that my roommate was the youngest of seven from a big Catholic family, and they thought that was really neat. They kept calling and asking about these people. They were really concerned that now that I had left, I was going to leave my religion too, and they wanted to make sure that I hit the Newman Center as much as possible.

Overanxious parents, even those whose own values reflect an appreciation of the richness of different cultures, may find themselves seeking out potential friends for their children. A freshman from suburban Atlanta exclaims mockingly:

> I can't believe my mother. She keeps asking me if I've gotten to know that nice Jewish girl from Bethesda

who lives across the hall. My parents have never even noticed if my friends were Jewish before!

In response to the plethora of new people, some students themselves initially cling to anyone who is remotely familiar—a long-lost buddy from fifth grade, a fellow Bostonian, a former cabin mate from summer camp. International students and students of color find it particularly comforting to make connections with others from their own backgrounds; indeed, they can be a lifeline to one another, and many schools plan special programs to help them meet.

An African-American junior recalls:

> There were only two black people on my freshmen floor, just me and Marysse, and only six in the whole building. I didn't experience us as a community. The floor did stuff together, but Marysse and I didn't. It's not that they excluded us, but drinking was a big thing freshman year . . . and that's what people did to socialize, and we didn't drink. It was just the nebulous, unidentified white people drinking on our floor. That was how they bonded, and we just didn't.

Some students respond with enthusiasm to the opportunity to meet so many new people and join the party crowd immediately. But even the most outgoing feel disoriented as well as excited by the fast pace and their new surroundings. The hallways and walkways reverberate with fleeting conversations as strangers make their introductions—"What's your name?" "Where are you from?" "What's your major?" The questions and answers are an endless echo.

In spite of efforts to concentrate, it is impossible to keep names and faces straight. Two students may engage in an impromptu half-hour conversation at the soft drink machine and walk away without knowing who the other is. Time seems distorted, the way it does to travelers in a distant country who are bombarded with countless new experiences in the course of a day. Nothing is connected to the routines and rhythms of life at home. It is exhilarating and exhausting.

There are a lot of choices to be made, and students are often concerned about making the right ones. Is it important to go to the orientation session on note taking or should I skip it and play softball in the quad? Should I wear black or tie dye? Would it be better to go to the freshman ice cream social or out for a pizza with the kids down the hall? Should I go to a French film with my roommate or party at the frats? What courses should I sign up for? What activities should I get involved in? Should I drink at the party? Should I or shouldn't I try out for the choir? Do I want to be called Peggy or Margaret or use my middle name instead?

Parents may receive frantic phone calls from confused and overstimulated sons or daughters who just days before brushed off attempts at last-minute advice, now wanting immediate right answers. The father who is a pragmatic business executive may be strongly tempted to respond from his own perspective to the question, "Do you think I should take cultural anthropology or economics?" If he can take a deep breath and then ask some probing questions, he will be teaching his child something about decision making and will help him move toward independence. Questions such as: "What do you see as the advantages and disadvantages of each?" and "How do the faculty compare?" are more effective than a direct answer. The mother who in her own college days was fiercely anti-Greek and receives a bubbling phone call from her daughter announcing, "I've gotten a bid from Pi Phi. Do you think I should join?" is challenged to pause and open a discussion that will help her daughter discover her own best answer.

This North Carolina mother reflects a year later on her handling of the sorority situation:

> I made the mistake of putting down sorority life when our daughter called. She did join anyway, but I never responded positively when she talked about it. It went against so many of my own values. But as time went on, I realized that it provided her with a structure for her social life that she needed—and also gave her better housing opportunities than she would have had on such a big campus. The bottom line was she had investigated all of this and had more information than we did to know what was best for her. I just regret that I wasn't more supportive at the time, and I've learned to trust her judgment more.

It is easy to succumb to the lure of simple right and wrong answers that these dilemmas seem to evoke. But these moments are a perfect opportunity for parents to promote and encourage independent decision making with an expression of support for whatever is decided.

At stake in the aggregate of these decisions is the freshman's sense of who he or she is going to be in this new place where the labels of high school and family and community no longer stick. What affiliations will he make? What groups will he become part of? What image of herself does she want to present? What commitments will she make? What is important? In the company of strangers, a clean slate opens up the possibility of developing a clearer identity—a more solid sense of self that is not merely a reflection of, or reaction to, parents and family expectations. It is exciting to think about the option of change, as well as frightening to think about the possibility of losing oneself. It is almost always disorienting, as exemplified by the comments of this Mills College sophomore:

When I was first at school I felt like I was floating. I kept having to remind myself who I was—what my name was, where I was from. I felt like I always had to explain, this is my name, what I do, who I am. I needed to assert this all the time. With all these strangers it was so discouraging; I had to start all over again. Everything I had in Memphis didn't matter. It took me several weeks to realize that who I was hadn't really changed. If I just went on living normally, people would discover who I am. I didn't have to keep putting it out like it was my resume.

A University of Rochester student from Omaha recalls:

In high school I was quiet and mild mannered. People saw me as an athlete and a scholar. My good friends saw the outgoing side of me, the clown, but that was reserved for them. It was fun coming to Rochester. A whole new beginning. Nobody knew Liza from Omaha and so I could start out anyway I wanted. I could be the clown or stay in my shell. I thought, If I want to make college something I'll remember, I want to meet as many people as possible and especially in the first week. It was a fresh start. I could have my own identity here. No stereotypes were attached and everyone was in the same boat. We were all academic type people and there had to be someone to break the ice and provide comic relief, which I did.

And a freshman from Haverford explains:

When I got to school, I decided to use my real name, Amelia. It's a name most people don't have, and it's

> more sophisticated than Amy. Amy had served me well when I wanted to blend into the woodwork. I thought I would be happy if I could bring Amy, but call her Amelia.

The issue of identity is predominant as freshmen find ways to present themselves to each other. Having left family and long-standing friends behind, they are anxious to make connections that will begin to fill the void. They communicate who they are by how they dress and what they do, by the music they listen to and the way they decorate their rooms. The music they select blares into the hall, a communiqué to passersby. It is an introduction, a way to break the ice, an excuse to wander in—a common language, drawing together like-minded admirers. It also fills this alien space with familiar sounds that entertained and soothed them back home.

Throughout their rooms, students scatter bits and pieces of home, a reminder to themselves and a message to others. Pictures of family and friends and pets, beloved stuffed animals, posters, and yearbooks take their places of honor. Even those who were miserable in high school or whose home life is precarious tend to bring some tangible part of their past for display.

Roommates stack up their beds double-decker style, or take them apart and put mattresses on the floor. They build lofts and hang kites from the ceiling. Some strive for a trendy look of neon signs and blacklights; others fill their space with sports memorabilia from their hometown favorite. One way or another, they create an ambiance and put their personal stamp on rooms formerly devoid of character.

Roommates who do this together face their first challenge: two strangers making the kinds of decisions usually reserved for intimate friends or couples. As they make plans about space and supplies and decor, they may have their first disagreements. These initial difficulties are a chance for them to begin to learn about accommodating each other's needs, about standing up for themselves and engaging in the art of compromise. Through dealing with each other they begin to develop skills that they will use in many other situations. And as the transformation of the room takes place, they also begin to build a bond between them; they feel more competent and independent. Parents who intervene and take charge of setting up the room before they leave, unwittingly deprive their children of an important opportunity, more important by far than the perfect rug and matching comforters.

Whether the formal orientation period lasts a day or a week, most upperclassmen look back on that time and smile at how naive, scared, and hyper they were. Emotions tend to be at a peak and change from moment to moment.

There are countless triumphs and defeats as students navigate the first few days of college life. They feel pulled in different directions. They suffer bouts of loneliness and homesickness, doubting that all these new people will ever measure up to their dearest friends at home. Everyone else looks happy and secure; it will take time to develop friendships and to find out that others share their doubts and feelings. Freshmen may enjoy the camaraderie and sociability of constant activities and impromptu get-togethers, but worry about how they will ever have privacy and time alone in such close quarters. Many liken it to summer camp. Others remark incredulously that their fellow classmates "act like high school kids."

While basking in this new parent-free zone, freshmen often resort to juvenile behavior and antics. These same students suddenly are in charge of "grown-up" tasks, arranging for allergy shots, opening a bank account, interviewing for work-study jobs. Perhaps at no other time is this crossroads of adolescence and emerging adult more evident. As one young woman put it, "All of a sudden I feel like I have to be independent. I feel like my parents. I feel old; the child is gone in a second."

Even the hallowed collegiate rituals are confusing to a freshman who as yet has no context in which to place them. A freshman walks out of the convocation ceremony, where the provost has spoken, turns to his roommate, and asks, "What's a provost?" His roommate shrugs his shoulders. Another looks with disbelief as a procession of faculty dressed in academic regalia, streams into the somber chapel; she whispers to the student next to her, "Do you think these people are our teachers?" Later another student quips, "I wonder what we should call them. Professor? Doctor? Your Majesty? Hey you?" And a student at Brown recalls:

> We have these gates at Brown. They're only opened twice, once at convocation and once at graduation. At convocation, the first day of classes, we all file through these gates in rows. I did it barefoot; I couldn't resist. There we are, all the freshmen with no idea what is going on. Some administrator I don't know is telling me what to do. It seemed impersonal and strange. There were all these people giving talks we had to listen to and we're the ones who don't know them. It was all done as if they were doing it for our own good, but it had no meaning to us.

Some students become so absorbed in the euphoria and intensity of their new lives that promises to call or write home are temporarily forgotten. They lose track of time, and when they do think about calling it's 2 a.m. As one college dean told a group of parents, "If your children don't call home for a week or so, it probably means that they are busy, healthy, and haven't run out of money yet." Some students, though, call a lot in the beginning—perhaps several times a day. They may want to talk about everything that is happening, or they may simply want to hear a parent's voice yet offer little information or insight in return. Occasionally, they tell just enough to set parents on edge. A Trinity student called home breathlessly a few hours after her arrival in San Antonio to report, "I'm in love with the guy who gave me a ride from the airport!"

DISORIENTATION: PARENTS' FIRST FEW WEEKS AT HOME

Of course, the world at home hasn't remained completely stable. A child's departure always has an impact on the parents who are left behind. Some feel the jolt at the moment of parting. Others find themselves reacting after the fact, their feelings taking them by surprise.

During the weeks before his son's departure, the father of a Lawrence University freshman had been trying to console his wife, who was having a difficult time. He repeatedly told her that she should focus on the positive aspect of the upcoming event, that they had been preparing their son for this day for eighteen years and now it was time for him to leave. He urged her to think of this as a time for celebration, for after all, they had a terrific son who was going off to a fine school. It was all very logical. But after they dropped their son off at Lawrence and were heading back home on the interstate, his wife looked over at him and noticed his tear-streaked face. He describes that unexpected moment:

> I guess it didn't really hit me 'til then. I did feel really good about Kurt and about the experience I think he's going to have at Lawrence. But there was no way around it. We had just been through a passage. My wife and I spent the next three hours driving through the cornfields, reminiscing about Kurt—both of us alternately laughing and crying.

The father of a University of Missouri freshman finds himself filled with emotion as he remembers the day of parting:

> After we left him, on the drive home, I came unglued. The whole summer, even the year, everything just snowballed until that point when we left the main campus. I came uncorked, and I started crying like I never cried in my life. My son—we always tell each other that we're buddies—and I was leaving my buddy behind.

A mother of three found that each child's leaving was different. She remembers most vividly the departure of her third:

> The last was the most difficult. In some ways it surprised me. I have a ritual—after they leave, I change the sheets and clean up their room. Jossie, the youngest, left a long, sentimental note and I found it under her pillow. I wept.

A mother from Cambridge, Massachusetts, whose only child moved into a dormitory just across the river at Boston College talks of the special challenges when a child leaves home, but doesn't leave town:

> Kids from far away had to plan ahead, pack everything, get it into a car and arrive with parents, set up the room, and within 24 to 48 hours the parents left. We spent at least a week setting up little by little and it was incredibly tense. She was anxious, I was anxious, and it kept on for days. We also didn't really have a ritual to launch this major experience—i.e. me driving off and our knowing she wouldn't see me for months. So the separation dragged on for days and we never really had closure.
>
> And after she left—that's when it really got hard. I thought about her constantly: How was she doing?

> Did she like her roommates? Was she trying to fit in or just running off to see her old high school friends who were still in town? Did she know how to use the ATM? In the beginning I would just call her casually and say I was in Brookline, or would be near campus, did she want to have lunch, or could I drop off some things she forgot. That was a mistake. She wanted the freedom to jump in and my calls kept reminding her I was nearby. I got the message quickly and stopped asking. Sometimes I felt like a stalker—just wanting a "sighting" of her.

There are many factors that affect parents' reactions—their own marital status; the size of the family; the birth order of the child or how pleasant he or she was to have around in those last few months before departure. Most parents feel mixed emotions after they have sent a child off to college. It is a bittersweet time of excitement and nostalgia, of weighing and evaluating gains and losses. Waves of feeling tend to emerge and recede at unpredictable times, when walking past a daughter's uncharacteristically neat bedroom or glancing at her baby picture on the wall, after a son's telephone calls or long-awaited e-mails describing his new friends. One father whose son and last child had gone to the University of Denver told of placing a pair of his son's old track shoes in the front hall for weeks to ease the hollowness he felt whenever he came home from work.

And an energetic newspaper publisher and mom exclaims:

> I was always surprised at when these kicks would come. After we had dropped her off and returned home, I burst into tears in the cereal aisle, because I realized I didn't have to buy low fat granola anymore.

Barbara Kohm, an educational consultant, writes her impressions after her last child left for college:

> I love the freedom my husband and I enjoy, and I love the quiet orderliness of a clean house. I love having my car to myself, and I love having the radio permanently set on the classical music station.
>
> At the same time I miss the exciting confusion that the children and their friends provided. I miss the dinner table discussions about parties, poetry, politics, and English assignments and the silly songs we sang as we did the dishes. I even miss helping them solve problems although my memory may be a little fuzzy here. I'm ready to go out to dinner more and to cook less, but I'm not sure I'm ready to have my primary parenting years behind me. What hurts the most is that for twenty-five years I've thought of motherhood as my main job. Now that job is reduced to a weekly phone call and an occasional piece of advice—although even that isn't needed very often. I have a hunch that this bittersweet rush of mixed emotions will never entirely go away, that it will linger for the rest of my life, not as an irritant, but as a reminder of the real depth and meaning of life.

Many women, including those who have long-standing, demanding careers, share this feeling that being a mother has been their primary role, and the bonds that they have formed with their children often make the separation process more difficult for them than they had anticipated. When her own daughter left for college, Pulitzer prize-winning columnist Ellen Goodman wrote:

> A long time ago, I thought that mothers who also had

> work that engaged their time and energy might avoid the cliché of an empty-nest syndrome. A child's departure once meant a mother's forced retirement from her only job. Many of us assumed that work would help protect us from that void. Now I doubt it.
>
> Those of us who have worked two shifts, lived two roles, have no less investment in our identity as parents, no less connection to our children. No less love. No less sense of loss.
>
> Tomorrow, for the first time in 18 years, the part of my brain that is always calculating time—school time, work time, dinner time—can let go of its stopwatch. The part of me that is as attuned to a child's schedule and needs as it is to a baby's cry in the night will no longer be operative. I don't know how easy it will be to unplug.[1]

For single parents of an only child, leave-taking may be particularly poignant. An attorney from Philadelphia writes:

> My daughter's father and I were divorced when she was only two years old, so we have been through a lot together. This made for a lot of intensity in our family dynamics. Put another way, there was lots of estrogen and very little "social diversity" in the home. It was just the two of us. So her departure for college was a profound change for the both of us.
>
> When we arrived on campus, things went normally—at first. But after we had gotten everything unpacked and organized, things started going a little haywire. First, she exploded about the fact that "we bought the wrong computer." The fact that this was the exact computer, down to the model and color, that she had begged her father and me to buy for her

as a graduation present, did not seem relevant. It went downhill from there. It was at this same point that I ceased to be my normal self. I began to feel what I can only describe as *discombobulated*. In fact, I clung to this word as the most accurate description of what I was feeling and continued to feel for several months after she left for college. Now I understand better with the perspective of time that what I experienced was a feeling of being severed from myself. Some part of me—and some part of my daughter—had not yet separated.

Releasing my daughter into the world to be who she really is requires some REAL letting go. It was like giving birth again. Less a physical letting go; one more in the mental, emotional and spiritual realms.

Just as the freshmen are orienting themselves to the college world they have entered, their families back home are changing old patterns and finding ways to adjust to the new configuration their own world has suddenly taken. Siblings' relationships change; the threesome that was always a study in shifting alliances becomes a united duo. A father suddenly finds himself the only male in a family of women; he'd never thought about his daughter's common bond with his wife before. A divorced mother finds herself living alone for the first time in her life; she alternately revels in her freedom and weeps at the solitude. A couple look at each other across the dinner table night after night, wondering what is left of their marriage, or cherishing the opportunity to talk at last without interruption. A widower's delight at each e-mail from his son is tempered by the reminder that he can't share it with his wife. The only child still at home challenges her parents not to be boring—to pay more attention to her now that a favorite brother is no longer there to joke and commiserate with her.

While parents are struggling with a sense of loss, a younger sibling may rejoice at the possibility of her new position in the family. A Los Angeles woman smiles as she recalls what happened the day after her first daughter left for the University of California at Santa Barbara:

> The next morning I got up very early and was engrossed in writing a long letter to Molly, trying to tell her all the things I'd forgotten to say, without letting on how much I missed her. I felt very emotional, crying as I was writing. Suddenly the bedroom door opened and in bounced Beth, my youngest, dressed totally in Molly's clothes!

In many households, as soon as the departing child walks out the door the rest of the family scrambles for the space that's suddenly available. Brothers and sisters who have shared rooms grab the chance to have one of their own. Empty nests are replaced with newly redecorated studies or exercise rooms filled with the latest equipment. Parents may later be surprised when their children are hurt or angry at finding their room redone or taken over; their reaction seems out of sync with their self-proclaimed independence. But when everything else is changing in their lives, their room and all their childhood memorabilia represent grounding and continuity. Clearly, cordoning off an underutilized room in an overcrowded apartment or house is impractical. But it is the wise parent who discusses these changes with sensitivity *before* they are carried out.

The period of launching children typically coincides with the normal developmental issues of middle age. Parents of college-age children are often concerned about elderly parents; they may be caught in the middle, assuming financial responsibility for parents at the same time that they are taking on the burden of college tuition. There is anxiety about finances, both present and future. No longer taking their health for granted, men and women become more concerned about staying fit and taking care of themselves. Stimulated in part by the excitement and possibility of their child's new adventure, they may be reevaluating their own careers, thinking about switching gears, about increasing or decreasing work or community commitments. Or they may be coming face to face with their own limitations and letting go of long-held dreams. The changes implicit in a child's leaving for college may heighten parents' awareness of other changes in their lives, and although still in home territory, they often feel a sense of disorientation themselves.

A Colorado father is struck by the depth of his feelings as he reflects: "For the longest time, I had defined myself as the father of young children. If Sara is becoming an adult, then what am I?"

And so at a time when children may be checking back for the reassurance of the routine and familiar, family members may be feeling shaky and off balance as they shift to accommodate the loss of one member. On the home front, senses are heightened and emotions more raw, swinging between elation and deep sadness as the reality of the loss becomes evident in the routines of an ordinary day—unconsciously setting the table for four when only three sit down for dinner, hearing the silence of an evening without the abrasive interruptions of the phone ringing, suddenly aware of the freed-up Saturdays that had been spent watching high school football games.

Young men and women ask for little more at this time than a steady and rooted home base to return to, just as they had many years ago when they hurried back from their adventures across the playground to find Mom and Dad sitting on the park bench where they left them. To provide this sanctuary and still stay out of the way is an artful balancing act. It requires sensitivity to the often confusing dynamics of separation and to the long journey the freshman has begun.

7

THE FRESHMAN YEAR

Academic Life and the College Scene

THE ACADEMIC YEAR ON COLLEGE AND UNIVERSITY campuses has its own predictable rhythm, but that rhythm—the markers and intervals—may be quite different from the one parents and children have grown used to at home. As parents pull sweaters out of mothballs, feeling renewed and invigorated by the clarity of cool autumn weather, their freshman sons and daughters may be approaching midterms, feeling especially jittery and vulnerable as they prepare for the first tangible measure of their college work. Campus traditions and rituals become part of the fabric of students' lives: fraternity and sorority rush, fall break, homecoming, winter carnival, registration for the next term, housing selection, reading period, and finals.

The particular markers and their exact timing vary from school to school, and the reactions to these events vary from student to student. But within all this variation there is a common flow, common rituals and patterns that pervade college campuses at particular times of the year. And since the campus environment is different from home, with different priorities and different cycles, it is no wonder that parents and children sometimes feel out of sync when they talk to each other across the miles of their separate worlds.

TO EVERY SEASON: THE RHYTHM OF THE FRESHMAN YEAR

During the first few weeks of school, the frenetic pace set during orientation continues. Classes begin, professors are sized up, and students approach their brand new syllabus for each course with good intentions and high expectations for success. They may shop for courses, sitting in on numerous classes before they actually finalize their schedules. Trying to integrate their own impressions with the collective wisdom of their advisor and the upperclassmen they talk to, freshmen often drop and add courses until a cutoff date forces them to make their first academic commitments. They tend to want certainty, perhaps believing that if they search long enough, they will find the perfect courses and the perfect schedule. "It was so confusing that first semester," recalls a current junior:

> When I came to school, my advisor told me to look at the course listings and just pick my courses. She told me I could drop and add later. I was already having enough trouble just having all these choices. I just wanted somebody to tell me what to do. Telling me that I could change my mind made it even worse. I was holding on to an old high school idea that you can't change your mind, that if you start something you have to finish it. And if I changed, I'd be responsible for that change, and what if I didn't make the right choice?

Beyond the classroom, freshmen are faced with an explosion of activity: parties and sporting events, concerts and plays, and a tempting array of co-curricular organizations all trying to lure new recruits—not to mention a seemingly endless series of impromptu get-togethers as students wander from room to room in the residence halls, listening to music together and talking and wondering how they will ever get any work done.

Everything is new—exciting or frightening, overwhelming or stimulating. Some students thrive on the onslaught of activity and choices, hyper but happy with the overstimulation. Others seem bewildered and overwhelmed and retreat into bouts of homesickness and self-doubt. In the midst of the whirl, there is no place to be alone. Students' reactions to school tend to be intense during these early weeks: they either love it or hate it or alternate between the two extremes, sometimes in the same day, sometimes even during the same phone call home. Almost unanimously, they complain about the institutional food, announcing that they can't find anything edible except salad and pizza.

Three or four weeks into the semester freshmen tend to settle down a bit, to come to the realization that this is not just, as one student put it, "summer camp with homework," and that they have made a long-term commitment. It is often a sobering time:

> I suddenly realized that I was staying—that this wasn't like camp or a vacation from home, that this was real life, and I got a funny sort of feeling. I had been swept along by the excitement of it, and I hadn't really let it sink in that this was now my home.

The euphoria of the first few weeks may turn to homesickness. Many students reach out to high school friends at other schools, and they wonder whether they will ever find comparable friends at college. IMing, texting, calling and even visits from campus to campus are common attempts to establish continuity in an ever-changing period of transition:

They long for the familiar touchstones of home. A freshman at the University of California Davis says with a bit of embarrassment:

> OK, I know it sounds crazy, but I use to go stand on the overpass to look at the I-80 when I got homesick for L.A. I just like the sight and sound of all the cars.

Students who were overwhelmed and homesick at first may find comfort in the familiarity they are beginning to feel with people and places and the day-to-day rhythms of life in college. They have taken the first of many steps in the year-long freshman task of finding a niche.

As classwork progresses, idealized expectations of intense intellectual discussions in the local coffeehouse give way to solitary sessions in the library or bouts of boredom in the classroom. Freshmen discover that long stretches of daytime with no classes and no assignments due the next day make it easy to succumb to the temptation to sleep late and check out the latest episode of "Lost" or sit in front of the computer checking social networking sites or gaming. For some, serious studying is limited to the middle of the night, the only time when, along with the brightness of daylight, the distractions temporarily disappear. Others find themselves filling every available hour studying, often inefficiently plowing through what appears to be an endless amount of reading, unable to decide when one is allowed to take time out to play.

> My first days at college were really really miserable, because here I was with this great big swath of time, and I was used to having this structure when I was in high school and that structure was totally out the

> window, and I think the first time I realized that nobody missed me at class—like I was in one of these 250 person lecture halls for one of my classes—and I could not go and could get the notes from somebody else. It didn't count against me and somehow it didn't seem like I was doing anything wrong, except for the fact that it cost me something like $50 a class.

During this second month of school, social life may also start to be tempered a bit as the pace slows down. First impressions begin to fade, and students who were wary at first learn that they can live together in spite of different backgrounds, values, or tastes in music and wall posters. Students who formed instant friendships during the first few weeks of school may find that the novelty and comfort of those relationships are starting to wear thin. The roommate who had been a constant companion during mealtimes and sojourns to the library may now seem more like a leech who is never out of the room and whose obsessive neatness is nerve-wracking.

No longer treating each other with the tolerance accorded strangers, roommates often have their first major disagreements at this time of the year, and complaints to residential life staff about roommate problems inevitably increase. Students gravitate toward loosely formed groups in their search for companionship and a sense of community. Freshmen who delighted in the news that they had a single, may feel isolated or lonely at times, and recognize the need to venture out of the room to become a part of the kinship of their floor. Most are still wondering just where they will fit in.

As the semester approaches its halfway point, first major papers are due and midterms are scheduled, and an air of tension envelops most campuses. Students move across diagonal pathways to and from libraries, labs, and studios, heads down, faces serious—even somber, carrying the weight of several academic texts in the ubiquitous backpack.

Many freshmen pull their first all-nighter during this time, a rite of passage—a time of desperately seeking to reclaim the many hours that seem to have disappeared during the previous weeks. They spend an inordinate amount of time studying and worrying about studying. Not surprisingly, the campus health service treats a constant stream of exhausted students complaining of sore throats, colds, and the flu. And the counseling service readies itself for the onslaught of students who are trying to cope with the emotional stresses that predictably emerge during this pressured time.

The aftermath of the first set of midterms often evokes a period of intense self-doubt. Students who sailed along effortlessly in high school may be shocked to realize that the success they had come to take for granted is no longer necessarily going to be theirs. The first failing grade, or even a C in a course, can be an affront to the confidence of many students, especially when their identity has been tied to their academic prowess. They may even start worrying that the admissions office made a mistake in accepting them and begin to think, This is the wrong school for me. Premeds who encounter a disappointing grade in biology or chemistry may panic and question their entire future.

Some students breathe a sigh of relief when they see the results of midterms. Intimidated by war stories from parents and high school teachers suggesting that they will no longer be able to get A's and B's when they reach college, those who do continue to do well feel the satisfaction of getting past the first academic hurdle of their college career. Whether or not their initial academic ventures have been successful, once they have moved beyond the midsemester point, most students begin to see the differences between the demands of high school work and the more sophisticated academic challenges of college. And at this point some of them begin to make the adjustments necessary for their academic success.

By late October, students start to talk eagerly about their Thanksgiving holiday plans. Some feel homesick for the first time. In numerous parts of the country, November brings signs of gloomy wintry weather, adding to the anticipation of the upcoming holiday and a break from campus life. For children of divorced families, the question of where to go for Thanksgiving often resurrects painful family conflicts and questions of allegiances. Some students who don't return home for the vacation struggle with an outbreak of homesickness, missing the familiar traditions of this family-oriented holiday. Others delight in the opportunity to be independent and try something different, whether it is a visit to a roommate's home, a trip to a nearby city, or cooking turkey with friends for the very first time. For international students, it's often an introduction to a classically American tradition.

Although many students can't wait to get home, once they arrive and check to see that the refrigerator is stocked and the old place looks pretty much the same, they are out the door for an extended round of visits to high school friends. Trying to explain their new worlds to each other, students begin to realize how much has happened to them in the few months since they left home. With the excitement of reunions and rounds of parties, it is often a confusing and disorienting time.

In spite of the brevity of their time at home, some students take this opportunity to let their parents know that college is changing them. As they try on different identities, students may surprise their parents with new hairstyles, modes of dress, accents, or food preferences. One bemused mother recounts:

> Three months ago all Tim would eat was spaghetti, hamburgers, and fries. When he came home for

> Thanksgiving I fixed all his favorite foods only to find out that all he wanted was tofu and brown rice.

Most students return to campus from Thanksgiving break to face several weeks of intense work, culminating in their first set of final exams. "It's hit-the-wall time," explained one student. "It can feel pretty grim in spite of all the campus preholiday traditions and hoopla. We all show up at these Christmas get-togethers tired as hell. But of course we manage to squeeze in our share of partying too."

As the days before winter break come closer, students plow through long hours of studying and writing final papers, trying to hold themselves together until the long-awaited holiday. Freshmen have a foot in both worlds, immersed in their studies and new college friends while fantasizing about going home, being taken care of, and reconnecting with old friends from high school.

Most students want nothing more than some time out when they arrive home for winter break. Parents are often dismayed by their first glimpse of their exam-weary son or daughter, with dark circles under red-rimmed eyes and ten pounds heavier—or lighter—than usual. The typically energetic freshman is likely to want to sleep or "veg out" in front of the TV for a few days and consume as much food as possible. Parents, meanwhile, energized by the hustle and bustle of the holiday season, may want their son or daughter to get moving, to participate actively in long-established family traditions. They may even feel angry at this apparent inertia and cynically question why they are spending so much money on education if these are the results. For a while, at this particular juncture, the rhythms of the calendar and academic years seem markedly mismatched.

Winter break is a much-needed refueling time for students. It is also a time that stirs up for parents and their temporarily returned offspring new struggles over separation and letting go.

Students often make emphatic attempts to assert their independence and establish their emerging identity. Coming home night after night at 4 a.m., sporting new tattoos and multicolored hair are some of the more visible manifestations. There are, of course, deeper and more subtle pushes and pulls, as students test values and limits and new ideas in the context of old, familiar ground. They struggle too with questions of intimacy, wondering if their new college friendships are truly meaningful and at the same time questioning if they will be able to, or want to, maintain their old friendships at home.

When the winter break is over and students return to school, the residence halls are filled with the excitement of coming together again. Animated meetings and greetings, warm reunions among friends and roommates, and eager attempts to catch up with each others' worlds are a telling contrast to the hesitant, self-conscious arrival on campus of this same group of freshmen the previous fall. For many students this is the moment of recognition that they actually belong to a community, that this place has become a focal point in their lives. For some, it feels like coming home. They have finally begun to believe that the place is theirs.

■

As they settle into the rhythm of the second semester, many students thrive on the comfort of knowing the ropes, of knowing where things are and who does what. They are often beginning to see their college friends as their close friends; many are giving up the illusion of the perfect high school group. They approach their coursework with a newfound confidence. Although still wavering in their attempts to manage time, they have learned something about pacing themselves and setting priorities. The sense of urgency and anxiety they felt first semester is replaced with the satisfaction of having more control over their lives, and as one student put it, "knowing what I have to do and what I can get away with."

Some students, however, feel let down and homesick when second semester begins. They may find it hard to readjust after being at home, comfortable and secure, with few responsibilities. The long list of academic demands looms ahead of them, and still feeling burned out from first semester, they wonder if they can survive the same cycle of papers and tests all over again. Those who did not do well first semester often feel a combination of self-doubt and determination to do better. Many students rethink their initial plans. Premeds and engineering students often question their choice as they plunge into the second round of courses in a rigorous curriculum. During this period, freshman deans hear from a lot of students who are thinking about transferring. Feeling lonely or perhaps uncommitted to anything at the school, they worry that they have made the wrong college choice. Some start to search out other schools on the Web and may even begin to fill out applications. Others make their first commitment to an activity outside the classroom, taking another step toward creating a niche for themselves.

In many parts of the country, the first two or three months of the semester coincide with dreary winter weather. Not surprisingly, students' moods often plunge with the temperature. Those from tropical climates may find their initial fascination with snow waning. This is the time of year in most schools when students have to make sophomore housing plans; they decide who they are going to live with and where they want to be. As they scramble to pair up or form groups of four or six for suites and apartments, inevitably some students end up feeling left out and unwanted. Midterms, which usually come at a particularly bleak time of the year, only exacerbate the situation. Most schools in cold climates plan special events and festivals to counter the frigid weather. And many students head south for a respite and the time-honored tradition of fun in the sun during spring break or join their peers in a week-long community service project, commonly called "alternative spring break." Others use this vacation time to explore summer job opportunities and set up interviews in their hometowns.

When spring finally arrives on campus, the social pace picks up in earnest. Students revel in their access to the outdoors, and impromptu Frisbee games, concerts, and parties pop up all over campus. This can be a wonderful time for students who are comfortable in their friendships or who have found romance. But for some, spring can trigger feelings of intense loneliness. As couples pair off, those who are unattached see a tableau of their classmates walking hand in hand amidst inviting greenery. It looks as though everyone is in love and carefree, making it all the more difficult for the many students who are neither.

Most freshmen agree that the second semester goes by more quickly than the first, and before they know it the end is in sight. They have a pile of papers to write, exams to study for, and a host of decisions to make: Do I store my things here or ship them home? How am I going to get home? And then there are the concerns about how to finance next year's college expenses and what to do during the summer. Students check out the financial aid office in search of the latest information on available money and go to the career office in search of summer jobs.

For most, the academic year ends with rushed good-byes and promises to friends to keep in touch over the summer. As soon as they have finished their last exam, tired and bedraggled students throw their belongings into suitcases and storage boxes. They depart a few at a time over the course of several days, in a very different fashion from their simultaneous and emotion-filled arrival the previous August or September. The last to go find themselves wandering through quiet hallways and lifeless rooms, perhaps realizing more than most how much their feelings about college are intertwined with their fellow students.

For many, the decision to go home for the summer raises familiar issues about separation, as well as independence, identity, and intimacy. Is it possible to go home and maintain a newfound, but still shaky, sense of independence? Is it feasible to hold on to a separate emerging identity and not fall back into the role of family peacemaker or jester or superstar? What will it be like to separate and leave behind intimate college friends, or a lover who is a constant companion?

Some students decide that they don't want to spend the summer at home. They may get jobs near the campus, surrounded by friends who have made a similar choice, all hoping to enjoy the college environment without the pressure of academic demands. Or they may choose to work abroad or at a resort far from home. Parents who had been looking forward to their child's return are often disturbed by such decisions, and it may be hard for them to accept that their child wants and needs this opportunity. Once again parents are challenged to let go.

By the time summer vacation rolls around, college freshmen have been away at school for approximately nine months. Their sense of time is likely to be very different from that of their parents. As one freshman put it, "Every day goes by so fast, but it feels like I've been here forever." They have met a whole new set of people; they have struggled with new ideas and knowledge and values. There have been countless firsts in all arenas of their lives. "My world has exploded," said a 19-year-old from Minneapolis. "There are so many new elements—I find it hard to figure out where my parents fit back into that."

In the context of parents' lifetimes, nine months have been but a moment, and in comparison to the universe of their college student offspring, theirs has remained relatively stable. Fitting back in is a given; parents expect their child to have matured, to be more reasonable, more considerate, and tell Mom and Dad where he or she is going each night and for how long. Their child's idea of independence is that he or she be trusted, left alone, and not accountable. The freshman year has ended, and the family has come together again, if only for a while. So much has changed; so much has stayed the same.

■

To follow the sequence of the freshman year from fall to summer in a linear fashion captures the peaks and valleys of the year, but misses the complexity of any given time. Simultaneously trying to adapt to academic demands, new social relationships, and the freedom and responsibility of the campus scene, college freshmen are deluged throughout the year with challenging experiences in all domains of their lives. The combined effect is more than the sum of the parts. Students don't have the luxury of compartmentalizing the challenges they face, or handling them sequentially. It is not possible to wait until homesickness is conquered, the roommate problem is resolved, and the noise and excessive drinking in the hall settle down before tackling the first big chemistry exam. Students have to try to handle everything all at once, and through the course of the year most of them do.

Yet, for parents to understand more about what the freshman is going through, it helps to examine separately each of the central elements of the freshman experience: academic life, friendship and social life, and today's campus scene.

ACADEMIC LIFE: THE FRESHMAN PERSPECTIVE

Paradoxically, the area of a college freshman's life that parents are the most interested in is the one students may speak of least. To transmit in writing or a phone call the excitement of new learning or the heady feeling after a provocative seminar with a talented professor is difficult at best. Moreover, for many students the academic side of life has been too closely associated with grades and expectations. A parent's question,

"How is your English class?" may be heard as "How are you doing in your English class?" or "Are you keeping up with the work in your English class?" As a result, a student may cut off the conversation with an abrupt "Fine" and move on to less threatening subjects.

Some students are turned on by their courses and long to share their excitement with their parents. Parents who give them the opportunity speak of discovering in their children a new and previously untapped curiosity about art or politics, philosophy or physics. Some students call home and spill forth their delight in a particularly brilliant lecture by a favorite professor, or their first glimpse of the connections between Renaissance art and literature. When a parent responds seriously or in jest by saying "What can you do with art history to put bread on the table?" or a student even senses that a parent's thoughts may be moving in that direction, the conversation turns flat and the wind is knocked out of the student's sails. But parents who set a tone of openness and interest, who reflect the enthusiasm they hear and ask for more details, may be rewarded by hearing about the best that college has to offer.

Questions such as, "What's your favorite class? Tell me about it." "What are you reading? What's the professor like?" convey the message, "I'm genuinely interested. I want to know what your new world is like, what you are learning, how you are maturing, and I appreciate you discovering your own interests, opinions, and strengths. I value your intellectual development and growing independence."

Parents can participate in a student's experience in other ways that show they care. One student who discovered women writers during her freshman year recalls:

> I read *The Awakening* and just loved it, and when I told my mom she went and got it and read it too, and

> we had this great discussion about it at Thanksgiving break.

Many students assert their independence by holding on to their new discoveries, however, protecting their new turf and emerging self from any infringement by family—perhaps fearing the pull back to an earlier, more passive academic self. Spending an evening discussing the pros and cons of environmental regulation or stem cell research can be exhilarating extensions of classroom learning—cherished private moments with fellow students. To question, to challenge, to explore established values are crucial steps in the educational process. But these new ideas are still unformed, and to share them with parents may open them up to criticism or scorn. The freshman daughter of two New York attorneys explains:

> I was brought up with the idea that you have to be able to back up your opinion with logical arguments, even about small things. So now, when I'm changing my opinions about things I think are important, like politics and art, I'm not ready to talk to my parents about it yet. It's not that they'll jump down my throat or anything. I just want to be clearer about what I think so I can talk to them on a more equal level.

Students frequently appreciate it when their parents express interest in their academic life, and it is not unusual to hear students complain about parents who fail to do so. But no matter how well-meaning and interested parents are, some will discover that their children do not want to talk about their courses. They want their parents to respect their need to keep this and other parts of their lives to themselves.

Not all students will find all, or perhaps any, of their freshman classes intellectually stimulating. A scenario familiar to many parents is one that starts with a student's phone call home complaining about one or more courses. Parents may have an instinctive reaction; they may be angry—at the child or the school; they may be disappointed; they may worry that their child is at the wrong school or taking the wrong courses; they may resent complaints when they are making sacrifices and spending so much money. The reality is that parents know little about what is actually going on and can't fix it no matter how much they wish they could. What parents can do is listen empathically and encourage their son or daughter to think of ways to improve a less-than-perfect situation. They might encourage them to talk to their advisor, to the professor or the freshman dean directly and to begin to investigate the course options for next semester.

Whether or not they talk to their parents about the academic side of their freshman experience, freshmen all struggle in one way or another with the gaps between expectation and reality. Initially, they may walk into intimidating surroundings, ranging from cavernous lecture halls where they are sentenced to anonymity to small seminar rooms where there is no place to hide. The professor, who the view book suggested would be a friendly sort who would get to know you on a first-name basis, may instead be a distant figure standing behind a lectern and speaking into a microphone. A freshman at Emory said, "Big classes were a real shock. You're nobody, not even a face, to the professor. In high school people knew who I was."

Large lecture classes are usually interspersed with small discussion sections led by TAs (teaching assistants), who teach to support their graduate work. A Berkeley senior recalled the first class she attended her freshman year, "I knew I was in trouble when I went to calculus and the teacher didn't speak English." Foreign graduate student TAs, whose command of English is limited, may be the only available resource people in a large, popular introductory freshman course.

Though many schools have taken steps to ensure that their TAs have adequate language skills, the fact remains that a disgruntled student who complains about not being able to understand the teacher may be dealing with a real and common problem. Although a parent's instinct may be to get angry along with the student, it is more useful to acknowledge his or her anger and then turn to brainstorming some ways to cope with the problem. Students may decide to seek out help from upperclassmen or fellow students or to get a tutor from the campus learning center. The student will have to be resourceful to find the best possible way to make the most of the situation, and it is helpful if parents encourage and support that resourcefulness, rather than try to take over the problem.

Not all freshman classes are so impersonal. Even large schools such as Cornell and UCLA offer freshman seminars with as few as fifteen students. Although designed to introduce freshmen to the process of intellectual inquiry in an intimate and non-threatening way, this format can be frightening in its own right. Many students find these small classes intellectually challenging and personally warm and inviting, but the expectation to participate in class is intimidating to some. The atmosphere of open inquiry and multiple points of view can be confusing for the less intellectually developed student who is searching for the right answer, and may conclude that, "It's better not to say anything unless it's something brilliant."

Occasionally, freshman seminars are taught by the stars of the faculty. At an increasing number of schools, full professors teach these small seminars, attracted by the enthusiasm and openness of first-year students. A faculty member at the University of Michigan expresses the delights of teaching the students in his freshman seminar:

> Freshmen are very passionate. They really want to learn and find out answers and think through ques-

> tions. It's their first taste of college. In that sense, it's very exciting. They have not been intellectually socialized as to how the discipline thinks about issues, so they bring a whole range of questions.[1]

A University of Michigan freshman, an Indian student born and raised in Zambia, describes her freshman seminar, "Writing about Cultural Communities, Ethnicity, and Imposed Categories," As part of her coursework, she explored her own aspirations and background, and the seminar became a transformative experience for her:

> Every time I wrote, I realized the people who had influenced me. By the end of the course, I felt a sense of wholeness. I knew I'd had all these experiences, but I never realized that's what I really am.

At some schools, such as Grinnell and Northwestern, every student participates in a freshman tutorial, designed to develop research and writing skills. Freshman seminars are often noted for their innovative topics or interdisciplinary approaches to more traditional fare: "Freedom and Authority," "Native American Music and Culture," "A Yen for Fly Fishing: Philosophy and Environmentalism from Mid-stream," and "Humans, Superhumans, and Posthumans," to name just a few. Many schools have adopted a course model known as University 101, developed by John N. Gardner at the University of South Carolina. These classes are designed to introduce freshmen to skills and resources that ease the transition from high school to college. It's not unusual for these seminars to become an important part of the student's life, evolving into a support group, an anchor of sorts for the freshman who feels adrift in an otherwise turbulent academic and social sea.

Opportunities for freshmen to take courses unavailable in most high schools are enticing—anthropology, philosophy, astronomy, management, marketing, communications, engineering, graphics—a smorgasbord of new academic treats. But for some, the course title that suggested an unknown, exotic realm in actuality turns out to be a bore. "*This* is philosophy?" one student moaned after three weeks of reading Plato. Somehow philosophy had brought to mind groups of eager and intense students questioning the meaning of life—*their* life, not Plato's. And introductory psychology classes are filled with young men and women who had anticipated dealing with the complexities of their own fascinating developing psyches, only to find themselves studying color wheels to learn about perception or mazes and rats to learn about conditioning. "What about people?" they lament. Typically, the introductory courses are just that—introductions to the basics of a discipline, exposing students to the inevitable frustrations that accompany first encounters with challenging materials.

"All classes look great in the course listings, but what goes on in the classroom is another story," sighed a cynical freshman two weeks before finals. His harsh comment can be attributed, in part, to his negative frame of mind at the time, but there is more than a hint of truth in his remark. All students learn that even the most wonderful courses have moments of tedium, that you have to memorize symbols and data and struggle with new methodology before you can use them creatively.

Most freshmen are surprised and confused by the level of sophistication that their professors expect from them. Moving beyond the more literal mode of high school, they are expected in college to be able to present and support complex arguments. Students who arrive at college secure in their abilities to read and write well find that now they are being asked to read more actively than they had in the past and to write not just reports, but analyses. They struggle with learning how to think and write critically; how to synthesize material; how to make connections between facts and theories and between different concepts in different courses. Even students who tutored others in high school find themselves trekking to the campus writing center for help with their papers.

A Cal Tech sophomore recalls:

> The problems in math and physics were on a different level, a higher level than what I was used to. The problems were much more intricate. You had to know the principles; you couldn't just go to a formula. It was frustrating, but stimulating to see if you could achieve a new level.

Students discover that scholars disagree with each other and that they must begin to rely on their own opinions, supporting them with coherent logical arguments. A brochure written for parents of Cornell University students describes an important transition freshmen have to make:

> Students who knew how to produce the "right" answers in high school are often confused and frustrated to find that the techniques which helped them succeed in the past are no longer adequate. After the first round of prelims, they will wonder what the professor is "looking for." But somehow or other, they will have started learning how to learn.

A dean of liberal arts describes a scenario she typically encounters with freshmen:

> Three students came in to see me because they were unhappy with the grades they had received. They had been asked to keep a journal, giving their reac-

> tions to major texts in American literature that they had read—Thoreau, Melville, Emerson, Hawthorne. The professor had said, "It doesn't matter *what* your opinion is." He just wanted a reaction, a reasoned response. He had written on their journals such comments as: "Good idea, can you give specific examples? What about the text gives you this opinion? Don't just say you don't like Transcendentalism. You have to engage the idea of Transcendentalism, and if you don't like it, that's fine, but you must do so on the basis of a reasoned argument."
>
> We are trying to help the young see what argument is, what evidence is, how to support an opinion. This is our principal goal, whether it's taught in history or philosophy. We're teaching different subjects, but this is the constant subtext: a level of analysis and an understanding of where intellectual authority comes from—how to have confidence in your own views.

Professors who teach freshmen are often deluged with questions about procedures and expectations. "All students want direction," said one professor of political science. "Freshmen just want a lot more direction than the others. They want to be safe, to be sure they are doing things right. And they really expect that there is a right way and a wrong way to do everything."

Students may work industriously, putting in long hours spinning their wheels, often on the wrong track. They compare notes with their peers and reinforce each other's ignorance, raising each other's anxiety level as well. They study for tests, trying to memorize an overwhelming amount of facts and figures, often concentrating on the details without a grounding or conceptual understanding of the theory. This can be a disaster, particularly in the physical sciences. Students are often engaged in what one bemused provost calls "intellectual bulimia—stuffing themselves with volumes of factual material and then regurgitating it back for the professor, maintaining for themselves little of nutritional value."

International students are often surprised by the informality and give-and-take of the American classroom. The difference in teaching techniques and expectations, as well as language, poses particular challenges for them. A Japanese student explained that in Japan, the teacher wrote everything on the board, "Here, I have to listen and decide what to write. Sometimes I compare notes with friends—they're totally different."

Many freshmen complain about ambiguity, and about professors who do not follow the syllabus. No longer required to do daily assignments as they were in high school, students are both relieved and unnerved by the freedom. A French professor describes the typical behavior of her freshman students:

> My freshmen are faced with long-term assignments and projects, many for the first time. When they are assigned a book, they ask, "How many pages a night do you think I should read?" For instance, when I assigned *Madame Bovary* to my third-level French class, I told them we would be discussing the book one period a week over an eight-week period. The freshmen in the class asked me which pages they should read for each class. They wanted me to be directive and tell them exactly what they were responsible for. I, on the other hand, want them to dig in and make discoveries for themselves at their own pace.

Without the routine of daily assignments and regular feedback about their performance, many freshmen feel adrift academically, especially during their first semester. When parents ask midway through the semester how students are doing in their courses, they are apt to answer, "I don't know." Students may be trying to evade the question, but more often than not, they really don't know. Or what they know is limited to their scores on a few tests or papers and is based more on their own hunches than on someone else's feedback. College may seem deceptively easy the first few months. Rarely is anyone checking on how thoroughly students are doing their work, or how much progress they are making on long-term projects. Some students welcome this newfound freedom to set their own rhythm and pace, while others find it difficult to function without external motivations and rewards.

Freshmen may put in many hours studying inefficiently. When they work inefficiently, they ask themselves, "Am I just plain dumb or inefficient? If inefficient, should I take the time to get organized, or is that a waste of time? If I take the time to get organized, how do I do that?"

Students find that they have to read some assignments two or three times just to understand them. But if they were to read everything two or three times, they'd never get through the semester. There are other assignments that they have to skim. A lot of freshmen don't trust themselves. They have to learn when to read things over, when to skim, and when to skip, and this takes time.

Learning how to manage time is the biggest academic hurdle of all. Procrastination runs rampant among freshmen. Faced with the challenge of new disciplines and the heightened expectations of college faculty, many students fall into the trap of perfectionism. Hesitating to hand in papers or assignments until they are "good enough," they fall further and further behind—sometimes leading to a failing grade or an incomplete. Students also procrastinate as a way of resisting courses they don't like or rebelling against authority of any kind, and end up sabotaging themselves. Some find the brinkmanship of last-minute cram sessions and all-nighters exhilarating, but a steady dose of these eventually takes its academic and personal toll. Some find it difficult to be motivated when they are unsure of their academic goals. And some students procrastinate simply because there are so many distractions, and they have not learned to resist the full range of seductive inducements to play now and work later.

In addition, their lack of experience with college-level courses makes it difficult to schedule study time. So much of what they are being asked to do is a "first." A junior at SUNY Buffalo looking back on her freshman year comments:

> Things always took longer than I planned. I was always frustrated. I had no idea how long it would take me to do a particular task. If you've never written a twenty-page paper before, how can you know how long it will take you? Plus, a lot of kids grow up having their own space to study, to play music, or to be quiet. In college it's hard to find a place to do any of those things. You have to write the kind of papers you've never had to write before, under conditions you've never had to deal with before.

Shirley Baker, Vice Chancellor for Scholarly Resources and Dean of University Libraries at Washington University, suggests:

> When students call home and want help with a paper, I wish their parents would remind them that they can contact a campus librarian who's in a better position to actually be of help. When students get stuck, they can help them sift through materials and find things that are hard to find.

For those whose identities have been closely tied to their academic success, the reality of competing with others as bright or brighter than themselves is a stunning shock.

A Columbia freshman reflects on his first few weeks of school:

> The thing that was kind of hard was the inadequacy issues that come with going into a wider pond. And you find yourself suddenly sitting in class with these kids who use GIGANTIC words, speak in full sentences in paragraph form. In my English class there were people who really needed to let everyone know that they knew their stuff. And the first week, we were analyzing Chaucer; we read the first line and hands would shoot up and this guy said I think this is analogous to this work by Virgil. And I said, like, Oh God. . . . After a while, people got to know one another and it turned into a dialogue instead of people throwing these academic bullets at the teacher.

Many students feel a responsibility to parents and to whole communities who have encouraged them—and the humiliation and sense of failure at not living up to these expectations can lead to a general lack of self-regard. For those students who see the world in polarities, even an A- or a B+ is seen as a failure, a blot on their past 4.0 record and their future GPA. A freshman at Yale lamented, "No one here feels special anymore. Kids need to know that they're still special to their parents, even if they're getting C's."

Whether or not they have excelled in the past, students worry about how they will be judged in this new setting. Will they lose the "specialness" they felt in high school, or will they once again move to the top of the pyramid? Will they finally get it together and do well after years of just getting by? Will they be found out as frauds and fail for the first time in their lives? Will they waste their parents' money by getting C's instead of proving their investment was worthwhile by getting A's? Will they ruin their GPA and be blown off track to professional or graduate school?

The pressure to excel comes from families, graduate schools, financial aid offices, professors, and peers; and often the greatest pressure comes from students themselves whose fragile sense of self-worth is tightly bound to external confirmation. In the academic domain, this confirmation takes the form of grades. From the mother of a University of Chicago freshman:

> When she first went to college, Elise was very glib. She'd call and say she didn't know why people had so much trouble adjusting. Then one night in the middle of first semester, she called home crying hysterically, which was out of character for her. My first thought was—she's pregnant. But no, that wasn't it. She had gotten a D on a test. The issue was her loss of identity as a high achiever.

Grades are an indicator of a student's academic success. And there is no denying that they will eventually influence students' chances for acceptance to graduate and professional schools and slots in corporate training programs. But parents who gauge their youngster's total college experience simply by looking at a list of letters miss the complexity of the educational enterprise.

Professors, after all, have different goals in mind when grading. The same paper may receive an A from one professor and a C from another. There are, to use the student lingo, "guaranteed A" courses; studio, lab, and reading courses; courses that are graded on a curve and others that are pass/fail. Some schools have chosen to ease the adjustment by forgoing grades for the first semester.

It is not unusual for students at even the most selective colleges to have a rocky freshman year. Deans and advisors often explain to parents that freshmen are likely to perform at a lower level than they did in high school. Each fall they make a common plea for patience and understanding and urge parents of entering freshmen not to put undue pressure on their children.

Unfortunately, some parents exacerbate their children's anxiety about performance, which is often high to begin with, by putting pressure on them to do well in everything. This attitude not only creates undue stress, it may inhibit students from taking academic risks; they may stick to courses in which they know they will get high grades, missing opportunities to take a course from a particularly brilliant teacher in an unfamiliar discipline or avoiding a quality class that is known to be difficult. Students benefit from their parents' encouragement to challenge themselves; those who know that Mom or Dad will be there if they temporarily fall on their face will have more courage to stretch their intellectual horizons.

A thoughtful senior, the editor of his university's newspaper and a newly chosen Rhodes Scholar, recalls his experience with grades and their limitations:

> Grades are not the only indication of how much effort or how much you're getting out of a class. I know that there were times when I have not done everything that I have had to do to get an A in a class but because I have chosen certain aspects of the class that were particularly exciting to me, latched on to these and maybe gone a bit further in those to the neglect of some other areas in the class, I haven't come up with the A on the test—maybe it's a B, maybe it's a C, but it's a so much more meaningful

> experience to me because I'm doing things that I've wanted to do.

Grades can be a barometer, however, when they are viewed in context. They can be a catalyst for discussion between students and parents. They may represent growth and progress, discipline and hard work, or innate talent. A sudden drop in grades may indicate emotional, social, or chemical dependency problems. Grades may soar and plunge as students fall in and out of love, as they become absorbed in campus activities or worry about problems at home. Grades that are consistently low may indicate that a student is taking too many courses or inappropriate ones. They may suggest that a student is feeling pressured to pursue a particular discipline or even that the student is at the wrong school.

Too much emphasis on grades, even high grades, can be disconcerting to students, and a parent's balanced sense of perspective is appreciated:

> Academically, I'm a hard worker—always done three days early. I'm challenged more at Haverford, but I'm doing as well as I did in high school. I hate talking about grades. As soon as you say them out loud, they become someone else's property—parents' and grandparents' accomplishments. It's nice to keep it quiet and feel kind of smug.

> I was so homesick first semester, I got really into my work. All I did was study, and I got straight A's. My parents were thrilled. Second semester I started to feel more at home. I made friends and got involved and my grades dropped. My parents wondered what was wrong.

Although the Family Educational Rights and Privacy Act (FERPA) was passed in 1974, parents of today's freshmen are often shocked to learn that they may not have access to their son's or daughter's grades. Colleges take a variety of approaches to the question of access and usually explain their policy in parent or student handbooks. Some schools will release grades to parents who can provide evidence that their children are financially dependent on them. At other schools, students have the option of signing a waiver that allows their grades to be sent home to parents.

As one student says:

> We have to sign a thing, saying I will let my parents see my grades. But if you don't sign it your parents will get a letter saying something like, "Doctor and Mrs. W: Your son, Nicholas, doesn't want you to see his grades." So it's a catch-22. My parents are so offended by that. They're paying all that money and they think they damn well better see my grades.

If grades have been a battleground upon which students have felt bruised and thwarted by parents in the past, then FERPA may be one more weapon they can use to assert some power in their struggle. For students who feel comfortable discussing grades with their parents, this barrier may never even become an issue, since conversations about their progress are shared regularly. One young woman, whose parents are divorced, says:

> My dad has always pressured me to get straight A's. I'm afraid he'll pull me out of school. That's my biggest fear. I don't tell him my grades; I lie through my teeth. I tell my mom everything. She can deal with anything I tell her. I think most students deal with

> grades the way I do. If a parent puts on lots of pressure about grades, they just don't tell them the truth.

Another freshman says:

> My parents are sacrificing so much to send me here. I'm working hard but so far my grades aren't so hot. I just don't want to disappoint them.

Freshmen are bound to get discouraged at various points during the year and question their ability to succeed. They may complain of stress and exhaustion and call home hoping for sympathy and support. Parents should realize that some stress is part of any college experience. The whole purpose of taking a course is to be challenged. But when stress is paralyzing, it is detrimental. Parents can help their children by listening, by asking them to describe what they are doing to cope, and by acknowledging that what they are going through is tough. Specifically, they also might ask them where they are studying and how they are dividing their time. Spending hour after hour trying to study in a noisy residence hall with one eye on the social scene outside the door is rarely effective. When challenged to think of alternatives, students often come up with imaginative options, such as finding secret study niches in the Asian Studies library, campus art gallery, or departmental lounge. And upperclassmen are usually happy to pass on some tips, enjoying the chance to demonstrate to freshmen the wisdom of their years.

A lot of students work themselves into a frenzy and call home before they have even tried to get help. A parent might assist by encouraging the student to take initiative—to seek help from a professor or TA, to get a tutor, or to take advantage of the academic learning center, the writing center or other academic or mental health support services. Some students have too much pride to ask for assistance. They may be embarrassed or so overwhelmed that they are immobilized. Or they may be so wrapped up in their own worries that they simply fail to see the help that is right in front of them. Many are completely oblivious to the support services available on campus or aren't aware that in most cases, they are free of charge. As one liberal arts dean put it, "When you are eighteen, nineteen or twenty, the world has a very narrow corridor. And sometimes all you can see is a mirror at the end of that corridor." A little parental encouragement may help students to open their eyes to the resources that are just around the corner, and remind them that the services wouldn't be there if the university didn't expect students would need to use them.

College students, struggling to assert their independence, often have the misguided notion that adults don't ask for help. A university administrator who directs a center for students with disabilities and assists students in developing effective learning strategies comments:

> Students arrive on campus with a newfound determination to do things on their own. But sometimes they do that to a fault. I tell students, "No one is going to present you with a plaque when you graduate that says, 'I did it ALL on my own.'" Rather, a more admirable skill to have is to know when to use resources and how to use them appropriately.

A good academic advisor can play a key role in the life of a college freshman. Though everyone agrees that good advising is important, advising programs on many campuses fail to measure up to their descriptions in the admissions literature. In some instances, advisors are faculty members saddled with what they consider an unrewarding bureaucratic task. Knowing little about departments outside their own, and caring even less, they take a laissez-faire approach and approve a student's schedule no questions asked. Students whose advisors are not accessible or helpful may be able to switch advisors—or turn to other resources on campus—deans, faculty members, or peer advisors for the academic insight and advice they need.

Often students find, however, that if they prepare for advising meetings, if they think through their options and formulate their questions before they meet with their advisor, the session will go much better. In order for an advisor to function well, the student has to be an active and engaged participant. One faculty advisor who takes her job very seriously explains her frustration when parents interfere with the advising relationship:

> When parents override a decision by a student and an advisor, it undermines the advisor and the student. For example, as a freshman advisor, I helped a student decide to drop a course in midsemester. The fifth course added pressure that wasn't necessary. The student wasn't organized enough to handle everything. His parents told him it wasn't appropriate to be a quitter, and they refused to let him drop the course. It made the student furious and frustrated, and it tainted our relationship. Ever since then I've been nervous about advising him. Even in crisis situations, generally I prefer the student to let me know rather than have the parents call. If parents sense, however, that their child is having a difficult problem and know that he or she won't talk to anyone, then—and only then—the parent might want to intervene. There have been times that I found out things after the fact and wish a parent had called—not to be directive and tell me what to do—but to say, "I'm concerned. My kid is in what looks like a bad situation."

Freshmen don't really expect or want their parents to solve their academic problems, but they do want them to care and to show that they are interested. A University of Vermont student's comments seem representative:

> I looked to my parents for support a lot freshman year. I needed to know that it was OK to tell them I was going through a hard time. I felt there was no way they could help me specifically. It didn't work when I asked for help with specific problems, because the specifics were all joined together in one giant process—sometimes it felt like one giant mess.
>
> What helped was to hear them show interest—show that they had faith in me. It was important to me that they be concerned that I wasn't doing well. I needed them to be calm, to listen, not to lecture. They were terrific and that really made a difference even though I had to work things out for myself on campus.

Throughout all the struggles and triumphs of the freshman year, students are sorting out what part academics are going to play in their lives. Will they devote most of their time to their studies and shoot for the top of the class? How important is academic success? What is academic success? They jockey for position with their peers and measure themselves against their own expectations.

Many who started the year with clear goals find themselves not nearly so certain in May. Others have discovered new intellectual passions and are beginning to look toward the future, wondering what they will make of it all. Armed with new ideas and abilities, they spend enormous amounts of time thinking about who they are and who they are becoming. Nothing looks quite as simple as it once did.

THE COLLEGE SCENE

> I needed to find the ground of my own personality. I'd spent too much time just being a student in high school, doing the things that people told me. Then I came to college and there was no one paying attention to me; I didn't have to answer to anybody. All of a sudden, I just felt afloat. Schoolwork didn't seem as important to me as becoming responsible in a different kind of way, finding out what kind of fabric I was made of, finding out what I could do—not just on paper. And that goes for relationships too. What kind of friend was I capable of being? How responsible can I be as a friend? There were a lot of things happening to me, and most of it wasn't what my parents seemed to care about. It had little to do with my courses and it was being denied by the official reality of the institution.

Caught in the web of his parents' and the college's reality, this introspective Northwestern senior looks back at his freshman year as a time when his primary learning took place outside of the classroom. But where was the official sanction for, or recognition of, the many days and nights spent dealing with the out-of-the-classroom decisions and dilemmas?

The college scene is often chaotic, exciting, and overstimulating, from time to time depressing and deflating, leading to bouts of intense introspection or episodes of carefree abandon. It is a rich tapestry of relationships, activities, and possibilities. And these are competing perpetually with the classroom experience for the student's attention and physical and emotional energy. There are abundant choices and, at first blush, seemingly endless—and joyous—freedoms. But freedom brings with it the burden of personal responsibility and all the attendant anxieties and possible consequences of difficult decisions.

Roommates, Friends, and Lovers

> I just can't concentrate. There are three of us rooming in a room meant for two and now Beth's got a boyfriend who spends the night almost every night. There's no privacy; I have to go to the bathroom to get undressed—to say nothing of the fact that they're having sex a few feet away from me. And my other roommate says I'm a prude because it bothers me. Am I a prude? Is there something wrong with me? Am I immature? When I sit down to study, all I can think about is how I'll handle it tonight when I go back to the room.

For most of us, our home is our sanctuary, the one place where some privacy can be found, where the rules and customs are known, if not always adhered to. At home, loud music might provoke a parental request to lower the volume or an angry outburst from a brother or sister to put on headphones. But in a college residence hall, the source of the blaring music or the roommate who borrows things unasked is barely an acquaintance, and students may be inhibited about asserting themselves with neighbors and recently acquired friends.

Parents are often shocked, dismayed, and angry to discover that the burden of change lies with their child, the one whose rights are being infringed upon. "We're paying for that room; there must be a policy about other people living there. Why don't they do something!"

The prevailing philosophy on college campuses today encourages young men and women to solve problems with little intervention from authorities. To live with a total stranger on a floor with all new acquaintances provides numerous challenges and opportunities for learning assertion and problem-solving skills. Residential life personnel help to set community standards on their floors, and act as coaches or facilitators of student interactions, intervening only after other avenues have been exhausted. As a result, students may spend a great deal of time trying to handle day-to-day interpersonal problems with their roommates and other residents of their floor.

Likened to an arranged marriage, college roommates, two strangers often matched by little more than their study habits and sleeping schedules, come together in a very small space that becomes the bedroom, study, living room, retreat, and playroom for each. When it is ideal, which is more the exception than the rule, students have a companion, company for dinner, someone to let off steam with, an instant cure for the first month's loneliness, and the potential for lifelong friendship.

Students find themselves living with roommates from different cultures. "At times, they misunderstand each other simply because their backgrounds are so different," says a counselor at the University of California's Irvine campus:

> Even in the initial getting-to-know-you conversations, they may unwittingly offend each other. For instance, black and white students may tend to talk openly about their families. But Asian students may think it's rude to inquire, "What does your father do? How do you get along with your sister?"

Sometimes differences in personal habits are more problematic than differences in backgrounds. A young man from a rural community in the South and a cosmopolitan San Franciscan may suit each other well if they both like to go to bed early and keep their rooms neat. But a student who has always had her own room may find it difficult to share space; and her roommate, one of six children, may be intolerant of her complaining. They may make awkward attempts at discussions about letting each other know if something bothers them. Some schools even have structured agreements for roommates to complete together to help ward off tension. Most students will struggle with the disagreements that are inevitable when two or more people live together in such close quarters.

An attractive, impeccably dressed freshman at the University of Pennsylvania's Wharton School recounts her first impression of her roommate:

> My roommate seemed very strange, tiny, glasses, braces, no make-up. She wore only army fatigues, and I was totally intimidated by her—and found out later that she was of me. We were very accommodating and compromising—otherwise it would have been a big hassle to change rooms. Much to the surprise of both of us, we eventually became great friends.

But lifestyles can be so different that accommodation is difficult, as this Montana mother recounts:

> Our daughter—an easy-going, freckle-faced, sweatpants-wearing ice hockey player from a rural western state—was paired with a child movie star and model from New York City, who arrived at school in a stretch limo with her designer luggage. "Roomie" wears designer clothes (size 2), obsesses about looks, smokes "to stay thin," and has a host of other habits that are incompatible with a student-athlete. When one is trying to get a full night's sleep the night before a big game, the other is primping and blow-drying her hair and getting ready to go out—at midnight. When "Roomie's" boyfriend came to visit, our daughter was banished to sleep in the lounge so that "Roomie" and her beau could have some privacy.

What? She can well afford a hotel! These girls have exactly one thing in common (they are both half Jewish)—and believe me, it isn't enough!

This Carnegie-Mellon freshman describes his frustration:

I need my sleep, and I'm a very light sleeper. He's a night person and a fine arts major, and he keeps the light on doing his projects late at night. He says he has no other place to go because all of his materials are in our room, but I just can't go to sleep with the noise and the light. It's finally gotten to the point that I'm barely speaking to him.

Or consider this vivacious freshman from the University of Texas:

Every time I come into the room, she's here staring at the TV. I've tried to be friendly, but she's sullen and uncommunicative. And she obviously doesn't like my friends, so I feel guilty whenever I have someone in the room. At first I kind of felt sorry for her because she seemed depressed, but now I'm just fed up. I want out.

And accommodation may raise fundamental questions of autonomy and compromise. How much of myself am I willing to give up in order to live peacefully with someone else?

We got along though we were so different. We had different friends and lifestyles. She'd go to parties; I'd stay in my room and play my guitar or visit with a few friends. We painted our room together and that bonded us and we put silly things on our door like—

> "We both throw up when we eat scallops, we have so much in common." I think she thought I was odd, but she liked me. But parts of me would disappear in order to get along with her—maybe to avoid conflict. Parts of me were dormant. I guess her side of the room influenced me.

Issues of competition arise as students measure themselves against this live-in rival:

> Why does he always have a girlfriend, and I can't get anyone to go out with me?

> Her parents give her anything she wants; she has so many fantastic clothes. I have a part-time job and wouldn't have the time to shop even if I had the money.

> I study constantly and get C's. He parties like an animal and gets A's.

> She's like a size 0 and keeps boxes of cookies in our room for days. I'm always on a diet, and having that food in the room and looking at her skinny body drives me up the wall.

These are the daily problems confronting students as they return home to the only private space available to them. Though some first year students have singles, most schools place freshmen in doubles or suites, and with the current popularity of residence hall living, three students are often squeezed into a room meant for two. Those who do have singles, and are outgoing and confident about initiating contact with students in neighboring rooms, are delighted to have this special place of their own. For the more introverted student, single rooms can exacerbate the isolation and loneliness they already feel. One problem is traded for another.

Introverts may also find the noise and constant activity of the residence hall scene more enervating than energizing:

> I'm an introvert; I need time being with myself in order to go out and deal with the world. So being in a dorm has been a challenge. Constantly music is being played, people are playing soccer in the hallway, and yes, people are either knocking on your door or calling you all the time. I live on a coed floor and, well, boys are loud. Then you have to worry about all the idiots who decide to do stupid things such as pulling toilets off the wall and flooding two floors or breaking windows and doors which your parents consequently must pay for.

Throughout the freshman year, parents are likely to receive unhappy phone calls about roommates and roommate problems. They may range from "He keeps messing with the things on my desk!" to "She's talking of suicide and I don't know what to do." Or from "She's the biggest slob!" to "He comes home drunk several nights a week!"

Parents often react to these calls with a for-or-against response. Some rally round with a modern Greek chorus, fanning the flames by getting angry along with the student. Or they call the residence director, the dean of students, or the president demanding a solution. Others, recalling sibling battles, may respond with a sarcastic "Well now *you* know what it's like to live with a slob!" or "What did you do to provoke him?"—responses that tend to end any communication, leaving the student feeling that their one lifeline has been cut.

Many parents speak of their frustration and feelings of helplessness, the bubble of this carefully chosen, expensive superschool burst by the reality of a difficult living situation and no administrator clamoring to fix it. Tossing their developing independence aside, some students plead with Mom and Dad to intervene so that they can rid themselves of the problem and get on with their lives. Under the circumstances, the temptation to do so is compelling, but this is a significant opportunity to encourage independent thought and action. College administrators agree that learning to live in a world full of differences is one of the most important lessons of the college years.

The most helpful parents are those who listen, acknowledge their child's feelings, and allow him or her to generate some options. Suggestions can be offered tentatively, as just one of several possible solutions, and students should be encouraged to seek out resources on campus such as counselors or student life personnel, who deal with similar situations routinely.

Parents can show support in more tangible ways as well. Survival kits of earplugs, eye-shades, or an iPod to blot out sights and sounds can provide a lift for a student. These are simple gestures, but powerful reminders that those back at the home front care and send their support.

Often students help each other out or come up with their own solutions. A young woman who spent several months grappling with the problem of a roommate with a live-in boyfriend, rebuffed her parents' suggestion to talk to the RA. Rather than stir up a potential conflict, she resorted temporarily to what current college students term "sexile":

> I knew I had to live on that floor for the rest of the year, and I didn't want to tattle to the RA and have my roommate and her friends angry at me. I had some really good friends who lived at the end of my floor—

> and on the nights when Randy was spending the night, I took a sleeping bag and slept on their floor. I did ask my RA to let me know of any room openings, and I moved second semester. It's funny—I was miserable at the time, but I'm sort of glad I went through it. I gained a lot of confidence just having to figure it all out.

In some cases, parents may feel so concerned for their child's well-being that a call directly to a professional on the residence staff is warranted. A dean of freshmen cites this example:

> We had a student who was being harassed by his suitemates. There was vandalism, theft, something was even set on fire. The student told his parents about it, and they told him to report it to the proper people in the residence halls. The parents had researched the proper procedures and encouraged their son to go through the appropriate channels. But he was unable to carry that out himself. He just wouldn't do it, or maybe I should say couldn't do it. The parents realized that, and they took over. It was important that they did what they did.

Calls of this nature are most effective when they are collaborative rather than accusatory in spirit, in spite of the frustration and anger parents might feel. A dean at Barnard reminds parents that "we are partners in this enterprise, not adversaries."

Friendships with roommates, floormates, and classmates begin to take shape in the first few months of school. Sorting out who will eventually emerge as good friends is part of the student's search for identity and becomes an important focus for freshmen who are, in fact, re-creating their lives in this new environment. There is a sense of promise and potential—an exhilaration accompanying the possibilities for new friendships with so many different kinds of people. At the same time there is a sense of profound loneliness and loss—an empty space left by old friends for whom no explanations are necessary. Students move back and forth between these two emotional states, now thriving on the excitement of new friendships, now retreating into times of quiet reflection and longing for the comfort of old, solid relationships.

After three months at Carleton, this young man makes the following observation:

> Social life here is chaotic. So much is going on in reality and in your mind all at the same time. You're searching to have different levels of friendship—intimate, close and just plain acquaintances. You spend time hanging out with lots of different people at once. You look for people like you think you want to be—punk, intellectual, or whatever. And all the while you're questioning whether you want to make new friends at all or if that means turning your back on your high school friends.

And an Amherst freshman asserts:

> I had friends I'd met at a summer program, and they were really intellectual and my roommates weren't at all—that was a schizophrenic thing. My roommates didn't get along with these other people, and I didn't know who I wanted to be with, and it was upsetting.

Perhaps this is another way of sorting out "who I am" questions—am I an intellectual or someone who likes *People* magazine and the Los Angeles Dodgers? Can I be both? Can I be friendly with different groups of people without losing out on both?

Some students find the identification with a group a secure substitute for missed family and friends. With their identity in such flux, it is not unusual for freshmen to stumble into a group simply based on its proximity. As an Oberlin freshman reflected on his initial choice of friends, it seemed almost arbitrary:

> Our floor quickly divided up into three or four cliques for the year. One clique was into country music and Karl Marx. My clique played a lot of cards. We were really into games of any kind, mostly head games, I'd say. Our conversations would be really twisted sometimes and manipulative. Then there was the third group—the musicians. Half of them were gay and the other half straight. And then there were some kids who hung out in limbo and went from group to group.

Students speak of their floor as a family—often traveling in packs, eating together, or going to a movie or local hangouts as a group. They refer to individual friends by name, set against a backdrop of characters on their floor, spoken of in the college student vernacular as "dorks" or "weirdos" yet with a tinge of affection, as if describing eccentric but beloved extended family. Some who felt like outsiders in high school now may experience a new sense of belonging to this accepting, inclusive group.

The diversity of the college campus is apparent in the microcosm of each residence hall floor. Students who have traveled the globe share space with those who have just left home for the first time. Some have been living "on their own" for years; others are tightly bound to parents and siblings and feel the stress of breaking away. Students who own BMWs mingle with those brought up in factory towns and inner city neighborhoods. Some students arrive on campus wise in the ways of sex, drugs, and alcohol, while others have been sheltered and are inexperienced. Whether sophisticated or naive when they arrive, almost all students will be exposed during the course of the freshman year to the problems of eating disorders and clinical depression, to alcohol and drug abuse, to unfamiliar religions and cultures, to alternative lifestyles. Students become familiar with the intimacies of people's lives in a way that they probably never will again outside the confines of family and very close personal friends. Many learn an appreciation for differences from these close associations that will last a lifetime. Certainly, there is a loss of innocence, and with that loss, a new maturity born of questioning and introspection that is often painful.

For many students, this environment is more disorienting than stimulating. Seeking the comfort of a familiar group identity, they may turn to Greek life or a religious, cultural, or political organization—a more homogeneous group whose identity is clearly associated with their own family values or perhaps just the opposite.

A young woman from the University of Kansas was grateful for early sorority rush:

> I rushed even before going to class. It was really good because I didn't know anybody; I got to meet a bunch of people. It was an intense first week of college, but it was worth it.

Though a strong connection to a group provides a feeling of stability to counteract the sense of uprootedness of the first semester, at a later time, this same group may become confining.

> Initially the people I hung out with and found I had the most in common with were the more conserva-

> tive. I took a turn toward a more conservative religion than my family's. My father's comments to my older sisters at college had been, "Are you studying and did you go to church on Sunday?"
>
> To me, it was, "Are you studying, and did you go to a Lutheran church on Sunday?" Ultimately I left the conservative church and went back to the Lutheran. As I became more comfortable, I started hanging out with a more diverse group of people.

Students also form friendships through the camaraderie and absorption of shared projects—working on the newspaper, singing in the choir, playing on the soccer team. Especially on large university campuses, joining student activities provides a shortcut to finding others with common interests.

These shared experiences may offer moments of sheer delight. "Sometimes we stay up most of the night to get the paper to press on time," said another freshman. "I feel closer to the paper staff than to any other group of people on campus."

Students on athletic teams are likely to find a ready-made family. Through long hours of practice and travel to out-of-town games, they form close relationships with teammates and coaches. A recent alumna of a national championship volleyball team looks back with fondness on her experience:

> Because I was recruited for the varsity volleyball team, I had to arrive early for preseason. My coach had asked each of the rookie players to write to one another over the summer. No sooner did we all meet face to face that we became attached at the hip. We were inseparable. It made sense because we were all in the same boat. We as a team were in pursuit of a national championship. We made a pledge to each other to take care of ourselves, to work hard, to win.

> When I struggled in a class, I could turn to one of the older girls on the team for help. When all the other first years on my floor were getting wild and crazy on a Thursday night, I could walk over to Emmy's dorm or to Chris's room. When I developed a crush on any guy at school, I could depend on my teammates to find out about him. I look back on my first semester in college and count my blessings that I was a member of that team. We came from all over the country and now live all over the country, yet the friendships that came from being a volleyball player are the strongest of my life.

In the midst of all the people and activities, loneliness is as normal to the freshman experience as the common cold, mono, and the flu. Whereas most students feel lonely some of the time, there are others who are truly isolated and without friends. These are often students who lack social skills and have dealt with social isolation throughout their adolescence. Hoping that college will make a difference, they may project their unhappiness onto the school, complaining that "these are not my kind of people." Some students who were loners in high school do discover a whole new world of peers with common interests and talents that may not have been available to them before. But more than likely a young man or woman who has not been able to form friendships in earlier years will have difficulty once again. Most colleges and universities provide free counseling or group experiences that deal with shyness or social skill building and support the development of the total student.

Cross-gender friendships are prevalent on today's campuses, a primary outgrowth of coed residence hall life. Though some parents worry about the repercussions of coed living, students are more likely to treat the members of the opposite sex on their floors as siblings, actually replicating the close relationship of missed family members, or perhaps enjoying the companionship of a "brother" or "sister" for the first time.

Some of these friendships do move into romantic relationships. The intimacy of shared late-night conversations about everything from future dreams to past traumas may lead to an intimacy born of sexual and romantic stirrings. Developmentally, these are often healthy, affirming relationships, having grown out of caring and natural ties, but they bring up new questions and anxieties. What will this do to our friendship, which is so precious? What will happen if or when we break up? Will it mean too much togetherness? Students even laughingly refer to a romantic relationship with someone on the same floor as "floorcest."

There are some students who move quickly into romantic relationships, often for the first time. There may be an intensity about the involvement that suggests a mutual dependency more than a mature sexual relationship. These partners may cling to each other and provide a secure haven that keeps them from engaging fully in their new environment.

A University of Miami junior recalls her freshman year:

> I began dating a graduate student the first week of school. I spent all my time with him and never got to know anyone. I barely even knew the people in the room next to me—I was just never around.

Most of these early relationships don't last much past freshman year, but they are still a vitally important part of that student's world and developing sexual identity. Some parents, suspecting that this may be just the first in a sequence of "serious relationships," dismiss it or minimize it. A freshman at Earlham describes her frustration when she calls home for support about her rocky relationship:

> At times when I call, they've tried to lessen what I'm saying. They think they're being really nice. They'll say, "Oh it's not that bad," and it *is* bad. I don't need to hear that. When they're good, they legitimize my feelings, but when they try to diminish a problem, I think they don't want to cope with the fact that their daughter's going through a rough time. All I want is some support and concern, not "Oh, it's just a college romance." It's not just a college romance. I'm having a nervous breakdown—don't you care? I'll end up calling my sister, but I like calling them first.

Some of these relationships challenge parental values as students become involved with classmates from different religions, races, and cultures. A freshman of Catholic descent, and the first member of her family to go to college, refrained from telling her parents about a relationship she knew would upset them:

> He was from Pakistan. They're going to kill me if the guy I marry isn't Catholic. If I told them I was involved with someone who's Muslim, it would just petrify them. They have a lot of racial prejudices. I just didn't want to inflict that on my relationship with them.

Students often talk about feeling torn and guilty, facing the dilemma of how to remain loyal to family while making independent decisions that are in conflict with established family norms.

> I've been aching to tell my somewhat overprotective mother that I drink on weekends and am practicing

> safe sex with my boyfriend of nine months—just to be honest with her. But I always felt like I couldn't, or when I tried to hint at it, she would just ignore me or change the subject. I was making responsible decisions and being careful with them. It was very frustrating and still is, because I feel like I am lying even though I'm aching to let her know that I'm being responsible about it.

Sometimes students are surprised by their parents' reactions, as this young woman, a freshman from Penn State explains:

> I had met a guy over the summer who came to visit me in October. We decided to go to an inn for the weekend. It was a big problem with my parents. My mom was my rock and had always been so liberal and accepting. And now all of a sudden she was uptight about my spending a weekend with a guy. I learned something; I tested my boundaries and got to my mom's limit. When I was little and had an argument with a parent, I would end up thinking they were right. This time I felt they were wrong. I had always looked up to her. It was painful for me.

Unwittingly this young woman had tested her mother's limits and run smack into a conflict. She stumbled into a situation that challenged her to make her own value judgments and establish her own code of behavior.

Sex, Drugs, and Alcohol

Throughout the freshman year students face many puzzling moments of personal decisions, confronting previously established values, taking risks, and making compromises—all moments that sap energy and time and often provide fertile soil for spurts in personal growth.

What are the unwritten rules of conduct in this place? Am I supposed to lose my virginity now that I'm in college? Am I supposed to pretend that I haven't lost it? Do I spend the weekend with my boyfriend in spite of what my parents think? Is hooking up OK with me? What exactly is hooking up? Do I say yes to pot and no to coke? Do I go along to the fraternity parties where the action is even though I hate them, or do I look for alternatives, out of the mainstream?

Many freshman who "acted out" in high school and are experienced with sex, drugs, and alcohol reexamine their earlier choices within the new context of college life. With the freedom to do as they choose, some continue to experiment, stretching the boundaries to their institutional limits. Others, with no parents to bump up against, are not as involved as their classmates in the experimentation that is part of the freshman scene. The high school "boozer" or "druggie" arrives on campus without a label; fellow students carry no expectations, and there is a chance to try out a new identity. "It is," said one student "a whole new ball game."

Some students, who have lived in highly structured and restrictive environments at home and arrive at college with little experience, go haywire when they are left with no external constraints. Lacking internal controls and a sense of moderation, they experiment and try everything—usually to excess.

Struggling to establish their own identities, some students take a blatantly rebellious stance. Their behavior sends a message that they are different from Mother and Dad; they are establishing their own moral turf. They may even tell their parents about their exploits. They call home and say, with the typical hyperbole of college freshmen, "Oh I'm totally out of it. I got completely wasted last night," or "I've been partying all week." One student described how much she liked to tell her mother shocking things. When asked why she enjoyed doing so, she replied, "Because Mom can't do a thing about it. She has no control over what I do."

Others try to hide their behavior, and their parents don't have a clue as to what is really going on. One Princeton student described what he called "a college student's nightmare—having your parents call when you're stoned":

> I remember having had several exams and coming back to a friend's room across the hall from mine and getting stoned. My phone rang, and I stumbled to it. It was my mother. It was the middle of the afternoon, and I was totally incoherent, and I knew it. The next day, my oldest brother called me because my mother had called him and said she thought I was studying too hard and would he talk to me. We had a good laugh when I told him what happened.

Actually most parents don't know what is really going on, and unsettling as this may be, it is a necessary part of the separation process. Students need privacy and an opportunity to establish their own limits and values. They need to experiment and handle the consequences. John Gardner, Senior Fellow at the University of South Carolina and the Executive Director of the Policy Center on the First Year of College at Brevard College, urges parents:

> Look at college as a laboratory for testing behaviors. Students have to figure out who they want to spend time with, what and when they want to eat, drink, and smoke—how much they want to sleep, socialize, and study. As students experiment, they are testing out the consequences of their behaviors. If they can't learn in an unfettered way, they'll test the same things

> out later when the stakes are much higher, when there aren't the built-in safety nets that exist in college.

There are times, of course, that students truly want their parents to be there for them or even to intervene. They send out signals that they are in trouble—a series of depressed phone calls home or aloof calls of the "everything's fine" variety; they may sound spacey or uncommunicative. Their grades may drop suddenly or their weight may change dramatically. They may be spending a lot of money they can't account for.

The director of student activities and orientation at a southern university comments:

> Parents need to look for signs, but they shouldn't jump to conclusions. If they have built a relationship through high school, they need to maintain it. Parents should confront their children in a positive way—express concern, not hysteria. They should ask about friends, about the weekend, about eating and sleeping. They should show that they care, but not interrogate.
>
> I think parents should confront their children if they find things that indicate drug use. They should take the time to explain their concern, but not cut off communication with a barrage of accusations. They shouldn't make assumptions, but should ask open-ended questions and listen. When parents know that their child is abusing drugs, they should seek professional help for the student either at home or at a counseling center on or near campus.

A young woman who is now a sophomore at an East Coast university found her parents' intervention during her freshman year particularly effective:

> One time last year my parents called me, and I was just really hung over. I wasn't bragging about it or happy about it, but that's just the way it was. I was in bed, and I said—"Look I can't talk to you right now. Let me call you back." When I called them back I was fine, and they didn't mention it. But then I did get a letter that said, "We are really concerned that at 12:30" or whatever time it was, "on a Sunday morning, you're hung over." And that was perfect! It didn't feel like they were bugging me. It was more like—"Hey, buddy, we're really worried about you." They were sort of acting like concerned friends.
>
> I think I was relieved when my parents said something. I was already a little worried about myself. When they brought it up, that opened up a chance for us to discuss what was going on. Some parents have a tendency not to say anything, and then you start to wonder, don't they care? How come they don't say anything? I'm not sure how parents are supposed to know when there's really something wrong. But I think they should follow their instincts and at least say they're worried. They shouldn't ignore it.

Many students who choose to experiment with sex, drugs, and alcohol are motivated by the desire to be part of a group, by a search for connection with their peers. There is a compelling camaraderie that develops as students come together over beer while they listen to music and talk. For students feeling unsure of their status in this new place, alcohol or other drugs are an easily accessible social lubricant. The lure of friendship and intimacy is powerful. One group of students brags about how wasted they were all weekend beginning with Thursday night "happy hour." Another talks about their mellow gathering, smoking dope and talking through the night.

International students and American students who grew up abroad are often shocked by the immaturity and irresponsibility of some American college students who drink excessively. One American freshman, a self-proclaimed "global nomad," whose family has lived in Cairo, Geneva and Paris, explains:

> I'm American, but spent all of high school in Paris. I just can't relate to the drinking and partying scene here. It seems ridiculous. I feel like I'm so past that. I tend to hang out with some of the juniors who live down the hall.

And a Taiwanese student notes:

> The novelty and freedom have worn out when I was in high school. I am not understanding why people go so crazy with these substances when they are for the first time in their life adults.

The drinking culture differs not only from group to group on campus, but from one campus to another as well. Walter Kimbrough, whose career has spanned a broad range of universities from Old Dominion to Georgia State and Emory, and is currently President of Philander Smith College in Little Rock, Arkansas, comments:

> The culture here is a little bit different. When students have parties, alcohol isn't the focal point; students don't expect alcohol to even be there. That's not typically a part of how African-American students socialize. This was evident even when I worked at other campuses. It doesn't surprise me that research studies on student alcohol use show that historically black colleges have lower percentages of binge drink-

ers and fewer major alcohol incidents. Of course, here at Philander Smith, we still do our alcohol awareness programs, particularly for newer students who are away from home for the first time.

An African-American student from the University of Chicago explains how he carries his family's values within him:

I was raised in an environment where drinking, especially underage, was frowned upon. A part of my decision not to drink is motivated by my religious background, but the bulk of it has to do with values that my parents instilled in me. I never want to be in a position where my judgment and ability to act is impaired. I have friends who drink and friends who don't. I find that I can easily interact with both. We are able to hang out and watch movies, play games, have conversations and even party without alcohol being a factor at all.

Some students are overwhelmed by the party scene and the constant inducements to participate. A University of Michigan freshman admitted that she had a lot of anxiety about this part of college life.

I was scared 'cause I hadn't been a big party girl or sexually active. I found a lot of others in the same boat. Things move a lot faster than in high school and since we all live in such close quarters, we see a lot more. I saw a lot more drugs than in high school. I could walk down the hall and smell marijuana. I never did start smoking dope, but a lot of my friends did—and I was surprised to realize that I liked them

> anyway—that I was much less judgmental than I had been in high school.

Many students drink moderately or don't drink at all, and most of them say that they don't feel the overt peer pressure they felt in high school.

> No one will make fun of you if you don't drink. But there is a kind of self-imposed pressure. If you feel shy or awkward in the first place, it's kind of hard not to drink if you're at a party.

> I don't drink and I don't want to hang out with people who do. When I go to a party I sip a little beer—just enough so I feel kind of mellow. I call it "drinking for buzz maintenance."

> A lot of the drinking we do is manageable, not like in high school. It's more about enjoying each other's company than it is about getting really hammered.

Drug usage tends to be more private than alcohol and usually takes place behind closed doors or at off-campus clubs. But on most campuses today, alcohol is visible to all. No matter what the college's official policy is, students are very resourceful when they want to drink. On weekends, parties seem to erupt spontaneously, and a keg is often the main drawing card.

For large numbers of students, the ethic is one of "work hard, play hard"—go to the library during the week and "drink to get drunk" on the weekend For many, drinking is a way to blow off steam, to get rid of social inhibitions, to prove that they are grown up. It is an integral part of their culture and inextricably tied with their social life and their sexual behavior.

There is pressure on both men and women to be knowledgeable and comfortable with sex. Rarely are sexual encounters between college students as spontaneous, smooth, and carefree as their parents might think. Almost no one is immune to the agonies of sexual growth.

A student from Boston Unversity muses:

> I think that a lot of people are really confused, and I must say I'm really confused. What is normal? How far should you go with someone? How much respect should you demand? And then you throw alcohol into all that . . .

Students worry about sexual attractiveness and performance, about finding a private place, and about the future of their relationship. They worry about the dangers of sexually transmitted diseases as well as pregnancy and how to integrate these clinical intrusions into their sex lives. Those who choose to remain virgins throughout their college years may question their own desirability or their sexual identity. "If everyone else is doing it, why aren't I? Is it simply that I'm not interested in sex without love, and I haven't fallen in love? Maybe there's something wrong with me." Those who feel sure of these choices based on moral or religious values may gravitate toward like-minded peers.

In spite of the decline of sexual stereotypes, there is still more peer pressure on a man who remains a virgin than there is on a woman. And many women are now the initiators of sex, so that some young men find themselves saying no, which is incongruent with their messages about manliness and may cause them to feel off balance and bewildered.

A student's evolving comfort as a sexual being goes hand in hand with his or her total maturing process. One young man about to graduate looks back on the changes in his attitude over the past four years with a new perspective and insight.

> My friends were mostly guys freshman year. At first it was like oh, wow, college! It went from girls and sex were something illicit, like drugs, or like alcohol, just going out of control and being really stupid and insensitive about it, to incorporating sex more and more into our personalities—having more respect for other people—respecting other people's lives and the way they behaved and learning how to live with people.

Issues of confusion over sexual identity are also common among college students. The dean of arts and sciences at one southeastern university comments:

> This struggle often interferes with academic achievement. Students are sent to me because of academics, and then they start talking. They are not sure about their sexual identity; they can't talk to their parents; some of them feel uncomfortable going to gay groups. What I do is listen. I'm not sure what parents can do, but I think they should know that many students are questioning their sexuality. Their own kids may be, and certainly they will be exposed to other kids who are.

Although homosexuality is far more open and aboveboard than in earlier generations, the stigma still remains. "Coming out" is usually a long and agonizing process. Some gay men and women who are clear about their sexual orientation before they come to college still have anxieties about how they will fit into this new environment.

■

Bombarded with new freedoms and responsibilities, at a time when they are trying to figure out who they are and how they can live on their own, freshmen behave in ways that are often disturbing to their peers as well as their parents. Their exhilaration is mixed with confusion, their experimentation tempered by responsibility. They are trying to incorporate new people, activities, and interests into their lives. They're expanding their academic horizons and learning new ways to learn.

So much seems to be happening at once. At times they appear very certain of who they are and what they think; at other times little about them seems to be integrated.

A dean from Macalaster College reflects on the freshman experience.

> The freshman year is about separation from family and home. It's about the questions, "Who am I?" and "How do I fit in?" It's about maintaining one's ego in a strange environment, learning to live with a roommate and handling freedom and responsibility. It's about making friends and finding a niche.

For parents, too, the freshman year is a rite of passage, a passage to a new relationship with their sons and daughters. *The Harvard Parents' Handbook* describes the essence of this major shift:

> For parents, the freedom freshmen enjoy can be hard to accept. So can recognizing how little you can now appropriately and directly do to shape the daily round of your son's or daughter's experiences or his or her life style choices, curricular, or career plans. . . . A young person is setting out on his or her own life's course. Don't try to hold the course you set and have been sailing together for seventeen

years. It is very hard to sail a ship with two pilots. Come along, by all means. But keep in mind that it is a new voyage, someone else's voyage. This way college can be the shared and happy embarkation it ought to be. . . .

8

IN AND OUT OF YOUR LIFE

CARRIE HAS THAT "NEW YORK LOOK." HER CLOTHES are from secondhand shops; they're always artfully arranged, never look studied, but seem a natural extension of her cameo face. She walks with assurance, her shoulders back, eyes straight ahead; she appears to know where she is going. A senior at Yale, she's a talented artist and enjoys exploring the rich resources of her hometown, New York City. She feels close to her parents, who have always supported her personal style and encouraged her independence.

It is obvious that Carrie's mother takes great delight in her daughter. She reminisces about Carrie's rocky start freshman year, and the unexpected ups and downs that followed:

> Carrie finished high school early and took courses at a college in the city in place of her senior year. She seemed ready to go away to school. In fact, she seemed more mature than most 18-year-olds. My husband and I drove her to school. I remember that she was anxious and obviously disappointed by the post-

ers of puppies and kittens that her roommate had already put up, but by the time we left, she seemed to be cheerfully settling in. John and I drove home thinking, This is it, we're on to the next phase of life.

The phone calls came as a surprise. There were lots of them, and they were always late at night. John slept through most of them, and I would listen for what seemed endless hours to her unhappiness. There were many tears and many tales of poor courses and loneliness. She was in one class with all seniors, the result of sloppy advising. It was way over her head, but she refused to change.

Finally, when she came home for Thanksgiving, the dam burst. She became nearly hysterical, and the three of us talked most of the night. When she finally went to sleep, John and I decided, This is not worth it; we'll withdraw her from school, send her for therapy, and she'll go to school here in the city.

The next morning when I began to tell Carrie what we had decided, I noticed the slightest flash of disappointment on her face. It was so tiny that only a mother would have seen it, and I knew instinctively that we were wrong, and that she was strong enough to get through this. She needed us to encourage her, not come to her rescue. I took a chance and said, "Carrie, this is all bullshit. You will go back. You can do it." She looked shocked and relieved all at the same time. The next day she returned to school on the train. And now she's a senior and will probably graduate with honors. That first trip home was the turnaround. But it was also just the beginning. At times it's been a roller-coaster existence. Carrie has been in and out of our lives in ways we never would have predicted when we blithely dropped her off in New Haven.

Throughout the freshman year and continuing through the rest of the college experience, young men and women move in and out of their parents' lives, often in fits and starts as crises or triumphs occur. When students become upperclassmen, the quantity and intensity of contacts usually lessen as they shift their support systems from home to school and become more adept at discovering resources for themselves. But the vicissitudes of life at home and at school bring unexpected turns of events, and the reentry of parents and children into each others' lives can be awkward and unsettling, as well as comforting and confirming.

For students who go to school a short distance from home, there is a sense of continuity as they drop back in for a quiet weekend, a family celebration, or a quick fix of TLC. Their parents, within a short drive of campus, may occasionally arrange to drop off a basket of fruit, or take their child's friends out for a much appreciated good meal.

A mother whose daughter lives in a residence hall just a few miles from home finds, however, that proximity brings its own special challenges:

> The hardest times were when she was having a problem and I wanted to jump in and help. She couldn't do something with her computer or she was having trouble doing some research, or she lost her student ID. She would tell me these things, usually by phone, but really didn't want me to help—just wanted to tell me, and it was excruciating not to drive over and help her "fix it."

For those who go to school far from home, contacts with family are reduced to vacations, occasional visits, phone calls, e-mails, or text messages. The experience of both students' and parents' lives during these years is reduced to images, frozen in time and often distorted and misunderstood like snapshots viewed out of context.

The impact of such slices of life reverberates across the miles in phone calls as parents take stock of their children's progress, happiness, and success—measuring their tone of voice and the contents that spill forth against an imaginary norm. How powerful these brief calls and texts and e-mail musings are, pouring out the emotion of a particular moment. Exuberant accounts of recent events, successes, or a general sense of their child's well-being can brighten up a parent's day. On the other hand, complaints, distresses, disappointments, and depression are delivered in shrill staccato or flat, gloomy conversations that interrupt peaceful evenings at home or invade an already overburdened parent's domain.

> The surprising thing has been that our daughter calls home as often as she does. She was so ready to go 2000 miles away and lead an independent life. We asked her to call us once a week, and we really didn't expect she would call more than that. But she began calling for the tiniest little things. And often—sometimes twice a day. She even asked my advice! (This is the girl, who in 9th grade made me walk 20 paces behind her in K-mart, lest I cause her any embarrassment.) Who knows why she calls so frequently? It could be that kids call home more, or that she misses us, or that her health problems have made her more aware that she needs our help and support. Whatever the reason, I am happy to talk to her.

A successful surgeon, the father of four, acknowledges that on Sundays, when he and his wife routinely speak to each child at various locations across the country, "At that moment we are only as happy as our least happy child."

But what of the hours before or the days after his phone calls? Is his daughter who sounded sad or distraught rejuvenated an hour later? Is his son's happy voice genuine or a reaction to an unspoken but imagined request to sound good-humored because Mom and Dad cannot tolerate sadness or depression?

A substantial number of students speak of protecting their parents from their disappointments and problems—some because they don't want to burden their parents who are sacrificing so much for their education, some because they are protecting themselves from their parents' lack of understanding and support.

> My dad made it very clear that he didn't want to hear from me when I was complaining or depressed. He's got all kinds of problems with his wife and stepdaughter, and if I sound down, he just gets mad and I end up feeling worse. So we have these stilted conversations because I have to pretend everything's fine.

> Every time I call home depressed, my mom either starts sounding depressed herself, or she says maybe I should come home, like I obviously can't handle things. That's the last thing I want to hear.

When students are feeling down, parents often react too quickly; they have difficulty assessing from afar how much this depressed message reflects the totality of their child's life. A

Californian at Boston University explains how frustrating it is when she simply wants some support and understanding, but her mother overreacts and responds as though her bad moments are the whole of her experience:

> I'll say one thing on the phone, like I'm tired or down, and my mother makes such a production of it. She spends the whole day picking tangerines from our tree and wrapping them up individually to send to me. She encloses a note, telling me she's worried about me, and my sister tells me that's all she and my dad talk about for three weeks.

And a freshman at Trinity College in Connecticut has difficulty communicating her low times to her mother without getting what she considers an overreaction or an underreaction:

> My mom is such a stoic. She just says, "You're fine," when I'm sick or depressed. It hurts her so much when there's something in my universe that she can't cure. All I want her to do when I'm depressed is to recognize it . . . to validate it. So when she says, "You don't sound too bad," I'll say, "You're not listening to me. I'm really, really down." And then she becomes convinced that I'm suicidal or deathly ill and starts calling every day. "Hi. Just calling to see if you're still alive."
>
> I can't just have a cold. . . . She either thinks it's nothing or it's mono for sure. All I want her to say is, "I'm sorry you have a bad sore throat, I know how miserable that can be."

Many students admit that they call home when they want to complain and tend to share their good times with friends:

> There's only so much you can complain around here, because everyone complains so much. I have four papers due. My friends' attitudes are, "So what!" They'll be bitching about their own heavy load . . . so you call home for pity.

Even when students do attempt to communicate both the ups and the downs to their parents, they find it impossible to capture the day-to-day pleasures of their new world in such brief sketches. A Pomona student explains:

> I feel like my parents only know what upsets me, like when I call home and say I'm failing something or I had a fight with my roommate. But when I say I went to a party last night and had a lot of fun, I don't think they have any idea how wonderful my life is here . . . how wonderful my friends are. I think my life is pretty rich, and I'm very secure. This is more of a natural environment than even being at home was for me. I'm much more in my own element with people I'm comfortable with and have a lot in common with.
>
> I have two separate worlds. I have another life here that's as full and complete as my life was at home. They're separate and distinct. I'm made aware of it when I talk to my parents. Even though when I was home, they didn't know a lot about my life. We were close, but I didn't tell them very personal things—they saw it; they saw people I spent time with. When I talk to them on the phone now they really have no conception of what my life is like. It's so disconnected.

And for a Bryn Mawr student from India, the physical distance, as well as the cultural differences implicit in her college experience, highlight the sense of disconnectedness:

> I've always shared everything with my parents. They're so far away now. I can't call them and tell them about everything. Especially when the work gets underway, I don't have the energy to sit down and write. It's impossible to let them know what my life is really like here. I realize I'm going to get out of here after four years without their ever having seen any of the rituals or the friends or anything that's become such a part of me at this point, and they won't ever know that, and that's hard, but there's nothing I can do about it.
>
> I'm used to communicating with my mother on a very adult level. I am a friend to her. I'm the eldest, but once I came here I became her little girl. All she can think of is taking care of me. So, this very intelligent, interesting woman—all she can say is, "Are you all right? Are you drinking your orange juice? Are you praying every day?" That's the extent of our conversations. When she writes, she writes as to a child.

The fact is that college students *are* no longer a regular part of their parents' lives. For most students the reality of the ever-widening gap between their experience and the world of their parents is fraught with conflicting feelings. Young people, as well as their parents, struggle with the balance between staying connected and letting go. At times college students revel in their separateness, keeping the delights and traumas of their lives at school to themselves. At other times they long to share their college world with the family at home, even as their worlds inevitably become more separate. Heady moments of independence and the adventure of expanding horizons give way to wistful desires to be taken care of and nurtured.

STAYING CONNECTED

How can parents keep in touch, yet still affirm their sons' and daughters' growing adulthood? There are a number of recommendations that students make again and again when they are asked what they would like their parents to do. Almost all students claim that they want attention and support from their parents—but not unsolicited advice. They want mail; the contents don't seem to matter as much as the simple, tangible connection to the life they have left behind. Even in this era of electronic communication, they still treasure the sight of a mailbox with a letter from home. They want care packages, and they talk with childlike delight about receiving bundles of food at exam time and inexpensive decorations for their rooms at holidays. Most prefer to talk on the phone to one parent at a time, and especially enjoy private conversations with siblings.

Students talk of their frustration with parents who call "only when they're angry," and the pain of rejection by parents who always seem too preoccupied to communicate at all. They dislike getting caught in the middle between divorced parents, and sometimes can't remember what they told to which parent.

Many say they love it when their parents make their plane reservations home for them at the end of the semester, when they are overloaded with exams and papers. These same students, however, complain when their parents are "too helpful," sending immediate replacements for lost sweatpants or gloves without being asked to do so, or sewing buttons on as soon as they arrive home for vacations. Though college students resent intrusions and parental attempts at control, they long to be understood, and contrary to their public claims, most of them do care what their parents think:

> When I call home excited to tell that I'm doing something independent, and I just want to tell them

> and they give me advice, it's deflating.
>
> I wish my mom would be more in tune sometimes with what's going on with me. Mention my friends by name; say hi to them so I know she's hearing what I'm telling her. I have my friends here, and she doesn't know as much about them as I'd like her to. That's hard. I guess it's part of growing up.
>
> Even if they don't approve, it's important to have their understanding. They're not going to approve of everything I do, just like I don't approve of everything they do. We're different people with different ideas about things. But I want them to try to understand where I'm coming from, and why I'm doing what I'm doing.
>
> I called home full of complaints last night. Mom just listened and listened. At one point she said, "Isn't growing up a bitch?" That was just great!

In their concern for their children's happiness, parents may unwittingly focus on their vulnerabilities. When the father of a young woman who has a tendency to procrastinate keeps asking her if she has had a productive week, or a shy young man's mother asks repeatedly if he's made any friends, the student's attempts to cope independently are undermined. By constantly bringing up a sensitive topic, the parent is sending the unspoken message: "I'm worried about you and don't think you can manage on your own." A sophomore at Emory comments:

> Everyone in our family has a weight problem. Before I came here my mother teased me about the freshman 40 instead of the freshman 10. When there is a

> weight problem in your family and the last thing your mother says before you go away is "Watch out for the freshman 40," that's really not a good thing.
>
> When I first got here I was paranoid about food. The first few weeks of school my mother asked at every phone conversation, "How is your weight doing?" Parents should be careful, because the number of bulimics at school seems to be amazingly large.

Parents may wonder why at times their children seem so accessible and at others, so distant. Moments of understanding and tenderness between them are treasured by both. And yet, as parents and children temporarily bridge the gap between their worlds, their sense of connection is tenuous. Although comforting to students, it can also feel threatening—a flashback to earlier times of childhood dependence.

Sometimes after periods of intense and intimate contact with parents, students pull back abruptly. Ambivalent about their own ability to be independent, they act out this ambivalence through bouts of silence or antagonism. They may stop calling or writing for weeks on end and be unresponsive to family attempts to communicate, claiming uncharacteristically that they have nothing to say. Some fight their separation battles on an intellectual level, haggling with parents over the phone about politics or values, testing themselves and establishing their autonomy. Some retreat silently in an attempt to extricate themselves from the knots that bind them to an alcoholic family member, or from battling parents who are vying for their allegiance. Or, finding it stressful to switch gears abruptly from being an independent college student to being the kid in the family, some decide to stay at school over brief vacations such as fall break or Thanksgiving.

Students may seem unpredictably elusive and remote for months at a time when college life takes them into realms never experienced by their parents. A young woman whose parents live in a working-class Irish enclave and have never left their home state talks about feeling guilty and frustrated as she tries to share with them the diversity of her college friends and the travels they have enjoyed together. Another student returns to his depressed neighborhood in East St. Louis and tries to imagine what it would be like to bring his neighborhood friends and college roommates together. He often feels like a stranger in both worlds, but he can't explain any of this to his parents, who wonder why their formerly gregarious son is suddenly so quiet.

A lesbian from an upper-middle-class competitive and traditional Long Island community deliberates over how to stay close to the family she loves and admires while rejecting their community and lifestyle. Though she goes to school less than 200 miles away, she rarely goes home, but worries that she is hurting her parents as she wrestles with redefining her relationship with them.

And still another student, from a Puerto Rican immigrant family, talks about the anger she felt toward her parents, especially during her freshman and sophomore years, because they didn't understand her life. She resented what she considered their limited aspirations and their attempts to limit her. She withdrew from them emotionally and physically. Now, as a senior, she has come to a renewed appreciation of her parents and realizes that if they hadn't done certain things, she never would have gone to college, that her own life would have been much more narrow. After a painful withdrawal, she has reclaimed her past and reentered their lives.

WHEN SOMETHING GOES WRONG

When something goes wrong, parents are forced to step back and see their children in new ways. Never was this more apparent than on September 11th, 2001. Today's college students were young children on that day when the world stood still and life in this country seemed to change forever. . . . Whether touched directly by the tragedy or reeling from the impact of the event, families across the country—and around the world— felt an incredible longing to be together.

Though this event shattered an illusion of safety that oceans had provided, frightening incidents more closely associated with the seemingly halcyon American campus have raised the anxiety of many parents. Virginia Tech and Northern Illinois University will long be linked with tragic campus shootings. Natural disasters such as Hurricane Katrina left many parents of college students in New Orleans panicky, out of touch and helpless as their sons and daughters coped with the chaos that followed. Though rare, these dramatic happenings have left frightening and vivid images embedded in our minds. And as a result, as mothers and fathers send children off to college, new questions have surfaced. Should my child go to school closer to home? Do I want her in New York or Chicago or in any major city? Will my Muslim or Jewish child be ostracized or in danger? In the event of an emergency, what kind of security systems are in place at my child's school? Will my international child be safe in the United States?

More often than not however, just when we feel the most protective of our children, they remind us of their resilience and ability to handle difficult situations. Faced with the challenging task of bearing painful family news from home, some parents withhold information, hoping to spare their loved ones. Students are vehement about being kept informed about problems or major crises and feel betrayed when they aren't. "I want the privilege to worry over someone I love," one young woman exclaimed angrily after learning of her father's serious illness when she arrived home for spring break. "It's a violation of trust not to tell me. I'll always be anxious about what might be happening that I don't know about. And it makes me feel very isolated and remote from everyone at home. What I know about, I can handle."

Though students make it clear that they want to know what is going on, parents still have to wrestle with how much to say and when to say it: Can the news wait until exams are over or is it important to tell her right away? Can I let him know what is happening without burdening him with details and my own anxiety? Should I call some official at the college? How can I use the system that is already in place to provide support during this troubled time? One mother received the traumatic diagnosis of a malignancy and impending surgery several days after her freshman daughter's arrival at William and Mary. Her sensitivity to her daughter's needs in the midst of her own crisis helped to ease this difficult time:

> Amanda went to school early for preseason hockey practice, so she was in an empty dorm with just her head resident. I told her I wanted her to tell people what was going on at home, and she agreed to talk to her head resident. I called the head resident myself and also her coach, the two people I knew she was having the most contact with. She wanted to come home, but I said, "No, you need to get started." I suggested that she come home in early November after the surgery, after people had flocked around, and when I knew I'd need cheering up.

Although parents strive to foster their children's independence, when things go wrong at school students still need to turn to them for support and counsel. Students who have felt the disgrace of being called up by the campus judicial board for academic or social improprieties are often too ashamed or frightened themselves to deal with their parents' disappointment or anger. Or, since on most campuses parents don't receive their child's grades, parents may not know that their son or daughter is in academic trouble until it is too late. It is not easy for parents to assess the severity of a problem from afar, but students do send them signals and clues, some of which are indirect pleas for attention.

Lori Tenser, Dean of First-Year Students at Wellesley, speaks from her experience working with college students who have been in trouble: "Many parents don't recognize how much kids want to please their parents. When kids face disappointments or failures, they find it so hard to tell them."

Calls from an unhappy child that invade the daily routine of a family back home range from bouts of homesickness to serious illness—from academic failure to a drug problem. During the first few months of school, homesickness calls are routine interruptions in many homes. In most cases they eventually wane, only to erupt once in a while at particularly stressful times. A Colorado College freshman explains:

> In the beginning of school, I called my parents every day. I was very homesick and I felt like I needed to talk to them. I felt a tremendous void inside of me and by talking to them I was able to fill that void. After about a month, I got into the pattern of school. I don't call them nearly as much anymore. Before, I loved talking to them. Now, I don't have as much to say to them, and when we're on the phone, I am easily distracted by others around me.

A divorced mother of five recalls her middle child's grueling first semester:

> At first she called nightly wanting to come home. I told her she couldn't, but could come for a weekend. She cried every night. She was really scared and kept

> telling me she missed the rainbows in her room and that she wanted to stay with me forever. I finally told her she could call two times a week unless there was an emergency and after the first semester we would talk about whether she would stay. She made it through the semester . . . we both did; it was tough. By second semester she had made a commitment to stay and had three and a half pretty good years after that.

There are, of course, the few exceptional cases that deans and counseling centers deal with each year when the rupture of leaving home is simply too great and the panic increases with each passing day. With the help of college administrators and counselors, parents and their children may have to come to the disappointing, but nor irrevocable, decision that a student should go home. Most youngsters will be able to separate from their parents eventually in their own way and at their own pace, some with the additional help of therapy. Many return to college after a year or two of either working or going to school closer to home.

It is bound to be difficult for parents when their children come home unexpectedly. This sudden switching of gears throws a wrench into the whole family system. Parents may feel let down or burdened by having to cope with their children's problems on a daily basis. While trying to provide their children with emotional support, parents are likely to be struggling themselves with a sense of remorse as they question what went wrong. This return to the fold certainly was not part of the original plan when, full of dreams and expectations, they sent their children off to college.

As they try to separate, young adults often test their parents' limits in painful and destructive ways. The more emotionally dependent they feel, the more dramatic the rupture is likely to be. "In our darkest moments, we felt vilified as parents," said one mother whose daughter left school abruptly during her freshman year. "We turned to our friends for support. It was comforting to be told that we were just human, that we'd done the best we could."

And from the father of a student who returned home halfway through his first semester:

> We had to keep letting Josh know that we cared about him. He got an apartment near where we live. He was belligerent and very hostile. When we heard from him we had to listen to the melody, not the words. The melody said, "I need to know you're around." The words said, "I don't need you."
>
> We all got into family therapy. It was important for us to have an outside person to bring us together when the ferment was so chaotic.

During the course of their college careers, all students inevitably face bouts of minor illness. When they become run down and suffer from colds and the flu, they understandably miss the comforts of home, the privacy, chicken soup, and coddling they may have been used to. They are likely to call when they are feeling their absolute worst, seeking a bit of mothering. The first time this happens, the parents may be caught off guard. The mother of a Creighton University freshman says with a smile:

> The second or third week of school, he called and said, "Mom, what do you do for a real bad earache?" What I wanted to say was, "You put the phone down and wait for your mother, and I'll be there in four hours."

Of course, she didn't say that, but told him instead to go to the health service, which on all campuses is equipped to handle common illnesses and injuries. Some students simply need—in addition to expressions of sympathy—a bit of encouragement from their parents to use these services and to take responsibility for their own well-being.

The calls that all parents dread are those that bring news of a child's serious illness or accident. Most parents expect the college to keep them informed of serious medical problems. The notion of what constitutes something serious, however, is a matter of opinion. It's not unusual for parents to find out about episodes such as a bicycle accident or a case of mononucleosis long after the fact. If students are coping well with the problem and have not been hospitalized, most colleges will not call home on their behalf. They may encourage students to do so, but will treat them as adults

When students do encounter serious medical problems, parents face the difficult situation of having to place their trust in unfamiliar medical caretakers and their child's own ability to follow through. One mother from Wyoming who prides herself on her ability to "let go" found herself reacting in unfamiliar ways to unexpected circumstances:

> All of my carefree confidence about sending my daughter out into the world evaporated when we had to deal with a serious health problem. I have been tremendously anxious about this and what it means for her sports career, her grades, and especially her long-term health. When our older child went to college I was happy to hear from him once a week. With this child, I want to communicate almost every day, to "keep my finger on the pulse." I am as neurotic as the best—or worst—of them.

In the course of the academic year, a certain number of students will have to be hospitalized with either a physical or psychological illness. It's usually best that one or both parents come at such times, unless the hospital stay is brief and not traumatic. Many students are hesitant to ask, but usually want their parents with them, even if they don't say so directly. After receiving news that her daughter had developed a severe kidney infection and might be put in the hospital, this mother wavered between her own intuition and her daughter's direct response:

> I asked if she wanted me to come down; she said, "No." About 11 p.m. the next night, she called crying. She was getting worse, and the hospital told her if she threw up again, they would admit her. Then she said the words, "Mommy, will you come down? I am scared." I was on the road at 6 a.m. the next morning. I had spoken to the doctor, and she told me I didn't really need to come down. I disagreed with her. My Katie needed me, and I was going to be there.

This is a time when parents can cooperate with administrators to give the support and encouragement a student will need. Adjustments will have to be made; perhaps a lighter course load or leave of absence will be in order. When a serious accident or illness temporarily sends a college student back to childlike dependency on parents, it may take a special effort for the family to separate again after the student has recovered.

Less dramatic than hospitalization, but equally demanding of a parent's attention, are students' comments, either direct or indirect, that they are worried about their own behavior. Students who hint at or tell their parents of eating disorders, alcohol and drug dependency, and other self-destructive and compulsive behavior want their parents to respond. They don't want them to panic or nag, but to know they are in trouble and to take them seriously, as this student from Ohio State asserts:

> It took me two years to get up the courage to tell my mother that I was bulimic. By that time I was frantic. She hardly responded—kind of blew it off—and never mentioned it again. I'm not sure if she just couldn't handle it or if she really just thought it was a phase and didn't realize how serious it is.

Another student, a sophomore at Columbia, describes her parents' head-on approach:

> When I came home over break, it was obvious that I had gained weight and wasn't keeping in shape or doing any sports like I usually do. And during the first week I was back, I was hung over two or three times. My parents were really worried about this drinking thing with me to the point where they made me see somebody about it. They sent me to my doctor, who discovered that I'd gained 12 pounds, which is a lot on a small frame. He also said I had an iron deficiency, which can happen from drinking.
>
> Maybe I was lucky that my parents picked up the signals, and that my doctor discovered I had anemia. Once my doctor figured out what was going on, I talked mostly to him. When my parents and doctor intervened it was kind of like I was pulling back from being totally responsible for myself. I guess I wasn't doing a very good job of it. There had to be some help.

Doctors in college clinics see an abundance of symptoms related to stress. When a student comes in four or five times complaining of headaches, stomachaches, or sleep difficulties and no organic problem surfaces, the physician is likely to view the symptom as a functional problem and may talk with the student about it, perhaps making a referral to a counselor or psychiatrist for evaluation.

Psychological concerns are often insidious, developing over time and perhaps not clearly troublesome until well under way. College students are often mercurial; they may use the word *depressed* when they simply mean tired or lonely, and they tend toward hyperbole, especially when describing their own moods. So it is particularly difficult for a parent to distinguish normal ups and downs from psychological distress that needs attention.

Just as parents are beginning to relax and enjoy the pleasure of thinking about their son as an independent, capable, well-functioning adult, they receive a frantic phone call from him—now anxious and frazzled, having lost all sense of perspective. Or they get a disturbing late-night call from a despondent daughter who is questioning the meaning of her life. After a sleepless night, the parents anxiously call back the next day only to find the same daughter about to leave for a touch football game, irritated by their overreaction.

Brief episodes of depression and anxiety are common among college students. Most will feel the extreme pressure of some aspect of college life sooner or later: always another book to read, another paper to write, another exam to take, another set of problems to do—it never seems to go away. Add to this a broken love affair, disappointing grades, the threat of losing a scholarship, being rejected by a fraternity—all losses that take their toll. Most youngsters will cope with their fears and disappointments and, given the time to grieve for their losses, will pick themselves up with remarkable resilience. Letting go of dreams, coming to terms with one's own limitations is, after all, part of the reality of being an adult. But losses may be particularly powerful at this stage of development.

In his insightful book, *College of the Overwhelmed*, Dr. Richard Kadison, Chief of the Mental Health Service at Harvard University, comments that late adolescence is often the time when depression first appears:

> When it hits, it's not something students are familiar with. It's not like the sore knee that they know acts up occasionally, and when it does at college they know what it is and what to do about it. Depression seems to come out of the blue, and its symptoms are such that whether the students are freshmen or seniors, they and their families and friends don't associate them with mental illness. We all have occasional sleep difficulties, changes in appetite, problems with concentration. But putting the constellation together and getting proper care makes the difference between an engaging, enjoyable college experience and a miserable one that often leads to leaves of absence or other ancillary problems.[1]

Some parents find it difficult to understand the intensity of some depressive episodes when there seems to be no momentous precipitating cause, especially if their child has not exhibited these symptoms before. Why does a young man become suicidal when he gets a C in physics? How can the ending of a two-month fling bring on such feelings of worthlessness and hopelessness? These are the young people who don't bounce back from their bouts of anxiety or depression, but who continue to sink deeper into a period of increasing despair.

Janet Loxley, psychologist and longtime member of the University of California at Irvine's Counseling Center acknowledges that many of the typical signs of depression may simply be normal behavior among college-age students. Changes in eating and sleeping patterns, withdrawal, low energy, and flat affect in conversation are a few of the common symptoms that may or may not signal trouble.

Dr. Loxley believes, however, that if parents notice a cluster of these kinds of changes in their child's behavior, they should pay attention:

> In addition to the other patterns I mentioned, a marked change in hygiene, not just long hair or weird clothing, is something I'd be concerned about. Other things of note are forced cheer—trying hard to look happy—a sense of apathy and lack of interest in peers, waking up early and not being able to go back to sleep. Contrary to what some people might expect, depressed people are unlikely to be sitting around crying all the time. It's more subtle than that; they often just demonstrate little energy or interest in the world around them.
>
> If parents are concerned that their son or daughter is depressed, they might start by asking a simple open-ended question such as, "What's going on?" When a kid says to a parent, "It's not going well; I don't have friends," the parent wants to make the kid feel better fast and is tempted to say things like, "Don't worry. It will get better." Or, "I know how you feel. I went through the same thing. Everyone does."
>
> What the kid needs instead is to know that he or she has been heard, that the parents heard that these things are problems. A parent might say, "I'm not 100 percent sure, but you sound kind of depressed to me. Do you want to talk about it?" Let the kid feel as though he has some room.

Dr. Loxley believes that it is fine for parents who are worried about a noncommunicative and seemingly depressed child to call up a housing official or dean and tentatively express concern, though their son or daughter will be initially displeased by their intervention. But parents shouldn't try to get the university officials to collude with them without telling their child. Dr. Loxley asserts:

> It's one thing to call the head resident in the dorm and say, "My daughter has been sleeping late every day, and I want to make sure she's up by eight each day—and don't tell her I called."
>
> It's a totally different matter to call and say, "I'm not certain that there's a problem, but I'm concerned about my daughter and told her I was going to call you. I'd appreciate it if you'd keep an eye on her and encourage her to use whatever resources you and she think might help her."

Depression is a complex topic, and its causes are still being debated. College students, whose identities are shaky to begin with, live in a highly charged and demanding environment. Some bring with them the added burden of family problems; some may have a predisposition to depression. And in the intense race for perfection that has preceded the "getting in" sweepstakes, students are on overdrive, conditioned to do it all and do it well, and many pay a price. It is no wonder that depression is the most common psychological problem among college students.

As a result of the dramatic improvement in psychopharmacological approaches to treating depression, an increasing number of students take antidepressants that allow them to function well in college. When students go off their medication and then call home for help, parents are faced with yet another challenge.

The mother of a freshman describes a phone call from her daughter a month into college:

> My stomach dropped when I heard her say, "Mom. Things aren't going so good. I really want to come home. You know that I'm not a student; in fact I really hate school. I should have never come here. I'm not going to classes. I can't do this without you pushing me out the door." She had in fact slept through her first exam. "I miss you. I miss the dog. I'm not going to make it. Please let me come home."
>
> As Caroline spoke, I held my breath so I wouldn't let on to her how scared I was. I listened, asked lots of questions, and tried to let her vent her worries. She had taken herself off her antidepressants the week before the phone call. I had to somehow convince her to go back on her meds, to respect her desire not to have "these chemicals in my body," and to help her regroup. We talked for a long time. She bought my metaphor about first semester being like making waffles. You sometimes burn the first waffle, but you don't throw out the batter; in other words, you are just learning about this college business, not to mention all of the adjustments, so don't give up yet. You'll screw up, but so does everyone else. I let out my breath by the end of the conversation. She said she would go back on her Zoloft. I cried when I got off the phone.

A number of students suffer severe psychological illnesses that require them to be hospitalized, and some eventually have to leave college. This is devastating to parents and activates intense feelings, from guilt and self-doubt to anger and resentment. These families suddenly find themselves catapulted into a world of mental health professionals that may be foreign and frightening. Parents are encouraged to learn as much as they can about the illness and to reach out to friends, counselors, or clergy at such a draining time so that they can get support for themselves and still be emotionally available to their child.

Phone calls bringing news of unexpected traumatic experiences are likely to catch parents off guard. A father of a University of Virginia sophomore tells of his helpless feelings when he and his wife received a phone call from their son in the middle of the night:

> Jay had gone to Washington to visit some of his high school friends at Georgetown for the weekend. On the way to a concert, they found themselves in the midst of a crowd running toward them, so they ran back to their car. Suddenly they were kicked to the ground by several policemen, their hands forced behind their backs, handcuffed, and Jay found himself with a gun pointing at his head. After much physical and verbal assault, they were let go when it was clear that they had been innocent bystanders. But the trauma had taken its toll.
>
> When Jay called he was clearly shaken, and we felt so helpless not being there with him. My wife wanted to pack up his things and bring him home. I told her this could have happened three blocks from us, and we can't protect him from it. Although Delores answered the phone, Jay just wanted to speak to me. I think it's a gender thing. There are certain things kids just are more comfortable talking to the parent of the same gender about.
>
> He worried about upsetting us. I was glad that we had inculcated into our kids that no matter what happens, we may not like it or what you may have done, but we are your parents and we need to know.

It helped us to talk to the parents of the other kids and to our pastor, and it helped Jay to talk to his friends. But when he was still feeling down several days later, we suggested that he also talk to someone at the counseling center.

It was important to take care of what we could—contacting the police, the university president, an attorney—to get some control. I told Jay, "It's not guaranteed that we'll get results, but we'll do what we can do, and then you need to get back to the normal pattern of your life at school and remain focused."

When Jay went away to college, I knew that something was likely to happen. These things happen to us and our loved ones all the time. I thought it more likely that he might be picked up in a small town or driving on a back street. This incident happened because he was in the wrong place at the wrong time, but also because he is an African-American male. I had told Jay of the fun times I used to have visiting my friends at other colleges, and then this happened. It ruined what should have been a happy time.

Remaining steady in the face of frightening or heartbreaking news draws upon all of a parent's resources. When a son calls to report that he has been in a car accident or a daughter describes a sexual assault by a fellow student, parents may respond out of their own anxiety rather than in ways that would be helpful to their child.

Though acquaintance rape and crime on campus are common topics for the headlines, nothing really prepares us to handle these situations when they happen to our own children. Startling evidence of our sons' and daughters' vulnerability is likely to stir up all of our most protective parental instincts. We're thrown off balance ourselves—frightened, sad, and angry about what has happened. We'd like to think that there's some way we can prevent something like this from ever happening again. And that's when we start asking the kind of questions that one student labeled the "Why did you? Why didn't you?" variety.

A young woman who was sexually assaulted by a classmate after a party explains what happened when she finally got up the nerve to call home and tell her mother about it.

> The first thing my mother hit me with, after she asked if I was OK, was "Why was he in your room? Were you drunk? Was he drunk?" I was raped, for God's sake!
>
> And then I had to deal with my father, who called me back that night and wanted the name of the guy. He wanted to call the dean and find out what the college was going to do about it.
>
> They just didn't get it! At that point, I didn't know exactly what I wanted, but I knew I didn't want to be blamed or rescued . . . just listened to and supported. I needed someone to help me figure out what *I* wanted to do.

Having experienced the helplessness, violation, and betrayal of acquaintance rape, a woman needs to regain control over her life—to make her own decision about reporting the incident or pressing charges. It's not unusual for a woman to wait weeks or even months before she recognizes an act of unwanted intercourse as rape, and it may take even longer for her to reveal it to someone else. Recovery from rape, or indeed from an attempted rape, is a long process. Most campuses now employ counselors who are specially trained to help students who have suffered this trauma.

When a young woman calls home to talk about what has happened to her, parents can help by encouraging her to use campus resources. Though times such as these may stretch us to our emotional limits as parents, our children need us to listen, not judge; to be patient, understanding, and supportive.

The director of the University of Michigan's Sexual Assault Prevention and Awareness Center offers parents the following advice:

> The first thing you should do is take two deep breaths, and then tell your daughter you have faith in her, and that you're really sorry this happened. Emphasize that it's not her fault, and that the decisions about what to do are hers, and that you'll support her through this.
>
> Then I think you should go get support yourself. The feeling of helplessness, especially for parents who live far from their daughter's school, is overwhelming. Supporting your daughter through this is very painful, and you're probably going to need help.
>
> In addition to counseling and support from friends, I highly recommend Linda Ledray's sensitive and informative book, *Recovering from Rape*.

Students often respond intensely to the problems and tragedies that occur around them. A fellow student's attempted suicide, a rape, a fatal accident—any tragedy that powerfully shatters the illusion of invulnerability that cloaks the lives of college students—is likely to create ripples of distress throughout the campus. "I used to feel so invincible," said one student after the death of a classmate in a car accident. "Now it's never going to be the same again."

College faculty and administrators are on the alert when there is a suicide on campus. Such an event triggers thoughts of suicide in other students, and there is often an increase in attempts during the weeks following. It's common for counselors to go into the residence halls to meet with groups of students, and for administrators to inform faculty about the potential fallout. Many students will turn to their parents; some will want to talk; some will need to cry. All need a calm presence when they're in the midst of such turmoil.

Students react, also, to the losses their classmates suffer. When one student's parents decide to get a divorce, his or her friends may start to feel anxious about the relationships of their own mothers and fathers. And when the parent of a classmate becomes seriously ill or dies, intimate friends, and even acquaintances who happen to live in the close quarters of the residence halls, feel the reverberations of the loss.

Some students become so enmeshed in the problems of their friends that they feel virtually taken over by a sense of responsibility to them—more responsibility than they can realistically handle.

> My roommate had a lot of problems; she was bulimic, and she talked about it all the time. I was becoming more like a parent than a friend. I got too entangled—and at times, I needed to get away physically.

Although students can often help and support each other through difficulties, some problems such as this one require professional intervention. In their concern for each other and desire to be helpful, young people are often unable to set appropriate boundaries. When parents become concerned about their child's overinvolvement with a depressed or suicidal friend, they might point out that their child's constant availability may be keeping the friend from getting the professional help that is actually needed.

WHEN PARENTS VISIT SCHOOL

Visits to students on their own turf have the potential for bringing new perspectives and delights—if parents are sensitive to their child's needs and agendas.

Some parents choose to visit on Parent and Family Weekends, specially planned occasions orchestrated to show off the college at its most hospitable. Others opt for a visit that fits more easily into their child's schedule or one that coincides with a particular event involving their youngster, such as a football game or a musical performance.

Most freshmen look forward to showing off their new home, new friends, and new selves to their families. They may look like the same young people who left home so recently, but the first few months of college seem like an eternity to them and they'd like their parents to take note and understand their lives. They may act surprisingly remote at first, suddenly feeling the vulnerability of their emerging independence. Or they may take charge, frenetically trying to introduce their parents to everyone and everything on campus.

A freshman at Bowdoin describes how she felt about her parents' first visit to campus:

> I was nervous and excited when my parents said they were coming for Parents' Weekend. I wanted to show them my world, to show them where I go biking and where I take people on admissions tours. It's my home. I wanted them to see it and like it.
>
> I wanted them to meet my friends, but not for too long—like I didn't want them to hang out in my room. I wanted them to see the faces behind the names I'd been talking about. But I was used to act-

> ing a certain way and kidding around with the guys next door. I was afraid Andrew and Rick would do something embarrassing in front of my parents—or that my parents would tell a dumb joke or tell a story about when I was little. At first it felt kind of weird to suddenly have all these parents around. But it all worked out fine. We kind of got back together as a family and had a fantastic time.

Not every freshman is this enthusiastic about parental visits. A senior from the Midwest recalls:

> My mom kept asking me about Parents' Weekend freshman year. And I kept putting her off. I guess I just wasn't ready for her to come visit yet—maybe because I'd only been there a few months, and it still didn't feel like my place. I wasn't sure what I wanted, but she must have picked up my uncertainty, and I'm grateful for that. She waited until sophomore year to visit, and by then it was great to have her here.

Students often worry about how to entertain their parents for the whole weekend. If parents let their son or daughter know that they don't expect to be with them every minute of the day, students may breathe a sigh of relief. There are often school-sponsored events specifically planned for parents that students aren't even aware of. A little flexibility goes a long way in making the weekend enjoyable for everybody.

Bubbles can burst when parents comment on the state of their child's room or clothes or shaggy hair. The weekend can turn sour if the visiting parent demands instant maturity and constant attention. Students expect to be able to continue their studying and social lives when their parents are in town. A delightful dinner together may deteriorate if parents are disappointed or angry when their child leaves for a party soon after the coffee has been served:

> I learned the hard way that Parents' Weekend didn't mean that Doug would be with me the whole time. He had a paper to work on, and he slept in for the parent breakfast Sunday morning.

> Tom and I realized that just as we had some rules and expectations when Heather came home for vacations, she had expectations of her own for us when we went to see her. We decided ahead of time that we were going to try to tune into her agenda instead of sticking to our own. For example, we were hoping to go to a class with her, but that clearly and emphatically was not OK with her. Once we got past the initial awkwardness, I felt almost euphoric seeing her in her world. I got a new sense of how in charge she is, of how much she feels at home there. Before we went I had questioned whether we could justify the cost of the trip. Now it's a high priority for us to visit her at school once a year.

One set of parents even found their son's messy room reassuring:

> When I saw his room was as much of a mess as his room at home, I knew he was comfortable here

A parent who didn't come to campus until her daughter's graduation said:

> I worried that she would feel alone on Parents' Weekends, but we had talked about it when she

> chose a school far away. We just couldn't afford the expense of the plane trips on top of what we were contributing for tuition. She seemed fine with it and always was included in dinners out with her friends' parents.

Both divorced and married parents talk about the particular pleasure of a solo visit to campus. A woman who recently spent a day with her son while on a business trip to Boston reflects:

> I ended up going on a long afternoon walk with Dan and his girlfriend, making a couple of stops along the way for ice cream and a cappuccino. Then Dan and I went biking along the Charles and topped off the evening at his apartment, where he cooked dinner and his apartment mates wandered in and out. The music was blaring and the phone kept ringing and I soaked in the whole scene in a way that just wouldn't have happened if my husband had been with us. When I came home and told Steve about our day, he was jealous and decided that he's going to treat himself to his own visit sometime during the year.

Students who live off campus talk with pride of sprucing up apartments and cooking meals for visiting dads and moms. It's an opportunity for them to show off firsthand another step in their growing competence. Although visits to college are wonderful opportunities for students to share their world with parents, most students still take great pleasure in old standby parental pampering, such as a care package from home or a special dinner out for them and their friends.

WHEN STUDENTS COME BACK HOME

Visits home and long-awaited vacations often crystallize the changes taking place across the miles. They evoke questions about relationships and highlight a student's growing independence and separation. They may be particularly complicated for the large number of students whose divorced parents live in different households, sometimes in separate cities. Even parents who have worked out custody and visitation arrangements long ago may suddenly find themselves locking horns over where their son or daughter will spend vacations.

And if parents divorce while their child is away at college, the student has to grapple with questions of allegiances at the same time he or she is trying to separate. It is a difficult combination. In the turmoil of their own distress, parents often minimize the blow of this news to their college-age children and may be surprised by the emotional fallout. College students still define themselves as part of a family, and the rupture to that family unit is usually a major jolt. They may be angry at their parents for splitting up, and although they may act cool about the whole situation, parents should not assume that their external reaction represents what they are feeling inside. It is important for parents to keep their antennae out for emotional reactions and to refrain from involving their child in their own conflicts.

"I've seen parents pull at a kid like a Gumby doll," said one director of residential life. "One kid who didn't want to face making the choice between the two of them went back to his home town for Thanksgiving and checked into a hotel with his brother."

A move to a new city can also be wrenching for college students, especially at vacation times. It makes separating more complicated and often has more of an impact on a youngster living away at school than parents realize. College students are at loose ends when returning home for vacations to a city without friends or familiar landmarks. Family rituals and traditions provide a sense of continuity and may be particularly important at such times. But young people may feel displaced when parents are their only link to this alien community. At a time when they are trying to separate, coming to a new home may throw them into an uncomfortable position of dependence. They may be testy or restless; they may want to leave and return to familiar places and high school friends. A sensitive and understanding parent will be flexible about vacation plans to accommodate this conflict.

A junior whose divorced parents have each moved twice since she started college comments:

> The worst time was freshman year when my mother moved out of the house I grew up in. I felt like a visitor when I went home. My mother's next move was to a whole different part of the country. After that move I did a lot of visiting over the vacation; I went to my boyfriend's house. My parents didn't care, but my grandparents did.
>
> Moving is a pain in the neck. Most of my stuff at my mother's place is in boxes. Things that are real important to me are here at school. School is more of a home than my official permanent address is.
>
> Home is wherever I am at this point. In a lot of ways it's at school 'cause that's where my closest friends are. If any place really feels like home, it's where my grandparents are. I think of them as family and spend part of each of my vacations with them.

The first vacations of a student's college career are usually the most intense for everyone involved. Students and parents, eager to see each other, feel an unfamiliar tentativeness as the family comes together again. A junior at Tufts recalls:

I didn't go home until Christmas freshman year. It was really awful. I remember lying in bed crying the first night and thinking, Sara, you're not the same Sara who left here. I had come home with a bad cold and I was up half the night feeling terrible and confused. The next morning Mom looked at me kind of sad and asked why I wasn't happy to be home. She looked so let down.

A sophomore at Yale recalls the feeling of living in two different worlds:

It feels like putting life on pause . . . rewinding . . . you get to see everyone, it's really cool. It's a destressor, but once you come back home you fall back into this other life. You have this momentary bubble in this other life and then you fly back into your new life again.

And a senior at Drake describes his reaction to his first Thanksgiving back home:

I wanted to get back and see my parents so badly, but when I actually got there, it was kind of a letdown 'cause I'd built up expectations of this grand homecoming and I'd step in the door, and it was a feeling of not having a place where I was comfortable anymore. Home was no longer home the way I knew it, and yet school was not home yet; I hadn't spent enough time there. It was really a lost feeling for a while.

"Where is my home?" may not be articulated, but in this time of transition there are moments of confusion:

> There was one time when I was home when I said to my sister at the dinner table, "Oh, I can't wait to go home," and my parents' faces just dropped, and I looked at them and I looked at my sister and I was like, Oh, my gosh, I just called college "home."

And from the father of a Colby freshman:

> We picked Andy up at the airport the day before Thanksgiving and, after the initial greetings and hugs, he just kept staring at us. As he got in the car, he looked at it and said, "Wow, our car—our same old car." He kept making remarks like that about all the familiar landmarks on the road back home, fast food restaurants he had frequented, even gas stations—anything he'd ever had any connection to.
>
> His first few hours at home, he kept walking around the house, noticing every detail. He kept saying how quiet it was, and how weird it was to have all this space for four people. It was like he was trying to drink it all in, like he was trying to convince himself that it was all real. It took a while before we could just settle in and be with each other.

When students return home, most of them expect to find everything just the way they left it, as though time had stopped while they were gone. They prefer to find their rooms untouched and their siblings and parents just the way they always were. Yet they also want their parents to recognize and respect that they have changed, that they have been living on their own and have become more independent. All this calls for a sense of balance—not to mention a sense of humor. And it is the rare family whose members do not find themselves trying to renegotiate relationships and expectations during these weeks between semesters.

Young people look at their families with the discerning eyes of outsiders, seeing, sometimes for the first time, qualities and dynamics they had never noticed before. They may be disillusioned at the less than perfect scene they see; it is likely to have been idealized during their months apart. Or, after observing the way their college friends or roommates interact with their families, they may appreciate aspects of their own home life that they had previously taken for granted. They cast disdainful glances at household changes, even simple improvements.

Some students react by being outwardly critical of family habits and patterns that have long been taken for granted: Why do we have to eat dinner at such an uncivilized hour? Why don't the women of this family stand up for themselves? Why do we have to go to church? So what if you and Dad are divorced—can't you at least be civil to each other?

They often bait their parents with newly learned, but as yet unintegrated, bits of philosophy and social consciousness. They bristle at parental attempts to control their comings and goings, their behavior, or their schedules. Having been used to the independence of college life, yet feeling uncertain about their adult status within the context of the family, they may take rigid stances and balk at any suggestions offered:

> It hadn't entered my mind that I'd have to ask to use the car or answer so many questions like "Where are you going?" "What time will you be home?" "Who will you be with?" "Call if you're not home by twelve-thirty." It was a chore.

> Can you believe it? My mother started getting upset about my shoes being left on the stairs. I mean, who cares!

> It's so weird after being independent to go home and have to be a son. What do you mean, clean up my room?

> My freshman year winter break, it was ten or ten-thirty at night, and I wanted to go out and get some coffee, and my mother said she didn't think it would be a good idea. We live in suburbia, not exactly dangerous. My mother said, "It's kind of late." I said, "It's ten-thirty. Are you insane?" And I walked out the door.

Parents may find it tricky to strike a balance between respecting their son's or daughter's emerging independence and wanting to run their household with some degree of order. They may need to modify some of their old rules in light of the increased freedom their child has become accustomed to. Everything becomes even more complicated when divorced parents have conflicting sets of guidelines in their separate homes. Each family has to negotiate its own set of expectations, but as one freshman dean says:

> There's bound to be some tension about rules and what needs to be said and done. Students are used to coming and going without reporting to anyone. I think it is fair for parents to expect the same things from their children that they would expect from a courteous guest. It's reasonable to expect them to pick up after themselves, and let you know whether or not they will be home for dinner and approximately when they will be in at night.

From the mother of a sophomore:

> You have to have a sense of humor when you awaken to the beep of the microwave and the hum of the dryer at 2 a.m., and realize that it's your son fixing a snack and doing his laundry at a time that's normal for him.

In some households there's a sense of self-consciousness about how to reenter each others' lives. Students describe parents who suddenly treat them so much as equals that they lose the special quality of their relationship:

> All of a sudden I'm just another person in the house. My parents think I want to be treated as an adult, like their equal. I'm tired of all this independence. I really needed to go home to my mom and have her be a mom. Instead she wants to be my pal.

Others say they feel smothered and long for more parental recognition of their evolving independence:

> I want my parents to treat me as an equal. They baby me and don't seem to realize that I don't want them to do everything for me.

By their very nature, vacations are times of relaxation and pleasure, and many people approach them with anticipation and heightened expectations. Parents who take their cues from their returning college offspring report delightful moments of rediscovery and joy. Recognizing that this is, in fact, their son's or daughter's vacation, not theirs, they take pleasure in watching their youngster get together with friends and do not mind when he or she spends endless hours just unwinding around the house.

But as students arrive home geared up for rest and reconnecting with high school friends, many parents have their own, very different agendas—fantasies of special family outings, three weeks of unscheduled time for productive summer job-hunting, intimate moments alone with a maturing son or daughter. Such expectations are a trap and may lead to disappointed parents and resentful offspring.

Some parents save up their serious conversations for vacation times; they have plans of heart-to-heart talks with their child about excessive partying, poor grades, summer plans, or, perhaps the most stressful subject of all, their child's future. All of these are legitimate concerns, but timing is important and, without caution, discussions can become lectures that will turn off even the most receptive young person.

Often a simple open-ended question such as "What's happening in your life?" or "How are things going?" gives students just the opportunity they've been waiting for to talk about what's on their minds. A young woman from Scripps remarks:

> It's tricky. I want my parents to know about my friends and what's going on with me, but if they ask too much it might feel intrusive. I think the best thing is for parents and kids to take some of the time when they're together over vacation to try to catch up.
>
> Anyway, over vacation my father made the biggest move he's ever made. He said, "So what's going on?" I let out a big sigh of relief and said, "I'm glad you asked. Let me tell you."
>
> We talked about four or five of my friends at school, including the guy I was dating, and we had never done that before in the year and a half I had been there. We had discussed what courses I was taking and the extracurriculars, but we hadn't discussed social life, which is a big part of my own life. It's difficult to have those kinds of conversations over the phone. For me it was the ideal situation; my mom

> and sisters had gone to the movies, and Dad and I were sitting by ourselves. It was just the two of us, and it's easier for me to talk to my parents one-on-one.

Some students plan to talk to their parents about issues of major concern during vacations rather than e-mail or by phone. A gay student from Iowa describes the painful process of coming out to his father during the winter vacation of his sophomore year.

> I'd always known I wasn't attracted to females, but I kept praying it would change. I kept hoping when I got to college I'd start over and things would be different. I did become very attracted to someone, but that someone was a male; I realized I couldn't fool myself anymore.
>
> My mother died when I was in high school. My dad and I have always been very close—which, by the way, destroys the stereotype about homosexuals having cold, distant, or absent fathers. I wanted to tell him, and I knew eventually that he would accept it, but I was still worried about his reaction.
>
> During Christmas break, I got my courage up and told him. Initially, he was very accepting, calm, and supportive. He said, "You're my son. I still love you. Nothing changes. I just want you to be happy."
>
> The first time I became involved with someone, however, he reversed a bit. He was very upset that I was comfortable with it and that I was really planning to go ahead and live my life this way. I hesitated bringing my friend home at spring vacation. After several phone conversations, my Dad seemed to have become more resolved. He said, "Of course, come

home and bring him. If he's someone you care about, I want to meet him."

This young man acknowledged that he had the "near-perfect coming out" and that many of his friends went through a much more traumatic time. Some have been banished from their families; the parents of others desperately try to find ways to "cure" their children through psychotherapy, religion, or by actively encouraging heterosexual relationships. And still others pretend they do not know and make it clear they do not want to talk about it. All of these negative responses lead to alienation and distancing between parent and child.

The student quoted above was sensitive to the shock and pain his father would go through. Both father and son had built a strong foundation of trust and communication, which allowed them to get through some tension-filled times and to become closer. They recognized that these first awkward conversations are part of an ongoing process—a process that began long ago with their evolving relationship and will continue as each moves through his own difficult journey ahead.

Parents often need information and support when their children confront them with the news that they are gay. Students find it encouraging when their parents take it upon themselves to become informed. *Beyond Acceptance*, by Carolyn Griffin and Marian and Arthur Wirth, and *Always My Child: A Parent's Guide to Understanding Your Gay, Lesbian, Bisexual, Transgendered or Questioning Son or Daughter*, by Kevin Jennings, are among several sensitive and informative books on the subject. And the national self-help organization, Parents and Friends of Lesbians and Gays (P-FLAG) has groups in all parts of the United States that have helped provide information as well as support for those in need.

For many parents, vacations are a bittersweet time. Just when they thought they had gotten used to a quieter household, it fills up again with the music and laughter and exuberance of college students. Their children's friends drop by and reminisce about their childhood capers and share tales of their current college exploits. Suddenly there isn't enough milk in the refrigerator and the phone rings every five minutes as plans for the evening are made and remade. The dinner table crackles with the excitement of newly discovered passions, academic and otherwise, and everything seems a bit livelier than it had been. Of course, the dinner table is also the setting for the replay of sibling bickering and volatile outbursts about trivial matters: Who gets the car tonight? What TV shows do we watch? What do you mean borrowing my sweater without asking? For most parents, however, the squabbles and the McDonald's wrappers in the car, and the pile of towels on the bathroom floor seem a small burden to bear compared to the joy of reconnecting as a family.

"But," says a Wisconsin mother of a sophomore and a senior, "even though it's great to have them back, there's a certain sadness. You realize that it will never be the same again; they are not totally home. They have a whole different world that is part of them, and they are only temporary visitors."

Another mother writes on an online message board for parents about her surprise at her emotional reaction to her sophomore son's leave-taking after his Thanksgiving break at home:

> Taking him to the airport this morning was very sad for me. More so than it was last year. Maybe because this trip home was so nice: very comfortable, no conflict. Then I walked past his room when I got back and saw that he had MADE HIS BED, even though we had to leave pretty early to get to the airport (he never makes his bed!), and I wept. I don't know why exactly.

And, indeed, most parents do find that as their children progress through their college years and become more separate, their visits home take on a distinctly different quality. Students' eagerness to return home and reconnect with family and friends freshman year typically gives way to a more tempered reentry in the years that follow.

A woman from Hawaii whose only child attends the University of Santa Clara in California found herself facing a whole new level of adjustment between her daughter's sophomore and junior years:

> It hit me during the summer that this may be her last summer home, the last time she'll be with us for a whole three months. The reality is that there are very few jobs here, and she probably won't be coming back here for a long period of time again.

Students may return less often or set clearer boundaries of privacy when they do come back. Sometimes their behavior is confusing, sometimes humorous, and sometimes painful. Many go through periods of strident distancing before they can reconnect comfortably with their parents on more mutual terms.

The father of a sophomore describes a discrepancy between the way his son relates to him over the phone and the way he wants to interact when he comes home for vacations:

> Kevin calls a lot from school when things are going well. He calls to complain about courses or girls who gave him the cold shoulder, almost anything that's on his mind. He describes how he's feeling—if he's depressed or anxious or questioning what he's doing there.
>
> Then when he gets home, all the things he needs to talk to us about when he's at school suddenly seem

> not to be issues anymore. But of course they still are. It's just, I think that he feels safer talking about them when he's at school. We can be a long-distance sounding board. But when he's in our house, he might be swallowed up by us. It's too threatening. He's very quiet here, and I think we need to respect that.

And the mother of an in-town student who lives in the residence halls reports:

> When Abby was a freshman, she used to come home every week to do her laundry, and she'd spend a lot of time talking to me. She said the washing machines weren't very good. This year she's a sophomore, and she never comes home to do her laundry. It's funny; they're the same washing machines as last year.

A divorced mother of two describes the abrupt change in her older daughter's behavior during the summer between her junior and senior years:

> Libby used to tell me everything. Sometimes I worried that she was too dependent on me as a confidante. Her father left home when she was 13, and she and I had some rocky years together. Anyway, we were very close. But last summer when she came home it was as though she put a curtain down between us. She barely spoke to me. I knew she'd been going through a hard time at school, but she didn't want to talk about that or anything else. It was really a strain having her around all summer and getting the silent treatment. But I kept telling myself that there was a method to her madness, that she really needed to pull back from me.

> Now that she's back at school, we've had a few good talks over the phone. It's not the same as it used to be, but at least we're talking again.

As students mature they increasingly look at their parents as separate people, not just Mom and Dad. After a long absence, they may see signs of aging they had never noticed before. They shed their self-absorption and begin to feel more empathy for the stresses and struggles of their parents' lives. A young woman, a junior at Washington University, observes:

> I've noticed changes in my parents lately, especially my dad. I think he's changing as he's watching his parents get old and is responding to things differently. My dad is going through the kind of changes my mom went through a few years ago when her parents died. Right now my dad's mother is very sick and his father is not doing well either. In the last six months my dad has had to take over the role of taking care of both of them. I think he feels the burden of a lot of responsibility. I also think he's analyzing what happened in his parents' lives and the way they dealt with him. I'm not sure what the outcome of that will be, but I've already seen a change. I think he's becoming more sensitive.
>
> I also think he's feeling very pressured, watching his parents get old before his eyes, and sometimes I feel some of that pressure. For instance, if I come home from school with an incomplete, it feels like a disappointment to him. I think he needs as few problems as possible. I think he needs nurturing. He's having to nurture his parents and his kids, and I think he needs some of that nurturing back.

The pleasures and pains of parenthood are highlighted during the periods throughout the college years when children reenter the household. There is the joy of seeing a child develop—listening to her describe the way she is going to improve the school literary magazine, or watching him explain to his little brother what archaeology is and why he is so excited about it. It is rewarding to see evidence of burgeoning intellectual capacities and self-confidence, which may have been apparent in e-mails and phone calls, but bring even greater delight to parents in the course of daily interaction.

When children return home with problems, however, their disappointments and pain become part of their parents' day-to-day existence too. It hurts to see a child in the throes of misery from a broken romance, or filled with self-doubt, or struggling with a weight problem. It is more difficult to separate your pain from theirs when they are at home; their unhappiness is a constant presence.

And parents are reminded, also, of bothersome traits in their children—traits that had faded temporarily from their memories in the glow of eagerly awaited texts and phone calls from their distant college offspring. They may find themselves worrying about behaviors they hadn't thought about for a while and wondering, "How can this budding engineer consistently leave the gas tank on empty and never replace the toilet paper on the roll?" Or, "She doesn't know how to lose an argument. How will she ever sustain a relationship or hold down a job?" Parental anxiety often gives way to renewed attempts to control, to take another stab at trying to "set this kid on the right track." In their more rational moments, parents know, of course, that such attempts are doomed to failure.

As students move through their college years, their early experiments begin to turn into commitments—and these commitments may be in conflict with parents' own dreams and values. The mother who was amused by her son's "granola stage" freshman year now has to come to terms with the fact that he has decided to become a forest ranger rather than a lawyer as originally planned. The father who hardly gave a second glance to the silent, sulking boyfriend his daughter brought home freshman and sophomore years begins to wonder if he is going to be a permanent fixture in the family. As they decide who they are and how they want to live their lives, students make choices about their majors and careers, about religion and values, and about intimate partners. When they return home, these loaded issues leap to the forefront and parents come face-to-face with the essence of letting go.

9

SOPHOMORE SLUMP AND THE YEARS BEYOND

> Did you feel when you first came to college that it all was so new and exciting, such a big change from home? By spring it began to be a little routine, and this fall here you are taking these courses and it's much the same and you don't really know what you're here for and you don't know why you're taking these courses rather than any other courses. You're sleeping a lot, but still always seem to feel tired. Maybe you're just blowing off—sitting in the library, staring at the same page for forty minutes; maybe you're going out and eating pizza when you know you should be doing your problem sets, but you just can't focus your attention.

"That sounds like me," a bewildered sophomore responds, wondering how his dean knows so much about his lethargic state these past few months. This dean of a highly respected and academically rigorous university is not a psychic, nor does she have informants waiting in the wings. She has just described the common phenomenon known as "sophomore slump" to a student she had summoned to her office for a discussion about a failing grade.

The sophomore slump doesn't always happen sophomore year; some experience a similar state during the second half of their freshman year or when they are juniors or seniors, and some don't experience it at all. But the sophomore year has particular characteristics that make it an unsettling time of self-doubt and vulnerability for many students.

What has happened to the energetic and enthusiastic freshmen of just a year before? What has happened to their intense and often quixotic responses to the college environment, that beckoning world with new intellectual vistas and few social restraints? One might expect the second year of college to be a repetition of the first, perhaps a bit more stable since the sophomore has the advantage of knowing the ropes. The sophomore slump, though a common colloquialism, comes as a surprise to both parents and their children.

Sophomores return to school without the anxiety and hoopla of orientation that launched them the year before. Most are happy to be back and eagerly seek out friends and old haunts. They bask in their sense of belonging as they watch the glassy-eyed freshmen stumble by. Once school is under way, the peaks and valleys of the academic year—marked off by exams, vacations, and traditional college events—are reassuringly familiar. But the second college year intrudes with new choices, new responsibilities, and new problems to solve. The world of the college sophomore is substantially different from that of the freshman—with spurts of growth and a lot of confusion.

From a parent:

> We looked forward to seeing him develop a passion for a course of study which truly engages him and makes him grow intellectually. In his sophomore year

> now, we are seeing bits of that happening. He loves his courses this semester and finds them exactly what he wants to study and integrally related to one another. As a down side of sophomore year, the bloom is off the rose.

From a second semester sophomore:

> I have calmed down a lot since freshman year. Alcohol is very open here, and I took full advantage of that. But I got that out of my system by sophomore year. I also feel like I have been exposed to a lot of issues that I was sheltered from growing up in a small midwestern town where everyone was white, middle class, etc. We didn't deal with racism, homosexuality, or depression, or anything else like that at home, which are all issues which have come up here.

And from a junior:

> Sophomore year everyone seems to be floating in different directions, yet no one really knows where they are going. I found that a good portion of my sophomore year was spent trying to figure out who I was and who my true friends were.

Sophomores, no longer the new kids on the block, are responsible for themselves in ways that they weren't the year before. They are expected to know the system by now, and they are often embarrassed to let others know when they don't. No one is eagerly showing them how to use the library or computer center or guiding them to the remote corners of the campus. Campus groups are no longer clamoring for their membership; and everyone assumes that sophomores know from their own experience what it means to belong to a particular fraternity, team, or club. No one has assigned them a roommate; the choices and the consequences are their own. If they don't get along, they can't chalk it up to a glitch in the computer matching system or the misguided whims of the residential life staff. They may feel confined by their friends from the previous year and the potential for making new friends no longer seems unlimited. Intimate relationships may suffer the strain of unexpected changes after a summer apart. Some sophomores move off-campus into apartments, undertaking a whole new range of tasks and responsibilities,and may miss being in the middle of campus activity.

As one administrator put it, "No one is loving you up anymore, whether it is the RA, an advisor, or your parents; and at the same time you're betwixt and between in your academic life."

Academically, sophomores know enough to recognize how little they know. Though they are developing the tools that will allow them to do the more creative work later on, they wonder if they will ever be able to master anything—whether they have what it takes to be as competent and knowledgeable as the juniors and seniors in their classes. They haven't yet delved into the meat of the substantive specialized courses, and in many schools they are still relegated to large lecture classes. If they haven't picked a major and affiliated with a particular department, they have no academic home. Those who have collected enough advanced placement credits to move into upper-level courses may have difficulty competing with the juniors and seniors who already know the academic ropes and can handle what one dean refers to as the "rapier cut and thrust of the classroom discussion and the put-downs that accompany it." These gifted students find their upper-level courses stimulating, but may feel inadequate and question their abilities, perhaps for the first time.

The freedoms that sophomores celebrated the previous year haunt them now. The choices may still seem overwhelming—choices of courses, friends, and activities; choices of politics, religion, and lifestyle; choices of stopping out, transferring, or spending a year abroad. But they think more about the consequences of their choices than they used to. Making one choice means relinquishing others; choosing means taking responsibility for the choice. All the while, time is running out. In most colleges and universities, by the end of sophomore year, students are expected to have chosen a major, and the pressure of career choice is not far behind.

THE SLUMP—MORE OR LESS

> I felt like a character in the Roadrunner cartoon—you know, running frantically full speed ahead, straight off of a cliff—and that awful moment when he looks down and realizes there's no ground under him—that he's just out there by himself in the middle of the air. That's how I felt most of sophomore year.

Forging ahead with enthusiasm and eagerness, students may discard—though often temporarily—the values their parents hold dear. Now, as they are pressured to make decisions about their own futures, many become aware of the void that is left. Though some youngsters attend religious or culturally homogeneous institutions that confirm family values, the majority of today's college students are surrounded by diverse points of view from their classmates and professors. They are exposed to many so-called right answers, all backed up by rational arguments. How can all these answers be true?

Many sophomores not only question their parents' values and choices, but the very possibility of making rational choices at all. As they move beyond a dualistic view of the world, one idea seems as worthwhile as the next. They feel off balance and disoriented; nothing seems solid. Seeking answers, they find only questions. Why am I taking this course? How can behaviorists and Freudians both be valid? I always thought physics was great, but why is physics better than philosophy? Why am I at this school? What difference will it make if I stay or transfer? What is the purpose of education? What is the meaning of my life?"

They describe their experience as "tenuous," "arbitrary," "meaningless." They describe themselves as "fragmented," "seasick," "rootless." Frequently students look inside themselves and feel lost and immobilized. Their reactions range from hedonistic escape to existential angst.

A Brandeis student recalls:

> Sophomore year everyone collapsed—or at least my friends and I did. It was a year of questioning. What's the point of doing anything in life? What does it all mean? What is this all about? "Being and Nothingness" was the name of the game.

Parents may be taken aback by unexpected phone calls from a normally upbeat child who is suddenly questioning the meaning of life. The mother of one sophomore recalls:

> Madeline called at midnight, talking about God and death. She's taking a course about aging and death, and she was distraught. After forty-five minutes of listening, I finally told her I just had to get some sleep. I suggested that she talk to someone there—a chaplain or counselor—and I'd call her the next day after I got home from work.

When asked about his sophomore year, a University of Chicago student responds:

> All through my sophomore year I was unhappy. I was losing sight of what it all meant. It was kind of a masturbatory philosophical question, because there really wasn't any answer to it. It was just, where am I headed—what does this mean? I got so wrapped up in trying to solve that one that I neglected the present. I was real unsure of myself. There weren't a whole lot of black-and-white standards to deal with. Nothing was concrete.
>
> It seemed like I was spinning my wheels with schoolwork. Nothing seemed to make much difference. I would turn in the token paper for the token class, making the points that they grade on. It wasn't doing me any good. It just seemed really trivial at the time, like a big spoon of cough medicine that everyone has to take at some time.

Some students, such as this young man, become paralyzed by their own introspection. Caught like a gerbil continually spinning the wheel in his cage, they may try to alleviate their anxiety with numbing devices: drugs, alcohol, computer games, or a series of meaningless sexual hookups Some look outside themselves and impulsively grab hold of a group or ideology for support—a fraternity, a women's center, a political group, or, for a few, the rigid structure of a cult. Others, aware of a general malaise but unable to pinpoint the source, decide to transfer or take time off, hoping to find solutions elsewhere. Even though many sophomores are caught off guard by periods of confusion and disenchantment, most continue to be actively engaged in their studies and social environment.

A young woman from Ohio, now a vibrant and self-confident junior, looks back on her sophomore year:

> I had done really well second semester freshman year, and I came back to school thinking I know how the system works now. But it was a real struggle. I thought, Now I'm just going to sail through with A's and B's the whole way. But I took classes I had no background in—computer science, accounting, Spanish. They were all tedious and time-consuming, and I felt very inadequate. Spanish was the first class I ever took where I studied and didn't see results.
>
> I had already decided to major in English, but I had a bad experience in the first E. Lit course I actually took. My professor's comments on my first paper basically said, "Learn to write or get out." I felt outclassed because there were a lot of seniors in the class. I felt there was a gaping hole between what I needed to know and what I knew. I went to talk to my professor, and he wasn't very reassuring about it.
>
> On top of this, I had been invited to participate in a Women's Leadership Training Institute. We met monthly and it brought up a lot of issues I was ready to deal with. Thank God for WLTI! But it also brought up problems in a relationship I was in. I became angry at my boyfriend as I became more aware of things. I started thinking, I'm a woman first, what does that mean?
>
> I started looking at what I wanted to do with my life. And how does my English major fit in? I think I spent the year saying, Is this what I'm cut out for? Does this tap into some wonderful resource I have in me, or am I just going to struggle along like this the whole way? I remember feeling tired a lot.

In the midst of all this questioning, students wonder whether the financial commitment they and their parents are making is worth it. Financial sacrifices and the specter of loans to be repaid weigh heavily on students who feel unmotivated and unproductive:

> My sophomore year was a very tenuous time for me. I was very frightened. I was afraid I was drifting apart from my friends at home. I wasn't quite sure where I was going, what direction. I had no solid ground to pin myself to intellectually. I was aware of time flying by. Tuition was going up each year. What did I have to show for it?

Some sophomores who don't feel the unsettling ennui of the slump describe an almost manic sense of excitement that can be unsettling in its own right. Each new course they take uncovers another academic possibility, another world waiting to be discovered. They ask themselves, Is this the department I want to settle in? Is this the subject I want to master? Or, stimulated by the interests of their classmates, they take up one hobby after another—playing the guitar five hours a day, then turning with equal intensity to ultimate Frisbee or lyric poetry.

A sophomore at Dartmouth describes her second year there as "fantastic," but adds:

> Sometimes my head is reeling from all the choices. When I look at the catalogue before registration I get excited—and confused. There's so much I want to study. My parents probably think I'm nuts each time I call home with a different idea about what I want to major in. Right now I'm into philosophy—eighteenth century. And I love Italian. Maybe I'll combine that with art history and spend time in Italy next year.

While all this is happening at school, students continue to loosen the ties to home. Loyalties shift from family and high school friends to college friends, suitemates, and lovers. Though new connections are beginning to replace the old, sophomores often talk about feeling lonely and adrift. They describe their feeling as a sense of aloneness in the world rather than a dearth of friends.

Disturbed by a feeling of rootlessness, students reach out to one another. Friendships that were formed freshman year may begin to deepen and thrive. Some unravel, however, as students continue to develop new interests and venture forth from the pack:

> I moved into a suite sophomore year. We were all good friends, and we thought, This is going to be so much fun living together. And the first two weeks were fun, but then each person got singled out—"Be mean to Sue week." It was a mess. We had a huge fight at the end.
>
> We'd been so similar freshman year. We were all freshmen in the same boat, all gained 10 pounds, all were homesick. We came back and we started to choose majors and meet more people and expand our circle of friends, and we didn't like each other's friends or the habit of smoking that one picked up—a lot of petty things—but we were establishing our own identities. Sophomore year I started solidifying the me that people know and the me that I know.

Longing for intimacy and continuity as well as new adventures, many students talk about their dashed expectations. During his sophomore year, a young man from New York City had started to hang out with a group of seniors who loved jazz as much as he did. They went out on weekends together to local clubs. At the end of the year, as his friends were about to graduate, he became increasingly distraught about the impending loss of companionship:

> I'm really down. It's depressing. It takes so much energy to start all over again. I'm not the kind of person who needs to have every other person say hello to me when I walk across campus. I just want to have one or two really close friends.

Questions of identity and intimacy are intertwined, as young men and women refine their definitions of themselves through their relationships with each other. They treasure the intimacy of being a couple, yet strive to protect themselves from getting lost in the twosome. Particularly when they live in the same dorm, sometimes even on the same floor, students struggle to be identified as individuals rather than one half of a whole. The constant, "Where's Becky?" that he hears as he walks down the hall, the guilt that she feels as she moves quickly past his door without stopping in—these incessant reminders echo in the thoughts of committed couples, and as a result, they may start to pull away from each other.

In all arenas of their lives, there is a pressure on sophomores to define themselves and begin to take a stand. A professor of Individual and Family Studies at the University of Delaware believes that the issue of control is at the crux of a lot of problems students face during sophomore year:

> Many feel little sense of control over their own destinies. They feel trapped by the choices they made freshman year—choices about friends, fraternities or sororities, roommates, and courses. They have to declare a major, but feel constrained by family and social agendas. They are pulled in different direc-

> tions, asked to make choices and live with the consequences.

Those not ready to make commitments are most vulnerable to the sophomore slump. For some this is an important though painful time. A sophomore turns to an online college message board for advice and support from his peers:

> This semester, I'm realizing that I really am not so enthusiastic about my major (classics); I'm not that good at it, and frankly I don't really care about getting better. I'm in advanced level classes, as I was last year, so nothing really changed in the level of difficulty. I used to want to go to grad school, but right now the thought of it makes me want to drop out, not because I don't want to work hard, but because the thought of spending the rest of my life obsessing over things like the different uses of the subjunctive just sounds awful.
>
> The problem is that I don't really have any idea what else I might want to do. Law school is a possibility, but I haven't really thought seriously about it at all. I almost feel like I should take a leave of absence, except that I don't have anything to do during that time off. But I don't think I'm making good use of my tuition money, particularly since I'm spending far more time working at my food service job than I am doing homework or going to class and I enjoy it more.
>
> Does anyone have any advice on how to break out of this slump?

At this vital and energetic stage of life, standing still and feeling stuck can be almost unbearable. Kenneth Keniston, noted author and social psychologist, wrote of the "enormous value placed upon change, transformation and movement" of young men and women, and their panic, "when confronted with the feeling of 'getting nowhere,' of 'being stuck in a rut,' or of 'not moving.'"[1]

In the past, young people projected their desire for motion outward toward social and political causes—the women's movement, the peace movement, the civil rights movement. The restlessness of youth was captured in books and film, from *On the Road* to *Easy Rider*, and in the alteration of self through transcendental meditation or psychedelic drugs. There is a reawakening on today's campuses of a commitment to social justice, an involvement in grassroots politics and an active approach to protecting the environment. Some of today's generation of students, however, channel their need for movement primarily into collecting academic and co-curricular credentials that will get them onto the fast track of career, status and power—a world of adulthood that some sophomores fear as the ultimate trap. And so they procrastinate, stagnate, and spin their wheels until they find it intolerable and begin to make decisions.

THE MAJOR DECISION

> I declared my English major in September and then spent the rest of my sophomore year investigating it.

> I changed from architecture to urban studies and sociology. I'd wanted to be an architect since sixth grade. It was hard to change. It was hard to lose the identity I'd built up over all those years. I didn't tell my parents about it until first semester junior year.

> I came to school with no set idea of what I wanted to major in. I had many interests and would call home

> every semester with a different thing. Last year, I even told my parents I was going to be a coal miner after I took a geology class where we explored caves and got to wear those funny hats with lights on them. And I took a philosophy class and I was going to be a philosopher, and then I was going to be a lawyer. It's a running joke with my parents— thinking, What's she going to be now? And I think that's very common.
>
> Working as an engineer seems great, but I'm not wild about engineering school so far. I love metalsmithing in the fine arts school more than anything else I've ever done here. But switching doesn't seem practical.

The pressure to choose a major starts as early as the sophomore and junior years in high school when students fill out the forms for the Preliminary Scholastic Aptitude Tests. At 15 and 16 years of age, students are asked to indicate their academic and career interests, and the computer code for undecided always seems to be double zero. Most college admissions offices request similar information from applicants, conveying the message that before students even come to college they are supposed to know what they want to study and what career they wish to pursue.

Parents can be heard apologizing to admissions officers on behalf of a child who "hasn't decided what he wants to do yet," as though being open to all kinds of possibilities is some sort of deficiency. In response to this parental anxiety, one admissions officer always asks the parent how old the child is, knowing full well that a prospective college student is likely to be 17 or 18. He then says incredulously, "Well, that seems perfectly normal to me. Most people don't know what they want to do with the rest of their lives when they are 17. Did you?" He advises students to think of themselves as *exploring* rather than *undecided.*

There are, of course, those rare young people, driven by their talents and passions, who know they are destined to become musicians or biomedical engineers or entrepreneurs. When one such student was asked by a professor if she still wanted to be a dancer, she looked at him with eyes flashing and said, "It's not a matter of what I want. It's a matter of what I am!"

Such commitment and certainty is exceptional among the young. Despite the careerist era in which we live, most entering college students are not sure what they want to study, and even those who claim they know are likely to change their minds.

But on most college campuses, the mythology prevails among sophomores that, "everybody else seems to know what they want to major in and what they want to do for the rest of their lives." Rumors run rampant about which departments are good and what the future holds in store for its graduates. Each campus has particular departments that are held in high esteem by students and others that command little respect. Some schools are stridently preprofessional; others are more supportive of the liberal arts. Everywhere, stereotypes abound. Choosing a major not only means choosing a course of study, it means selecting a niche on campus—assuming an identity as "an intellectual philosopher," "a pragmatic preprofessional," or "a far-out artist." When students meet each other, one of the first questions they ask is, "What's your major?" And the response elicits a set of assumptions, an initial code for sizing each other up.

> I found myself not wanting to be a doctor, not wanting to be a lawyer, not wanting to be an engineer and not wanting to be a teacher, which meant that there was absolutely no job for me. My parents sent me to school saying, Try things; try everything, don't limit

> yourself to one specific thing—I wasn't pre-med or pre-law—I was simply pre-Ken.

Business and engineering students complain about being stereotyped by their peers in the humanities and social sciences who make assumptions about their motivation: "I get tired of everyone making comments about me going for the big bucks," said a sophomore in engineering. "I'm in engineering because that's what I'm good at and that's what I like."

In making a decision about a major, students weigh their own interests with concerns about status and image and future opportunities. What will the job market be like when I graduate? Will I be able to pay off my student loans? What kind of reaction will I get when I tell people I'm majoring in Early Childhood Education? They may feel pulled in different directions by parents and peers and faculty, all trying to help—all sure that they know what's best for the student.

Those students who enter the university with a specific career goal in mind pick the major that fits their career choice. That seems simple enough. But often the career goal of an 18-year-old is based more on image than a realistic understanding of the demands of the course of study and the career itself. When a physical therapy student who wants to help people, but doesn't like science, looks ahead to the long sequence of required science courses; or an engineering student realizes that an aptitude for mathematics isn't necessarily synonymous with an interest in engineering, a change is in the offing. That change can be upsetting, particularly when the student is uncertain about what to study instead. And parents are often upset when their child makes an alternative choice based more on passion for the subject than pragmatic career preparation. Students and parents worry about time lost, about getting "off the track" when time is precious and tuition costs are high.

Some parents feel just the opposite. Although they want their children to have employment when they graduate, they are worried that they will miss the point of an undergraduate education by being too focused too soon. This father of a Cornell sophomore voices his concern:

> In my generation, my fellow students talked about big issues and took courses to explore ideas so when Connor wanted to transfer out of liberal arts and into the hotel school so he'd have a ready career in four years, I didn't know what to say that would convince him of the value of time spent thinking. That, to me, is what college should be about—never again in your life do you really get to do that.

Premeds who change their minds—and many of them do—often have a particularly difficult time giving up their identity as premeds. Long after they've decided that they're not interested in the studies or the career, or realized that they simply don't stand a chance of gaining admission to medical school, many students struggle with finding new academic and career goals.

Some of these students, referred to by one administrator as "prenatal premeds," had never actually made a choice to be premed in the first place. They may have been successful in high school science, and swept along by the enthusiasm of their teachers and parents, they began to think of themselves as premed. Or they may have come from a family of physicians and merely assumed that they would follow in the family tradition. When these students decide to change, they are taking a big step in separating from their parents and asserting their independence.

Unfortunately, some parents make it difficult for them to do so. Perhaps finding it painful to give up the dream of "my child, the doctor," and failing to separate their own goals from those of their son or daughter, they refuse to accept the impending change of plans. Some parents respond with accusations or sighs of disappointment; others go as far as threatening not to pay tuition for any course of study except one leading to medical school.

A former premed describes her change of heart and her father's subsequent disappointment:

> I was a gung ho premed, but I started changing my mind first semester. Competition here was really fierce. I think that little spark in me started to dull and when I'd go to these classes with two or three hundred people, half had already had AP chemistry, and I was struggling for the first time.
>
> I had a couple of so-called friends tell me the wrong way to do problems before first semester finals. They thought it was funny and said, "Oh well, we're cutthroat premeds." I started realizing that part of my excitement about premed was connected to my father's thrill that I had decided to go preprofessional. I started realizing I wasn't totally doing this for myself. I started looking around and began to realize I'd enjoy and do better in psychology and sociology. And that's what I've double-majored in, much to my father's chagrin. He still keeps telling me I'd make a good psychiatrist.

Many parents, wanting to assure their son or daughter a secure and satisfying life, exert a tremendous pressure on students to follow a clear-cut professional route. Even parents who simply give offhand suggestions have more influence than they realize. Students often experience their comments as demands. Aside from explicit expectations, there are often implicit family norms. If the parents are successful in a particular field, they set expectations by their example. So do older siblings, whether they realize it or not.

It is not surprising that discussions about majors lead to the question "What are you going to do with that?" And when the proposed major is a subject like comparative literature or history, the question is often asked with an air of obvious skepticism. Indeed, many students who become enamored of a liberal arts discipline ask the question of themselves.

They are, in a sense, asking themselves the wrong question. Parents might encourage students to ask themselves instead, "What kind of an impact will these studies have on me? Who might I become, how might I view the world, and what skills might I develop if I begin to master this particular discipline?"

Students tend to attach an enormous importance to choice of a major. They are reluctant to believe it when their deans or advisors tell them that there is no right major and that in most cases their major will not determine their career. As a dean at George Washington University comments:

> An important part of intellectual development is beginning to have some sense of mastery over a body of material, to be able to get your arms around a discipline.
>
> In any discipline you will learn to make reasoned judgments, to develop fundamental intellectual skills—to analyze, synthesize, and express yourself. What we are giving students is power, the tools to teach themselves a new subject during the rest of their lives, the ability to approach a new mass of material and say, "OK, how do I start?" That's the real-world skill that a major is all about.

Some students are comfortable with exploring. They may take a long time to decide on a major and enjoy the academic journey. Others are so anxious about making their choice that they are reluctant to experiment. Professor Marion Hyson of George Mason University says:

> Many students find it hard to justify to themselves or their parents the value of taking anthropology or musicology. I wish they could see that the period of time they're settling on a major is not just spinning wheels. They're developing skills of pursuing certain kinds of inquiry and self-expression. As sophomores, some start to make connections in their minds between fields of studies and disciplines. That can be very exciting in itself.

For some students, however, lack of a focus is so uncomfortable that they may find it hard to concentrate on their studies. They complain about being unmotivated and may consider leaving school. They desperately want to make a decision, to have a goal. One dean suggests that these students invest in temporary choices. She urges them to "try out" their interests and tells them:

> If you think you're interested in psychology, try it out. Get into it. Really get into it. Take several psych courses. Work in a child development center. If you don't like it, come back and we'll talk about it. Negative choices are terribly important. Being able to shut doors is just wonderful. Sometimes when we close doors, we open others. Sometimes when we narrow the perspective somewhat, we can move on.

With all this talk about majors, it is important to remember that a major usually constitutes about a third of the courses a student will take in college. For most students, especially in liberal arts, there is plenty of opportunity to plan a curriculum that complements and supplements the courses in the major department. More students today are choosing double majors, or a combination major and minor. They are combining business and English literature, Chinese and environmental studies, sociology and computer science. They are straddling the humanities and technology; they are pursuing their intellectual passions and practical skills. Most colleges and universities, mindful of the liberal arts/preprofessional dichotomy, promote numerous opportunities to combine the two.

Professor James Madison is the director of Indiana University's LAMP (Liberal Arts and Management Program), which provides students with an opportunity to integrate liberal arts and business within a small close-knit community. He is a strong advocate of this innovative approach to twenty-first century education:

> We accept into LAMP high achieving motivated sophomores who want to major in the liberal arts—anything from biochemistry to theatre and drama—yet realize that management and business skills are useful—and may be for some careers—essential. We start with a foundation of a liberal arts education; we combine it with a half a dozen classes of business skills and a highlight of the program are the LAMP seminars. Students take a seminar each year which builds skills in writing, quantitative analysis, and working together as a team.

Internships and cooperative education programs offer students hands-on experience while still in school. And career-related part-time and summer jobs have become an increasingly important supplement to academic studies.

A junior math major at Duke who was actively involved in the performing arts had no idea what to do after graduation until she found a summer job in the education department of a major symphony orchestra, and loved it. Arts administration seemed to combine her organizational skills and facility with numbers with her interest in the arts. Upon her return to school in her senior year, she was able to gain administrative experience by doing an internship with a local dance festival and producing the campus fall musical rather than acting in it. By using her imagination and initiative, along with the resources of the university and community, this young woman was free to immerse herself in the intellectual challenge of higher mathematics while developing marketable skills for a career in arts administration.

This kind of inventiveness is common among today's students. A student with a double major in Spanish and international relations interned one summer at the International Trade Administration in Washington and was invited to do research for them the following academic year. An economics major who took a year off to work at the Chicago Stock Exchange returned to finish his academic work while interning in the production department of a public television station.

The anxieties that students feel about entering the job market can't be dismissed. For those whose academic interests lean toward the humanities and social sciences, internships, jobs, and student activities provide a means of developing career-related experience. These opportunities free students to pursue majors that truly interest them and to make an academic commitment.

MORE DECISIONS

It was February—cold and bleak outside. I was cooking a pot roast when the phone rang.

It was Betsy calling from Skidmore.

"Are you OK?" I had just talked to her two days before.

"Yes, fine. But I forgot to talk to you about a few things." She sounded exuberant. I relaxed.

"I've decided about next year, but I don't think you'll like it."

So much for relaxing.

"Instead of spending my junior year in England,"—she plans on majoring in English—"I want to go to Italy and study art. I talked to someone in the Syracuse program and she loves it, and you get the language training and live with an Italian family."

I was both jealous and concerned.

"It's your choice, of course, but you've always had so much trouble with languages, and what about your requirements for your English major?" I hated my words which were bursting her bubble.

"I'll take care of that. Don't worry. And another thing—spring vacation? I could come home or stay here and ski or Les invited me to New York to stay with him." Was this the time to mention that she still hadn't gotten a job to pay for her living expenses? Better leave it alone.

"I think I want to work on a ranch this summer."

"What about the camp job you interviewed for?"

"It's not enough money, and I really want to work on a ranch."

"Did you have any particular ranch in mind?" My mind was beginning to swirl and the pot roast was burning.

"Well no, but I'm talking to people."

"You'd better check that out soon because if you wait you'll end up like last summer."

"What was wrong with last summer?"

"You didn't make much money and you were bored with your job."

"I was not!" The exuberance was definitely gone.

When I hung up the phone I was wondering where I went wrong.

When I repeated the conversation to her father, he said, "Terrific. That's Betsy! England was safe. Italy's an adventure—the same with this summer."

He responded to her spirit. *I* kept placing barriers in her way.

And by the way, she did go to Italy, she never mentioned the ranch again, and she came home for spring vacation.

This is one mother's account of a typical conversation with her sophomore daughter. Overwhelmed and disconcerted by her daughter's barrage of options, she was reeling by the time she hung up the phone. Although she thinks of herself as a supportive and encouraging mother, her instinctive reaction had been to pull back in face of the onslaught and to point out all the potential pitfalls of her daughter's list of possibilities. Not a particularly helpful response, but one that many parents succumb to at some time during their child's college career.

Sophomores often call home with an ever-changing set of ideas and plans that may seem like the "whim of the week" to their bewildered parents. Just as parents have gotten used to the idea that their son is going to spend second semester in Washington on a political science internship, he calls home and says he has scratched that idea and is now planning to stay at school and switch his major to Spanish. Last week's request for permission to take a semester off turns into this week's decision to transfer to a larger school instead.

Summer vacations are also filled with possibilities. Today's career-anxious students want to fill their resumes with meaningful summer experiences, and many eschew yesterday's popular summer jobs of the camp counselor and lifeguard genre for positions in financial institutions, research labs, non-profit or government agencies or corporations. Most aim to make as much as possible while simultaneously propelling their career development. Some combine an unpaid internship by day with waiting tables at night.

The plethora of choices that face today's college students is often overwhelming to their parents as well as themselves: from internships in Africa to a semester at sea; double majors and joint degrees; stopping out and dropping out; a year abroad or an exchange at another university; graduating in three years or a fifth year of undergraduate study; staying put and making do or transferring to a different school.

Many parents assume that their child will go off to college for four years, pick a major and stick with it, come home and work in the summer, and graduate at the end of the fourth year, moving directly to graduate school or a professional job. However, most of today's students are approaching their education with a creativity that reflects their own needs and the demands of the rapidly changing society in which they live.

Stopping Out

"Stopping out" is not a euphemism for dropping out or running away, but a viable alternative for many students who want to spend a semester or year away from school. A student may take time off, or stop out, for any number of reasons—to find an academic focus or sense of purpose, to earn money, to contribute something to others, to get experience that will be valuable later on. Although the most common time for stopping out is during the junior year, students may decide to take time off at any time in their college career.

Many colleges and universities have begun to acknowledge

these periods of time out in an institutional way. A Williams College handbook for parents states:

> Such time away, especially when viewed as a time for self-evaluation and reassessment, can be more beneficial for a student than a half-hearted commitment to academics. The college urges students to spend their time off positively and constructively.

Parents may view the decision to take time off as a failure, a deviation from the norm. And those parents who feel constrained by the financial and emotional obligations of their middle years may find it difficult to listen with patience to the many enticing choices their child is contemplating. When parents haven't taken a vacation in years because of college expenses or obligations to an aging parent, their son or daughter's dilemma about whether to spend a year in Germany or to travel with a children's theatre troupe may seem like a frivolous indulgence.

In spite of her father's skepticism, a sophomore at Brown exudes a dazzling sense of possibility as she describes a string of alternative routes for the coming year:

> I wanted to go abroad with the American Field Service for a year after high school. My parents didn't want me to. I'm definitely going to do something different after my sophomore year. I go crazy when I feel like I'm just a student and not "living." It's so frustrating. I'd like to take a semester at home at Case Western. I know Cleveland and I can integrate being a student with my volunteer work in the community. Or maybe I can go to Bryn Mawr. I almost went there and I'd like to see what it would be like. I'd like to drive or bike across the country. I'd like to go to

> Central or South America. I'd like to have a significant job.

This young woman, excited and unfocused, needs a calm and patient listener who might help her begin to channel her energy. She may not yet realize that there is no best answer, but in finding the better answer she will learn to make commitments and to live with the regrets of roads not taken. She will certainly be more motivated to follow her own path than the one chosen by her parents.

Many students feel the personal pressure to succeed, to produce, to be responsible, to pay off loans, but are not quite ready to face such grown-up commitments. Some, like the woman above, see their education through a wider lens and want to grasp opportunities that are now available to them. Many have a hard time articulating why they want to leave and may turn parents off before any discussion begins. "At more than a thousand-dollar increase in tuition each year, he can go 'find himself' after he finishes!" one father exclaimed.

Parents who give an unqualified no to a request for time off, without an opportunity to explore alternatives, may stymie their child's growth inadvertently rather than encourage it. A job or internship is just what some students need to find the sense of direction that eludes them on campus. For others, merely having unpressured time for reflection is enough for them to become refreshed and clearer about their personal and professional goals. There is, of course, a fine line between bumming around doing nothing and pausing for some time to gain self-understanding. Financial pressures are of concern to most families, and a student who is serious about taking time off should be prepared to grapple with the dollars-and-cents aspects of this decision. By assuming financial responsibility, even through a mindless job, students enjoy an increased sense of independence, while stepping back from the academic world to get a new perspective.

A University of Michigan student describes what happened when he took a break from school and moved back home:

> Living at home this semester really hasn't been the big exclamation point in the book of life by any means. Living with my parents again is a weird thing. From their point of view I came home because I had something I wanted them to help me out with. I think they thought I'd be sitting down and talking to them for hours at a time. They were apprehensive; they worried about me. But I just wanted to get a job and hang out by myself for a while. I needed to clean out my system and get reoriented—to stop and think. A degree is something to work for; it's not an end in itself, but it does figure significantly. Like you have to do the work in order to get it. I'd been kind of missing that crucial point.
>
> When I was at school, I really didn't spend much time by myself except when I was sleeping. At home, when I'm not with my family, I'm on my own. It just gives me a lot of latitude for thinking and ironing out things—coming up with new ideas and perspectives. It's a good feeling to wash all this excess off the top of your skull. I'm enjoying it. I like figuring out things about myself. I think stopping out was probably the best thing I could have done.

Setting aside time for thoughtful face-to-face conversations about taking time off can clarify the issues at hand for both parent and child. And without such discussions, parents may find that their attempts to direct their son or child on the traditional four-year path backfire. Sometimes open, flexible discussions about taking time off lead to a change of heart on the part of the student. The mother of a University of Wisconsin sophomore relates:

> My son was rooming with someone first semester this year who didn't like school. He clearly had an influence on Peter who called home right after he returned to Madison in January and said, "I think I'm going to leave school for a while."
>
> I told him I didn't think it made sense or was practical to leave school in the middle of the sophomore year. I put my foot down, knowing that he was probably looking for some kind of limits at that point. If my daughter had called and said the same thing, I might have reacted differently. I threw out some options and said, "You might want to take off next year and work, or try photography which you love, or transfer to another school." I tried to give him reasons for my opinions and some options to consider. I tried to combine the guidelines with leeway, so he could eventually make the best decision for himself.
>
> I also knew that like so many sophomores he was concerned about picking a major. It had gotten to be a joke over winter break. Everyone who saw him asked the same question, "What are you going to major in?" He got really fed up with the repetition of that question, and eventually started to answer very fliply—to smart off by saying, "Sanskrit," or some such thing. The truth was he really didn't know.
>
> I suggested he go to the counseling center to talk about choosing a major. He started to get a handle on his interest, and before long it became quite clear to him that he wanted to major in journalism. The

> counselor he talked to suggested that he start to work on the newspaper, which he did. After that we never heard any more about his desire to leave school. We weren't against his taking time off; we just didn't want him to do it for the wrong reasons.

The mother of a Lafayette student who stopped out cautions:

> The original reasons they give may not be the real ones. Our son told us what he thought we'd want to hear. "I'm wasting your money; I don't have a sense of purpose."
>
> True, he hadn't been very happy there; he had no idea what he wanted to do, and he had to declare a major by the end of sophomore year. But he also wanted to earn enough money to buy some expensive musical equipment. And underneath that goal was his need to establish his independence.
>
> He lived at home, because it wasn't financially feasible for him not to, but he paid much of his way, gas for the car, the phone bill, that sort of thing. He worked two jobs and found them boring. And he missed Lafayette and visited there several different weekends. He began to appreciate college more. And he realized that his college degree is a union card. That's the hard and fast reality, and he doesn't want to go through life without one.

Of course, many parents fear that once their youngster leaves school, he or she may never return to graduate. Although this is always a possibility, most students who do return after a leave of absence perform at higher levels than they did before they left. The change of pace triggers renewed enthusiasm, and sense of purpose, and commitment to their formal education when they return.

The dean of a highly competitive liberal arts college comments:

> I think I have never known a case where the student took time off and returned to the same institution and didn't do better. I think they find out it's no fun to work in an unskilled job. They return more mature, with a better sense of who they are and about the world of work.

In retrospect, many parents who had originally opposed the idea, look back at their children's time off positively. A Brandeis senior recalls with a wry grin:

> I took a year off—worked on construction for six months and then went to Europe with the money I'd earned. My father was desperate about it. He was so afraid I would never finish. Now he thinks it was wonderful. He tells all his friends about this adventuresome thing I did.

Some students don't finish. A college education is not for everyone, and some youngsters make the decision to turn their sights to other pursuits—part-time study, vocational or technical training, apprenticeships or opportunities to develop artistic talents, to name a few. Others who feel locked into the university or a particular field of study in an attempt to meet parental expectations may go through the motions of getting an education but, lacking the interest or talent, ultimately fail or leave. For them college has not been a rich, expansive field of possibility but a confining prison that has rendered them unmotivated and thwarted. Most students who leave school don't make the decision lightly. They still want and need their parents' emotional support at the same time that they long for acknowledgment of their separateness. This is a challenge for parents who must let go of their own dreams for their child and accept instead the alternative route he or she has chosen.

Moving Off-Campus

Though living in the residence halls is back in vogue, a lot of upperclassmen contemplate moving to an apartment off-campus. At many universities apartment living has become as much a part of campus life as pizza and beer.

Some students make the move because they have to; there simply isn't enough room for them in the dorms. Others, discovering that sharing an apartment and cooking one's own meals can be cheaper than the room and board plan on campus, make the move to save money. Some, tired of the lack of privacy in the residence halls, seek space, quiet and a haven from the constant social scene. Still others crave the independence that apartment living symbolizes and see the move as another step toward the adult world.

Parents who spent four years at a residential college where everyone lived on-campus may be surprised when their son or daughter calls with the news that a move to an apartment is in the offing. The next surprise may come with the mention of an apartment mate of the opposite sex, since coed living is common off-campus as well as on. Though some parents may have difficulty believing it, most of these arrangements are based on friendship, practicality, and serendipity. Women often feel safer and worry less about security when there are men in the apartment. For many, sharing apartment space with the opposite sex simply seems a natural extension of coed dormitory living.

Sometimes the decision to move into an apartment is based on a student's commitment to a small group of friends. These groups usually come together with high expectations of community and intimacy, hoping to create their own home away from home. Other students who barely know each other join together in haphazard ways, united only by their common desire to share space. They expect little more of each other than basic civility.

Once they make the decision to move off campus, there are a lot of questions students should ask before signing a lease. Most schools have an off-campus housing office that helps students navigate this transition and make informed choices. For instance, Macalester's off-campus webpage is filled with questions to ask and tips to think about, ranging from issues of security to terms of the lease and tenant rights and responsibilities. The University of Vermont also offers a workshop addressing these topics and giving students the opportunity to discuss them with knowledgeable professionals.

All students who make the switch from residence hall to apartment life face the daily challenges of independent living. Paying rent on time, keeping the common living spaces clean, and buying food for a relatively balanced diet require time, thought, and action. At a time when much of their world seems tenuous and unsettled, taking care of themselves in the most basic, pedestrian ways can help students assume more control of their lives.

Many students muddle through and feel increasingly self-reliant. No lecture on nutrition from a parent is as likely to change a student's eating habits as opening the refrigerator once again to find it stocked only with diet soda, beer, and left-over spaghetti. And after seeing their funds erode at the campus dining halls, students begin to plan ahead and pack lunches for themselves. Arguments with roommates must be worked out without the help of an RA, and students learn to negotiate and share household responsibilities. Seniors often remark that the experience of living in an apartment reduces their pregraduation jitters, that it makes the transition into the real world look a bit less traumatic.

But apartment living requires adjustments that may add to an already overloaded schedule. The freedom of living on one's own is accompanied by the burden of responsibility. And if a student is weighed down with schoolwork, co-curricular pursuits, or a part-time job, the additional responsibility of taking care of an apartment may prove to be too much. Some students enjoy the space of off-campus housing, but feel isolated and cut off from college life. They miss the easy availability of friends and the ever-present stimulation that dormitory life provides. The decision about whether to move off-campus has to be weighed in the context of everything else going on in the student's life at the same time.

A vivacious young woman, now in her junior year, remarks:

> I moved into an apartment sophomore year. I had opted for an apartment because I wanted my own room. I'd never had a room of my own. I'm a vegetarian, and I thought meals would be easier for me if I could cook myself, and I wanted the adventure of an apartment.
>
> But I felt really isolated. I met no one. By the end of the year, I was working at a snail's pace in my architecture classes. I had gotten more involved in outside activities, and I was in a stressful, serious relationship. So this year I decided to become an RA and move back into the dorms. The money I save by being an RA takes some of the financial pressure off as well.

Transferring and Other Alternatives

Almost all students contemplate transferring at some point during their first two years of college—some fleetingly, others giving it serious thought. Disappointing classes, broken friendships or romances, the sheer exhaustion of a demanding schedule, all lead to periods of confusion and doubt. A change of scenery, a fresh start, is a tempting solution—a magical "right" answer to a complicated question. The grass and the ivy look greener somewhere else. The schools not chosen remain the perfect place pictured in the viewbooks.

One dean, familiar with these disgruntled reactions says:

> It becomes a question of, are you running away from something here—loneliness or confusion—or are you moving toward something that isn't available here? Much of what I ask them revolves around what kind of a person they are and what kind of a person they want to be. Being bored isn't an acceptable answer; it's up to them to change this.
>
> Some students stay simply out of a sense of obligation. They don't do anything to change the situation, and they're the ones I call the "what-ifs." What if I had done this instead? What if I had gone there? Others go through the questioning period and then really make a niche for themselves here. They get involved in the newspaper or a committee, go to lectures, seek out the community at large. They have a successful time.

Sometimes it is clear that transferring will answer a specific need. Discovering an interest in occupational therapy at a school without an OT department, feeling overwhelmed and lost at a large university and longing for the sense of community that a small campus affords, missing the stimulation of an urban center after time spent in a rural setting—these are clearly concerns that can be rectified by going to a different school. But when students speak of transferring to a school that is a rubber stamp of the one they are in, or are searching for a nonexistent perfect place, chances are they are seeking solutions that exist right under their noses. Given the opportunity to think this important decision through, it may become evident that starting over in a new place has its own set of challenges. Parents can help by asking open-ended questions, listening patiently, and allowing their child to discover his or her own solution.

A gay student from a small rural town had chosen his Ivy League school because it was adjacent to a large city. Set near a sophisticated urban setting, he thought there would be a large gay and lesbian population at the school. He was upset when he hadn't found the "out" community he had expected, and rashly responded by telling his parents that he thought he would transfer to Florida Atlantic University in South Beach, a school located in the center of a large gay community. His parents were stunned that he would so readily give up the school of his dreams, but it made them realize how isolated he felt. They listened patiently as he expressed his disappointment, and decided that having a car would give him some freedom to get into the city; he finally decided to stay. Within six months, he had found his niche at school and was glad that he hadn't acted on an impulse.

A New Jersey father talks with pride of his son's growth as he wrestled with the decision about whether to transfer:

> Gordon complained a lot about St. Lawrence. The kids weren't "like him"; he didn't like his classes. He was convinced that he had made the wrong decision and that there was a right school somewhere out there for him; he just had to find it. But his sophomore year he moved into a theme house; it was a political awareness house, and it gave him a niche. He had housemates with similar interests. He also

> really got into skiing. It was a turning point for him. The school still wasn't all that he had hoped for, but he began to see that he could make the difference.

Parents' reactions to a talk of transferring are often proportional to the amount of time they invested in the original college selection process. One mother recalls:

> She came home and said, "I hate this place." I'd been telling everyone how much she loved it. I guess when I think about it, she hadn't really said much.
>
> I was angry. I thought, Here we go again. I'd put all that energy into helping her get into what I thought was the right place, and now I was wrong. I felt one of the reasons she had ended up there was because of me.
>
> I told her, "OK. If you can find a school that will take you, and you make the arrangements, do it." And this time around she did everything herself.

The process of transferring offers another opportunity for a young person to make an independent, reasoned, and informed decision. The mother above insisted that her child take the initiative this time. When her daughter went to a school of her own choosing, she found that she was in for a big adjustment, but one that she was willing to tackle.

Some students decide not to transfer, but opt for a semester or a year in a different setting or different kind of institution. A young woman from Wellesley College was able to look at her all-women institution with new and appreciative eyes after a year at coed Williams. A Beloit student, feeling confined by her small, sheltered surroundings, chose to study at an urban university on the East Coast, and returned from her adventure to enjoy the familiarity and warmth of her friendly campus for the last year.

Students have opportunities of enormous variety, ranging from semesters of study with policy makers and lobbyists in Washington to programs in urban education in major cities or wilderness studies at field stations in remote locations. The most popular choice of alternative study still seems to be study abroad, usually in the junior year. It is an option that affords yet another confusing but tempting array of possibilities.

Study Abroad

> In Saint Louis, I got my education through books and lectures. In Fiji, I got my education through conversations and adventures. I learned about religion by listening to my host father entertain a group of bishops. I learned about conducting anthropological fieldwork by doing fieldwork with Indo-Fijian farmers. I learned by doing things I never thought I would or could do.

> Studying abroad in Madagascar was without a doubt the best learning experience for me during my four years in college. I am a chemistry/environmental studies double major and the program in Madagascar focused on ecology and conservation. I knew I wanted to go to a country where I could use my background in French. Certainly the classes did not compare to those of Grinnell in terms of rigor, but the experiential learning proved to be incredible.

Bolstered by a spirit of adventure and a recognition of the growing interdependent global economy, more and more students are taking advantage of the unique opportunities for international study. According to Open Doors, 2007, the annual report on international education published by the Institute of

International Education, 223,534 U.S. students studied abroad for academic credit, an astonishing increase of 150 percent over the past ten years. Only 5.5 percent spend the full year abroad, the norm a generation ago. The majority of today's students opt for shorter experiences—in the summer, during January terms, on internships or service learning expeditions—and increasingly they are selecting more non-traditional destinations—in the Far East, Middle East, Africa and Latin America.[2]

The experience of studying abroad provides the opportunity to enlarge young people's vision of the world, of the United States, and of themselves. It proves to be a pivotal life experience for some, a splendid adventure for others, but it is not for everyone. Before students decide where to go, they face the dilemma of whether to go.

In some cases, the decision is made for them. Many programs and universities require a minimum grade-point average; in certain disciplines, such as engineering and business, a prescribed study in sequence makes it difficult, if not impossible, to take a full semester during the academic year for a credited period of study abroad; language requirements eliminate many underprepared students; family obligations and financial restraints prevent others from going. Meanwhile, for some, especially language or international relations majors, study abroad is an integral part of the curriculum.

For many students, the decision to go abroad during the academic year presents a tug-of-war. They weigh the alternatives and ask themselves a lot of questions: Should I grab this once-in-a-lifetime opportunity? If I go, I can't transfer. Should I transfer instead? If I stay, I'll have a good shot at being editor of the paper senior year, or maybe president of the fraternity. Do I want to give that up? Studying abroad will look good on my resume, but will I fall behind in the job search? Can I afford it? Will my financial aid transfer? What's going to happen to Jane and me if we're so far apart? Do I have the guts to go?

Some students have the misguided notion that study abroad will magically solve academic or social problems, that the added stimulation of exotic new cultures will cure the state of confusion, stagnation, or ennui that they are currently experiencing. It is true that many students find study abroad programs stimulating and the catalyst for personal growth, but those who choose them to escape from unhappy circumstances are likely to bring their problems with them or simply postpone them for a time.

Students need not make this decision to study abroad in a vacuum. They talk to friends, faculty, and advisors, and upperclassmen who have spent a semester or year abroad are usually delighted to share the pleasures or disappointments of their own experience. For information about the programs themselves, they turn to a study abroad office or an overseas program advisor, who has been designated to provide this service. These offices and campus libraries are filled with practical information as well as the predictable alluring posters and beckoning brochures. The seemingly endless array of available programs can feel both stimulating and overwhelming—especially to the unfocused sophomore.

All programs are not created equal, and glossy brochures can be misleading. Faculty and study abroad counselors can point the way to tried-and-true programs that are approved by their university, and help students select courses of study and experiences best suited to them. The websites of most programs provide specific information. Many programs offer names of recent alumni—as well as their parents—who are available for phone or e-mail chats about their experience. A particularly good resource—filled with information and sound advice—is the CIEE (Council on International Education Exchange). Their website (www.ciee.org) includes an excellent section specifically for parents, providing information ranging from practical tips about "pre-departure do's," adjustment issues, health and emergency communication plans.

Students are often surprised to learn that in most cases their financial aid award follows them when they choose to study abroad. There are also special scholarships available offered by a variety of organizations. Before students and parents make a final decision about the financial feasibility of study abroad, the extra costs such as travel and a potentially unfavorable exchange rate need to be figured into the equation.

The decision to go abroad stirs up feelings reminiscent of the initial departure for college. Parents, as well as their children, get caught up in the anticipation and anxiety of the upcoming journey:

> I'm worried that she'll lose her passport or mess up her money or miss her train—the same things I always worried about with Nancy.

> He is so much more into getting ready for this than when he went to college—scattered, but much more organized. But he seems like such a naive little kid sometimes. My fear is that he will not pay attention to his surroundings and something dangerous will happen.

This mother describes the turmoil preceding her son's departure. Though she can laugh at it in retrospect, it wasn't so funny at the time:

> Before he left for Mongolia, our son was so unbearable that we cheered when he left. For the last couple of weeks he was home, he had reverted to an angry 11-year-old child. He was ornery, surly, uncooperative and uncommunicative; his misery permeated every corner of the house. We had no success in trying to get him to talk about what was bothering him. Indeed, we just didn't "get it."

This is a young man who had everything going for him—good grades, good looks, wonderful friends, significant mountaineering accomplishments, and a mature relationship with a girlfriend whom we adore. It simply hadn't occurred to us that he would get anxious or fall apart at this stage in his life.

The night before his departure, he finally broke down. He was standing in the middle of his room, amid piles of stuff—clothes, books, sleeping bag, camping gear, gifts for home-stay families, and a five-month supply of contact lens solution, which is unavailable in Mongolia. Not a single thing was packed. He was so overwhelmed. I suggested he start with the things he wouldn't be needing for the first week or two and put them in the bottom of the duffel. He shouted at me that he had no idea what he would or wouldn't need and that was the whole problem! He was utterly paralyzed. Surely, I suggested gingerly, he wouldn't need five bottles of contact lens solution in the first week; why not put four of them in the bottom of the duffel? He got it all done, left in the morning, and we cheered. We knew he would be fine as soon as he left home, and we haven't worried about him since. And we learned a thing or two about the anxiety that goes with a semester abroad.

These are the voices of parents as their children leave home again, but this time for distant and unknown places. Thrown into a heightened state of anxiety and excitement, families play out the themes of separation once more, the discordant tensions of disengagement and the unexpected pangs of loss.

Once the initial weeks of study abroad are under way, some parents are the recipients of more descriptive letters or e-mails than they ever received from campus. Students' messages and blogs are full of vivid impressions of places and sights and discoveries about themselves and the world. They are also a connection for students who are struggling with loneliness and the exhaustion that comes from trying to communicate all day in another language. Paradoxically, the distance of an ocean may provide a desire for connection—a connection readily available from many parts of the globe via cell phone or e-mail or Skype.

A Miami University junior wrote from Denmark, "Would you please send me any bits of advice for when I get lonely and depressed? Don't worry. I can handle it from this far away."

And a young woman who has recently returned from a semester in Kenya recounts :

> I told my parents so much by e-mail. I knew they'd save my e-mails, so it was a way for me to share stuff with them and have something tangible to reflect on when I got back. We didn't talk by phone much. I found that talking to them sort of kept me from being totally present in Kenya. I needed to stay in my world there—to speak Swahili—and I needed to know I could take care of myself.
>
> My mom followed my journey to different parts of Kenya as I moved around for home stays—she'd look up the exact places where I was—and she'd read about it. So she had a background, which helped so much in our e-mails to each other. To have her open to learning from me was so awesome.

Students' growing self assurance breeds a new respect from their parents. Young men and women speak of the confidence born of weeks of traveling on their own, of the capacity to manage their own finances in a foreign currency, and of the uphill struggle to master another language—often a lonely and arduous task. A junior in a Spanish-speaking program in Madrid lived with a local family and learned the language slowly and tediously:

> When people talk to me, I have to watch them, their gestures, anything I can pick up. Every time I have a conversation, I first have to translate what's being said into English and then go through it again before I speak. I have to plan out whatever I say, a meal or a favor; it can't be spontaneous. I have to have complete concentration all the time. I'm so tired at night, I just flop into bed.

By the middle of her second semester, however, her confidence grew along with her competence, and her messages to her family were joyful:

> All of a sudden, everything is beginning to click, and if it continues like this, all those months of struggling and shyness will be worth it to say the least. God, it's the most amazing feeling to achieve something like this and to have fun doing it.

Most students go through periods of intense loneliness and even depression at some point during their time abroad. As the semester wears on, long, gray Paris winters begin to feel interminable; Costa Rican diets heavy on rice and beans seem more monotonous than intriguing; and living with a family in a remote village feels more isolating than exotic. Students are stretched to adapt to cultures dramatically different from their own, as this student who spent a semester in Nepal illustrates:

> I felt uncomfortable many times in Nepal. For instance the first time I got my period there, I had to

> announce to my whole family that I was menstruating—there is a menstruation taboo. I had to sit outside the family circle—and couldn't touch the food. I became an untouchable. At first this was so hard for me. And there was no place I could go to hide or cry. I realized that this was part of the culture—part of a culture I had wanted to experience—and now I think that experience has let me feel confident that I can work with people of other cultures—that my perceptions aren't the only ones—that I can change my perceptions.

The students who thrive the most seem to be those who are receptive to the culture, without too many preconceived expectations. An ability to make friends easily, to be uninhibited in trying out an imperfect command of a foreign language, to be able to tolerate occasional periods of intense loneliness—these capacities all tend to enhance the study abroad experience.

Parents who are able to go abroad for a visit have the pleasure of witnessing firsthand their child's growing language skill, maturity, and cultural immersion. These are treasured times when the tables are turned and their son or daughter becomes a much appreciated and admired guide, interpreter, or art historian.

Whether they go for a summer, a semester or a year, students return home with remnants of a new culture—a British accent, the colorful fabrics of a Nigerian wardrobe, a subscription to *Le Figaro*, or a passion for Chinese poetry. Identity issues broaden from "myself as a woman" or an engineering student or an advocate for social causes to "myself as an American," an American who has discovered Norwegian roots, a Japanese-American devoted to his Japanese heritage, or an American who is part of a world community. Just as students discover the flaws in their own families when they see them from a distance, many young people view the United States through the critical eyes of their new international friends. They miss the friends, families, and lovers who had become a part of their lives in another land.

A student returning from South America recalls:

> I was gone for a year in Colombia, and I had really assimilated. I had a life there and I felt Colombian. I didn't just change countries, I changed identities. The last two weeks there were terribly emotional. I couldn't bear the thought of leaving my country.

Many suffer reverse culture shock when they are reunited with their families and their friends at school. A senior describes the period of reentry after a return from Norway:

> I felt so totally alone; it was a terrible loneliness until October or November. No one could understand what I had been through—what my life was like. I was a different person there from who I was when I left sophomore year. And when I came back to school, I expected the world had stopped because I wasn't here. And to think my friends here lived without me, and they have their friends, and everyone else is doing their own thing, and I don't have my niche anymore.

But more long-lasting than the adjustments of reentry, they return with a new perspective, a worldview that replaces the self-absorption of their earlier identity quest, and a new sense of their own ability to handle life on their own.

COMMITMENTS ON CAMPUS: *JUNIOR AND SENIOR YEARS*

> I see a big difference between sophomore and junior years. The main thing for me is I know how to solve

> problems. I know how to dig deeper and find resources. That goes for academics too. I know how to approach academic problems.
>
> Juniors and seniors have made a place for themselves. We've got a major and a definite set of friends we'll be calling up in forty years and asking, "How are the grandchildren?"
>
> I trust my own opinions a lot more than I did freshman or sophomore years. I feel freer to disagree with faculty or drop a class if I want to.
>
> I'm more realistic about what I can and can't do. I've channeled my commitments and don't try to do everything. I manage my time better and make sure I eat and sleep right. Sometimes my work comes second. My main priority right now is the lighting for the spring production.

Junior and senior years are a time of consolidation. No longer trying on a series of roles, juniors and seniors have a more solid sense of their own identity. Most have settled into a social niche on campus that confirms who they are and what they value. They have staked out an academic home in their major department. Now it is their turn to assume the campus leadership positions they may have aspired to as freshmen and sophomores.

As they become more aware of their own limits and talents, they wrestle with trade-offs, with the pros and cons of one choice over another. Whereas their earlier choices were made in the spirit of exploration, rebellion, or testing extremes, the commitments of upperclassmen are those they claim for themselves. Some opt for a balanced lifestyle, dividing their time among part-time jobs and academic, social, and extracurricular pursuits. Others choose to put most of their energy into one arena of campus life and narrow their focus.

Those who immerse themselves in academics discover the rewards of scholarship. Their sense of self-confidence grows along with their insight and competence in their discipline. They develop the skills of critical inquiry and delve into research and analysis. No longer satisfied by the "right answer" of an external authority, they respond to the challenge of ambiguity. They read original sources and struggle to form and justify their own viewpoints. They measure their success in academic terms, and their scholarly pursuits are an essential part of their identity.

Some "hang out" in departmental lounges, endlessly drinking coffee and testing their emerging skills in discussion and debate with their classmates. They may become involved in departmental politics or undergraduate organizations that revolve around an academic discipline. Relationships with faculty change, as students leave behind the formality of the large lecture halls for the more intimate seminar rooms, laboratories, and studios of upper-level classes. Some seize the chance to work as a research assistant for an admired professor; if they are fortunate, the professor takes on the role of mentor, guiding and encouraging their intellectual growth.

Although co-curricular involvement is meant to supplement academic life, for many upperclassmen, what goes on beyond the walls of the classroom has become their first priority. The sports editor of the college paper dashing to meet a deadline feels the rush of excitement as he joins his coterie of fellow journalists in a common pursuit. No journalism class could measure up to this laboratory of learning. No fraternity bond could be stronger than the one he feels in this community. A junior who had enjoyed singing in a campus choir in prior years, now spends many evenings at rehearsals with a small madrigal group and is taking lessons in the flute as a result of her growing interest in early music. As a computer science major, she has found the complexities of sophisticated programming intriguing, but she considers the friends who share her passion for music to be her college family.

Sometimes campus activities give students their first taste of a potential for leadership. Whether their commitment is to an athletic team , a sorority, a religious group, or a service organization, they have the chance to develop lifelong skills and a sense of themselves as people who can effect change.

A young faculty member reflects on her own college experience:

> Participating in Delta Sigma Theta sorority was a highlight of my undergraduate career. I had been in awe of the amazing women in the sorority before I sought to be a part of it. They were campus leaders in student government, in the arts and community service. Sororities and fraternities have a unique legacy in American history and service to the Black community. The undergraduate chapter at Spelman College did a lot to foster my leadership training. It was through the sorority that I learned about program planning and development, mentoring, time management and networking.

A senior from Portland, Oregon, looks back at the impact that campus involvement had on her:

> I joined the undergraduate English society sophomore year. I liked going to its poetry readings and figured I might as well get involved. Before I knew it I was in charge of pulling together a panel for one of the meetings. I had to call alumni and ask them if

> they'd be willing to participate. I was scared to death calling all those important people. But I did it, and then on the night of the program I introduced them and moderated the panel. It was the first time I thought of myself as a leader, and I liked it. That was just the beginning.
>
> By junior year it all started to come together. I was elected president of the English society and got involved in campus politics. I was invited to participate in a retreat for campus leaders run by the student affairs staff, and I was knocked out by it. We learned everything from assertion skills to how to lead a meeting. I got to know kids I never would have met otherwise. And I got to know the guy who's the director of student activities and he's had a big influence on me ever since. They kept talking about empowerment, and I understood what they meant because I was starting to feel it. Right now I'm running for president of student government. It's the first time in a long time that a woman has run for the top office.

Whether this young woman wins her election is less important than the process that got her there. There is only one student government president at every school, but all students have an opportunity to learn through their involvement in campus and community life.

The journey from the fragmented and disconnected state of the sophomore slump to the engagement and commitments a year or two later is not the same for everyone. But by the time they are seniors, most students have a greater sense of their own competence in and out of the classroom. They know more about who they are and what they believe in. They have found a place in the community that has become their home.

10

THE END IS THE BEGINNING

THE FAMILIAR RITUAL OF DEPARTURE IN EARLY fall—the journey back to campus, reentry one more time—the beginning of senior year. By now it seems so natural, this coming and going, this moving in and out of the family orbit. Students casually pack their life's belongings into the back of a car and drive off to school. Or they hop on a bus or a plane with the confidence of those who know where they are heading.

Seniors are at the top of the heap now. They are the team captains and newspaper editors, the leaders of campus organizations, and the enlightened voices in the classroom. Though some revel in that knowledge for the entire year, most are acutely aware that their position is tenuous. At some point they are struck by the realization that, "I'm a senior. This is it—the end."

The year is filled with a series of last times: the last convocation, homecoming weekend, basketball game, fraternity rush, winter term, midterm, final. Never will life be quite so ritualized again. And the dawning of the reality that "This is it" brings on a flurry of "last chance" activity. There is a sense of urgency, of time running out. Some students throw themselves into a host of endeavors as they try to make the most of college opportunities. They spend precious time with their circle of friends, hang out with professors, explore the surrounding city or countryside. And with graduation a mere eight or ten courses away, encounters with the academic catalogue take on a new significance. As they juggle their schedules, they are no longer just choosing courses; they are relinquishing the possibility of taking that seminar on Shakespeare's sonnets, or that fantastic course on film, or that once-in-a-lifetime chance to study with a renowned professor.

Some seniors use this year to take an assortment of courses they have always wanted to take—courses they consider fun. Some fill in their liberal arts curriculum with courses in accounting and Web development, practical courses they see as an entry to the job market. And others streamline their academic and co-curricular involvement, focusing on an honors thesis or a science research project, a music recital, or a drama production. This represents the culmination of years of effort, and for these students the sense of accomplishment has a tangible by-product.

A graduating civil engineering student beams with pride when describing the final structural design project that he did with a team of three students:

> We were told by the faculty, "You will design a bridge over the Mississippi River and you will design everything. You will design every bolt, every plate, every girder, every beam, every cable, every piece of cement. You will design the whole thing, and then you will present it to us, and we will tell you if it is good."
>
> This is the one class that pulls it all together. For the past two or three years I've been saying, All this theory, all this pragmatic, dogmatic stuff—as long as I can put out a good structural design proj-

> ect, I'll be satisfied. Now I know I can do this. Look at this bridge! You present this thing, and you have a professional engineer saying, "That's a good bridge."

And this graduating senior looks back at her growth from freshman to senior year, culminating with her thesis:

> Doing a senior honors thesis was very rewarding because it gave me the chance to work so closely with a faculty member, and it allowed me to become so immersed in one topic, but it was such hard work. The most rewarding thing is looking back at the trouble I had in my first year—how uncomfortable, unconfident, and overwhelmed I was—and realizing that during that time, even though I didn't know it, I was doing the "work" I had to do in order to become who I am now.

Linda Salamon, Professor of English and Human Sciences at George Washington University, is a proponent of honors theses and senior projects:

> No matter what the field, I see value in a sustained piece of work over a long period of time. A research effort and synthesis demonstrates to students, not so much that they can master a particular discipline, but that they can use skills of inquiry, analysis, and sometimes creative imagination as well. It's a culminating experience for students who do it. When they call their parents in the midst of it, moaning "I'll never finish," or "This is a giant monster," parents shouldn't worry. They should just encourage them.

For some students the sense of mastery is not tied to a thesis or particular project; it is more internal, less accessible to public display. They exude a sense of joy in their intellectual development. A Chinese studies major at Middlebury exclaims:

> I feel on the top of the world. Academically it is my best year. I feel as though I can do anything. My professors agree with what I say, or if they disagree, I realize I can argue with them. I've taken lots of classes specific to my field, and I've spent a year studying and traveling in China. I don't depend on gut feelings anymore; I can back up what I say with sources and cogent reasoning. Whatever I say has some validity to it. I know I can say something without making a fool of myself.

And a graduating history major, while enjoying the richness of his senior studies, realizes that the end of his college experience marks the beginning of his commitment to learning for the rest of his life:

> Since I've found something that interests me, that I want to learn about, this year has been incredible for me academically. I want to take classes on my own until I'm 60 or 80 because now I realize there's so much more to learn, and I'll study because I enjoy it and not because I have to. There's a reason for it. It won't be for a distribution requirement; it won't be for my major or for my minor; it will be because I'm interested and I really want to know.

Lacking a crystal ball to predict their future, seniors look back, sometimes wistfully, often with amazement, at the accrued accomplishments and changing perspectives of past months and years:

> I keep having these total flashbacks of four years. I can just picture myself waiting in line as a freshman, not knowing what to do next, staring at the map, trying to figure it out. I've done so many things, been so many places, met so many people. I've done some really crazy things. I think about how it's all progressed and how much I've matured.
>
> College opened my eyes to life and what happens—good and bad. I had no idea how bad things could get—or how good—or how different people can be. In high school it was almost like a mold that everyone fits into. Last year my floor had a lot of international students and I lived with people from countries I didn't even know existed. I learned about everything from food—like how Latin people don't eat much peanut butter—to how Pakistani people get married, to dances and clothing and a little bit of language. It's made me much more tolerant—more open-minded. Not many things surprise me anymore.
>
> When I came to college I saw everything as black and white. I was idealistic—but I didn't really know what to do with my idealism. I was much more judgmental. Like when I came back home during break freshman year, I thought my old high school friends were so conservative—so provincial. Now I have come to see things as less black and white—there's a lot more gray. I still don't know exactly what I'm going to do, but I know I want to work for social change. My experience with community service, my

> semester in Nepal, my honors thesis in American Culture Studies on Welfare Reform—all these have given me a lot more perspective.
>
> It's hard to believe it now, but before I came here I was so close to my parents that I actually felt scared to be away from my mom. Everyone always said we're so much alike. As time went on—I saw things about my parents I hadn't noticed before. You know how when you go out of the country you notice things about your own country when you come back. That's how it was when I went home. My parents gave me the space to be critical of them—and that made it easier for me. It also made it easier that they have their own lives, their own interests, work and community. They aren't trying to live through me—and I can be different from them—even though we still basically have the same values and I love and respect them more than ever.
>
> Somewhere I had this assumption that things would be taken care of at this stage—that I would cancel the newspaper and cancel the phone service and pack up all my personal problems and blithely move on to start life anew in another city. All of a sudden I realized that it was not going to be quite so simple. I see the complexities of things so much more now. It's not that my life is more complex. I guess I'm just more aware of the complexities. No more good, bad—right, wrong. It's harder this way. My mom says it's all just part of growing up.

Many express frustration, and regrets as well—thoughts of lost opportunity and squandered time. They often describe such thoughts, however, with newly acquired perspective on their total college experience:

> At the beginning of the year and part of this semester, I would kick myself about, oh God, I wish I'd done that, and I did so much wrong in college—but I guess part of growing up is knowing there are going to be regrets. There are things you're going to mess up—then realizing why you didn't do things as well as you could have and learning from that.

Some students have to come to terms with the fact that they haven't done well in college. Occasionally, students who've scraped by with C's and D's fail in their final semester. Unable to graduate with their class, they face summer school and an anticlimactic finish. This is a difficult scenario for everyone involved. An academic dean who deals with this each spring reminds parents:

> The student knows this is a failure—it's a failure in the biggest task he's undertaken in life to date. And he needs his parents to be there for him. Parents should remember, it's not their own failure.

Senior year is a time of intensity and contradiction—of the highs of accomplishments and the lows of dreams unfulfilled—of the comfort of familiarity and the anxiety of the unknown looming ahead. For many, there is a sense of things coming together, of goals reached, of efforts rewarded. And yet, standing at the top of the mountain, there is scarcely time to admire the view. Self-confidence becomes shaky as thoughts of the future invade the present.

As seniors make forays into the world beyond the campus, the question, "What's next?" is never far from their thoughts.

Some who are doing internships in a brokerage house or TV station, in a juvenile court or an art gallery, wonder throughout—is this what I want to do next year? For as long as they can remember, their occupation has been student, and September has meant going back to school. But now September conjures up either a blank, a void, or transient images of where they will be, whom they'll be with, or what they'll be doing a year from now. Some hedge their bets and apply to graduate school and for jobs simultaneously. Some become immobilized and do nothing. Still others make a conscious decision to concentrate on school and postpone the search until after graduation.

Although many eventually will seek advanced degrees, the majority of today's college seniors face the tensions and uncertainties of searching for their first job in a period of downsizing and rapidly shifting employment opportunities. Dressed in their interview suits, future bankers and corporate trainees run—or wobble on newly purchased high heels—from an oriental philosophy class to a meeting with a recruiter from Bank of America. They write resumes with online career programs and practice their interviewing skills in front of a video camera.

Those aspiring to attend graduate or professional schools write applications and compare their entrance test scores with an intensity reminiscent of their former bouts with SATs. Others who have no idea what they want to do are sure that everyone else does. Waves of panic sweep over most seniors periodically, sometimes triggered by a friend's job offer—or their own rejection letter.

At just the time that students may be feeling vulnerable and looking to their parents for reassurance, many parents become anxious as well. Instead of providing a calming perspective, they often inadvertently add their own worries to those of their children. Separation issues resurface as they look forward to the end of tuition bills, but wonder if these will be replaced by other burdens, financial and emotional. What if he doesn't get a job? What if she doesn't get a fellowship? What if he wants to come back home to live?

Even those who have been avid supporters of a broad liberal arts education may get the jitters about job prospects when the end is in sight. Fathers who had been uninvolved in the brouhaha of "getting in" four years before suddenly call inquiring about on-campus interviews by major corporations. "I know you don't want to work for Proctor and Gamble, but perhaps you should have a contingency plan in case newspaper writing doesn't work out." Mothers give unsolicited advice about how to dress and act in interviews. Parents who just months before bragged of their daughter's independent travel on another continent now worry that she will be unable to figure out the next step in her own future.

Parents who forge ahead as if the job hunt is their own are often puzzled by their offspring's negative reaction when they call to announce that they have set up an interview for him with a friend or client. Others are more subtle, hinting, "I saw a great new book on resume writing in the store."

A senior from Dallas describes the added burden of her parents' interrogating phone calls:

> My parents have been more involved than ever this year. They call wanting information. "How's it going? How're you doing? Have you heard from this school? Have you heard from that school? What are you doing this summer? Do you have a job? Do you have a place to stay?"
>
> It's hard. I already expect a lot from myself. Then to be bombarded with questions by them makes it harder. I want to say, "Look Mom, look, Dad, I know how important this all is." They don't seem to understand that I am aware, that I do know what's impor-

> tant. I wish they'd say stuff like, "We know that you're going through a lot. We know it's tough." Or ask, "Are you nervous? Are you scared?" They seem to just be concerned with the facts.

A senior from Phoenix adds:

> I think for my parents what's been tough is that they haven't been here—haven't been part of my world. When they ask me lots of questions, I feel affronted. Like when I was applying for a Fulbright, my mom asked me what I thought was a ridiculous question about a recommendation. I got really short with her, and we had a big fight. She doesn't realize that I know you have to prepare for things.

A young woman whose parents are questioning her desire to join Teach for America before going to medical school tries to see things from their point of view:

> They haven't been able to hear the conversations I have with friends—and with interviewers—about why I'm doing what I'm doing. If my parents were able to be here—to listen in on an interview—and hear an interviewer ask me questions—and then hear my answers—it would be different. I've done my homework. I need these two years with TFA to be the person I want to become. I want my parents to trust that decision

Although every senior seems to have at least one friend who has landed the perfect job in the perfect place at a higher-than-hoped-for salary, the majority of students do not have everything wrapped up by graduation. It is not unusual for seniors to leave campus after commencement stating as one student did, "My life is one big *if*. Nothing is solid right now."

The ambiguity and uncertainty of not knowing, however, is frustrating, and students appreciate parents who acknowledge this without trying to rush in and solve the problem for them or prod them into instant action.

Understanding and encouragement does not imply a light dismissal of the problem either. An engineering student who, much to his surprise and disappointment, was without a job at graduation found his parents' buoyant optimism more stressful than helpful: "They don't seem to understand that I'm really scared about not having a job. And it doesn't help when they tell me it's no big deal."

Knowing that they will soon be on their own, seniors are emphatic about maintaining their sense of autonomy. A former premed who discovered Spanish and international relations during her sophomore year called home with excitement when offered an opportunity to do an internship for Amnesty International after graduation—unpaid. Her mother, a nurse, was shocked and mystified at the news that her talented and bright daughter was planning to return home to live and work at a menial job to pay expenses, while participating in an unpaid internship:

> To my mom, this internship is kind of a black hole. When I called her and told her about it, there was silence at the other end of the phone. I knew she was upset. To her, it's no payoff for all the work I've done. To me, it is the foundation for moving on to something else. It's very important.
>
> When I switched from premed to Spanish in the middle of sophomore year, that was a hard thing to do because Mom wasn't happy about it. When I went away to Mexico junior year, it was the first major

> thing I did without her approval. And it was the best year I've ever had.
>
> Now this internship is an opportunity to build a foundation for what I want to do in international relations. For my mom, it's a culmination of all the changes I've made. She's realizing that I'm going to be doing stuff like this forever, and that's hard for her to handle. She doesn't understand the international opportunities of jobs, and what I can do and why I want to travel. My mom grew up in Cleveland and never left; it was an environment where you either went to nursing school or you became a teacher—something traditional with a name or a title. And I'm never going to have that. I don't want to have it. She was divorced and worries about my security. If I'm not something with a title, that's very insecure to her. To me, it's not. To me, it's exciting.

Though this young woman longed to maintain the close, loving relationship she and her mother had always enjoyed, she was determined to pursue her own goals. The week after she had called her mother about the internship she wrote to her and essentially laid it on the line. Her confidence in her own identity, in who she has become, is evident:

> I wrote an intense letter, spilling my guts, and said, basically, accept me as I am. I said, Would you like me to come home to the suburbs and become a secretary and live there for the rest of my life? That won't be me. It's not me; it's not who I've become. You sent me off to college to do well, and I have—and I took advantage of the opportunities and I grew, and I traveled, and I learned. And now here I am at the point of graduating. I am who I am because of what college

> has done to me and what I've done during college, and it's too late now. I can't change that. College is in me.

What a tribute to all college can and should be—the sheer joy of a student's discovery of the expansive world around her and ultimately of her own expanding self. But as parents, we often cringe when it is our own child who is taking the more adventuresome, less traveled path—or any path that differs from our hopes and expectations. We carry our own agendas—a dentist, whose real passion has been an involvement in Jewish volunteer activities, has a strong investment in his daughter becoming a rabbi. A mother who is a computer programmer has dreams of law school for her daughter. A doctor sees a medical career as the only acceptable route for his son. A bus driver makes sacrifices for the dream of his daughter, the future engineer. But the would-be engineer discovers TV production, and the doctor's son opts for a graduate degree in classics. The dentist's daughter forgoes rabbinical school for a career as a Jewish educator, and the young woman whose mother had visions of law school makes a commitment to biotechnology.

Our children will go their separate ways, and so they should. They have become who they are, not who we would have them be. As graduation draws near and students declare their financial independence, both parents and children feel the balance of power shifting between them. Money has, after all, been the one tie that has continued to bind, often unacknowledged, but inevitably present in the background.

In many families, issues of money are still under negotiation. Some students have put themselves through college; many have taken out loans and are facing substantial debts. Others worry about building a financial base so that they can go to graduate school in the future. Still others are in the throes of a job hunt. And questions arise for both parents and their children. Who will pay off the loans? Can I retain my independence and live at home? How long am I willing to help subsidize my kid? Who's going to pay for graduate school? If he lives at home, should I charge him room and board?

Each family has to weigh its own financial realities, values, and needs. Those who talk openly about money matters—expectations and limits—avoid disappointment and resentment at a later date. There are, of course, no hard and fast rules. One student who supported herself all through college decides to live at home so that she can pay off her loans. She is confident and secure in her independence, and her parents, who were unable to pay for college, welcome the chance to be of help. Another senior turns down his parents' offer to pay for graduate school, even though he knows it will be several years before he can pay for it himself. He's convinced that the financial ties are too threatening to his autonomy.

A graduating senior reveals that her world feels a bit precarious right now:

> When I left for college . . . moneywise, it was a little scary. You don't know if you're financially dependent or financially independent or somewhere in between. I'm experiencing that right now as I'm about to go out into the real world. I want to be financially independent, and college has been a good time to learn that . . . like my parents paid for my tuition, and I paid for everything else. But, if I have to be completely financially independent, I kind of freak out about it.

By the time they are seniors, most students have stopped turning to their parents for their primary emotional support, and turn first to their friends and lovers. For many, the heart of college life, especially during these last months, centers around a cherished group of friends. Much of their undergraduate experience is tied up in a mutual history of heartaches and treasured memories.

As the school year comes to a close, students are aware of the impending separation from those who have become so central to their lives. They plan outings and weekend getaways; some look forward to traveling together before settling into the routine of a job or graduate school; others hope to keep a thread of continuity in their lives by joining forces to live together after graduation.

They look to these trusted friends for confirmation of their decisions and validation of their identity. An about-to-graduate senior from the University of Wisconsin confides:

> I went through a stage three months ago of being very remorseful about leaving my security blanket, which this university has become. My friends know Lisa. They know what she stands for, what she does. I'm accepted here. I dread going out into the real world and having to reestablish myself and reintroduce myself. My self-confidence is wavering. I've decided to stay in Madison for the summer, live with a good friend, and send out applications.

Those whose plans will clearly take them far away from friends anticipate the grieving process that lies ahead. A young woman who intends to return home to Minnesota before entering divinity school notes:

> Part of me dreads after graduation, when I've left all my friends and I go home and get depressed and my parents are going to say, "It's not that bad—get yourself together"—and I'm going to say, "No, let me be depressed. It's OK for me to feel bad."

Those who plan to work after graduation worry about leaving behind a world in which they have been surrounded by people their own age—where it's always easy to find someone to talk to about politics or music or whatever. And there's always something to do—parties, lectures, concerts. And they're usually free! As the time to part approaches, they make plans to keep in touch, and joke about the reunions they'll have in the as yet unimaginable future. Those who have stayed in close touch with high school friends reassure themselves that they'll do the same with their friends from college. A senior on her way to medical school says laughingly:

> I know I'll keep up with my friends here. And I know that if I get married, my little kids are going to meet their little kids. There's no doubt in my mind that's going to happen. And now I understand that anywhere I go, I'll be able to make new friends, but that it's going to take time.

The unspoken intentions of romantic partnerships must now be addressed. Graduation brings a convenient end to some of these twosomes; commitment was only to this time and place. But for many students, conflicts of identity and intimacy are brought clearly into focus at this juncture. Choices are many, and decisions are often painful and poignant: Should I give up the chance to work on Wall Street and pick up whatever I can in Ann Arbor while she goes to grad school? Will our relationship withstand the strain if he's in D.C. and I'm in Tampa? If we compromise and go to the only law school that accepted both of us, will we end up resenting each other?

Some parents are surprised to find that couples who appear to be very much in love put career priorities ahead of personal ones. Many young men and women acknowledge that their priority is to establish a more solid sense of themselves beyond the campus world before they make a long-term commitment to someone else.

After an intense year-and-a-half relationship, a future graduate student in education finds herself at a crossroads:

> The past twenty years I've been my parents' child, and even at college, you're not a full adult. And I'm getting out, and here I have a chance to be me, and that's most important. I love Sean a lot, but after twenty years, it's time for me now; it's time for me to do what's best for me. And if what's best for him is going to coincide with that, well that's great, that's fantastic. But he's not the most important thing in my life right now. I don't expect to be the most important thing in his life either.

Parents may be caught off guard when they find that their child is making plans to live with a partner. What may look like impulsive, cavalier behavior may actually represent a carefully thought out decision. A senior at Dartmouth explains that his parents were taken aback when he called to tell them that he and his girlfriend were moving to San Francisco together:

> I had intentionally not told my parents much about our relationship. I didn't tell them anything until it was a fait accompli. It ended up being more of a scene than it would have been otherwise. They were very upset because they had no idea how important she was to me. I hadn't told them. In trying to avoid confrontation earlier in the year, I brought on more. I underestimated them. After all, I'm the fifth child, and nothing I could have done would have been a

> surprise. If I had to do it over, I would have let them know more along the way.

In the midst of all this planning for the future, saying good-bye to dear friends, wrapping up the last round of papers and finals, the pressure mounts. A chemistry major from Puerto Rico recounts:

> This is probably the most confusing time in my life. Everything is up in the air. I haven't heard yet from med school in Puerto Rico or if I have a job here. I'm packing up four years worth of stuff, but I don't know where I'm going to be. I'm still under pressure in one class—a take-home exam I have to finish by tomorrow. My parents have a new house. Nothing's solid, past or future. It's nine days before graduation, and I never thought it'd be like this.

Even those with definitive plans begin to feel disoriented, to experience waves of highs and lows as the countdown to graduation begins. When they finish their last exams, everything comes to a halt. "It's like coming off of drugs," said an engineering student from a highly competitive university:

> You've spent four years of intense pressure, day in and day out, and your body had become used to such incredibly high levels of stress. I keep thinking, What do I have to do? What's my homework? I've got to race to get this done. And then I remember, it's over.

And while her parents are focused on her getting a job, this student has very different things on her mind:

> It's a weird time, like I can't imagine having any deadlines anymore. No more semesters. I just don't

> know how to plan anything after graduation. I want to take a road trip with a friend for a week. I'm not really nervous about not having a job. I know I'll get a job in the fashion industry. I've been working every summer since high school, and I've made so many connections in that industry, it's ridiculous. But it's scary to think about everything being so open-ended, like I'd like to go to Spain, but I can't just take off for Spain without a job . . . but once I get a job, I can't go to Spain. How do you build breaks—time for fun—in your life? I can't imagine it.

On the brink of adulthood, these young men and women retreat to realms of childlike playfulness. "I've done a lot of crazy things with my friends," said a business student in his final weeks. "Nothing harmful. Just absurd. Like walking six miles to White Castle for a hamburger last weekend." The campus takes on an air of celebration, a spontaneous round of parties and picnics, barefoot smiling students cavorting with friends among the ubiquitous campus canines chasing sticks and Frisbees, scantily clad seniors lazing in the sun—a week's hiatus before the finale.

Students put finishing touches on plans for the big day—graduation. Groups of friends make arrangements for cocktail parties and brunches and look forward to introducing their parents to each other on their own turf. For a number of students from divorced families, graduation stirs up the pain of unresolved family conflicts. Some of them anticipate having to orchestrate the comings and goings of parents, stepparents, and grandparents who barely speak to each other. They talk about feeling trapped and resent the burden of having to hold things together on their special day. For many children of divorced parents, however, this isn't a problem. Their parents put their own conflicts aside and come together to share the joy of this milestone in their child's life.

■

When graduation day finally arrives, the campus is at its most resplendent, lawns clipped and bushes pruned. Instant gardens have sprung up in newly planted flower beds. The carillon rings out familiar tunes, and with luck the weather cooperates to produce the picture-book aura of the admission office's most enticing brochure.

Parents, some with young children in tow, or with grandparents on their arm, view the proceedings through the eyes of omnipresent video and cell phone cameras. Reflecting the diversity of the graduating class, assembled guests sport turbans and veils, three-piece suits, cowboy boots.

The students congregate, a sea of black robes and mortarboards. Beneath the solemnity of academic garb, they express their individuality with Hawaiian shirts and shorts, purple sandals and red hightops, sunglasses of every imaginable color. Atop their mortarboards they have taped champagne glasses, pinwheels, a mysterious Chinese symbol, a sign that says, "Hire me." They carry everything from bottles of champagne, balloons, and flowers, to a stuffed Snoopy dressed in full graduation regalia. As they line up for the processional, groups of friends join each other, expressing disbelief that this day has finally come. Their irreverent humor hints at their anxiety and belies the formality of the ritual: "I was once a waiter. I can do it again!" "I think I'll pick my grad school by what cool color robes and hoods they have; I like Stanford hoods myself." "It's with all of you guys that I got my best education. Good luck, we're getting out of here!"

The ceremony starts with a roll of drums or flair of trumpets, followed by the color and pageantry of a medieval academic procession. The music builds to the familiar strains of "Pomp and Circumstance"—guaranteed to send chills up the spines of even the most jaded of graduation-goers.

Among the speeches and musical interludes, and conferring of honorary degrees, there are the familiar phrases that invite the assembled graduates to "enter the company of educated men and women." The final words are greeted with cheers, popping champagne corks, tossed mortarboards, the release of balloons into the sky.

The grandeur and pageantry of this final college ritual is ephemeral; it remains only in the memory and faded family albums. What endures is less dramatic and unfolds over time.

In the words of a brand new graduate:

> It's not like right after graduation time stops and you just stand there and look at this big event—and this big white light comes out of the sky and says—"Sandy, you're 21! Look into the past at your life. Look forward at your future."
>
> You just take off your cap and gown, and it's still the quad.
>
> The place hasn't changed, but I have. Four years ago I wouldn't have understood this, but I feel like I'm leaving college with so many more questions than when I came in—and that's great. I know what the questions are and how to go about finding the answers.

As the recessional sounds, our children march out with arms around each other. We stand aside and watch them from a distance, catching a glimpse of the world that has been theirs for four years. We feel pride and joy and tenderness—but we also know that this is their moment, that they are creating their own futures.

RESOURCES FOR PARENTS AND STUDENTS

We've put together the following list of resources as a starting point for parents who want to seek out additional information. We have focused on websites and books that we and many parents have found useful, including a variety of resources targeted to specific populations and students. Our list is not meant to be exhaustive. There is an ever-changing body of helpful information available to parents of today's college students. Exploration of many of the resources here can lead to untold treasures on bookstore and library shelves or in the endless links of the Internet.

ADMISSIONS

College Board

www.collegeboard.com/parents

An excellent website from the same people who gave you the SATs. Tips on how to use the Web for admission and financial aid information, advice for parents and students, and links to many other related websites.

College Navigator

nces.ed.gov/collegenavigator

U.S. Department of Education website. Contains a comprehensive interactive index of colleges and provides detailed information about each individual institution.

Heath Resource Center

www.heath.gwu.edu

A national clearinghouse on postsecondary education for individuals with disabilities. There are links to other resources as well.

Publications

International Student Handbook 2009. New York: College Board, 2008.

Loveland, Elaina. *Creative Colleges: A Guide for Student Actors, Artists, Dancers, Musicians and Writers*. Belmont, CA: SuperCollege, 2008.

Pope, Loren. *Colleges That Change Lives: 40 Schools That Will Change the Way You Think about Colleges*. New York: Penguin Books, 2006.

Peterson's *Colleges for Students with Learning Disabilities or ADD*, 8th ed. Princeton, NJ: Peterson's Guides, 2006

Weinstein, Miriam. *Making a Difference Colleges: Distinctive Colleges to Make a Better World*. Fairfax, CA: Sageworks Press, 2006

FINANCIAL AID

FAFSA

www.fafsa.ed.gov

U.S. Department of Education online version of the free application for federal student aid with helpful step-by-step instructions.

Fastweb

www.fastweb.com

The Internet's largest free scholarship search.

Finaid

www.finaid.org

A comprehensive information resource for students seeking ways to finance their education. Offers "how to" guidance on securing financial aid. Includes cost and savings calculators.

United Negro College Fund

www.uncf.org/ForStudents/scholarship.asp

Offers and administers an array of scholarship, internship and fellowship opportunities.

Publications

Beckham, Barry, ed. *Beckham's Guide to Scholarships for Black and Minority Students*, 6th ed. Silver Spring, MD: Beckham Pubns. 2008.

Massoni, Wayne. *The Athletic Recruiting & Scholarship Guide*, Lafayette, LA: Mazz Marketing Inc., 2005.

ALCOHOL AND DRUG ABUSE

NIAAA (National Institute on Alcohol Abuse and Alcoholism)

www.collegedrinkingprevention.gov

A Web resource from NIAAA for comprehensive research-based information on issues related to alcohol abuse and binge drinking among college students.

"What Parents Need to Know About College Drinking"

www.collegedrinkingprevention.gov/reports/parents/default.aspx

This is the parents brochure from the National Institute on Alcohol Abuse and Alcoholism's report "A Call to Action: Changing the Culture of Drinking at U.S. Colleges."

U.S. Department of Education: Higher Education Center

www.higheredcenter.org/services/audiences/parents

Contains information and resources for parents on talking to their son/daughter about alcohol and drug use. Also contains links to publications, programs, and intervention resources.

CULTS

Cult Studies Association

www.icsahome.com

Provides information and educational resources related to identifying, responding to, and addressing situations related to cult organizations.

Cult Clinic

www.cultclinic.org

(212) 632-4640

The Cult Hotline and Clinic offers counseling, consultation, and referrals for families and friends of cult members. Services are offered to people of all religious, ethnic and racial backgrounds.

EATING DISORDERS

National Eating Disorders Association

www.nationaleatingdisorders.org

Publications

Siegel, Michelle, Judith Brisman, Margot Weinshel. *Surviving an Eating Disorder: Strategies for Families and Friends*, 3rd ed. New York: Collins Living, 2009.

GAP YEAR, STOPPING OUT, TIME OFF, OR TRANSFERRING

The College Board

www.collegeboard.com/parents/csearch/know-the-options/21375.html

An article from College Board entitled, "Should Your Child Take a Year Off?"

PLANETGapYear.com

www.planetgapyear.com

A website designed to help students contemplate and plan for a gap year or time off. Features a blog as well as collection of stories about the experiences of students who have chosen to take a gap year. Contains a special section for parents.

Publications

Haigler, Karl & Rae Nelson. *The Gap-Year Advantage: Helping Your Child Benefit from Time Off Before or During College*. New York: St. Martin's Griffin, 2005.

GAY, LESBIAN, BISEXUAL, AND TRANSGENDERED INDIVIDUALS

Parents, Family and Friends of Lesbians and Gays

www.pflag.org

PFLAG is a support, education and advocacy organization for the parents, families and friends of gay, lesbian, bisexual and transgender persons. The organization runs support groups around the country and provides opportunities for dialogue about sexual orientation, gender, identity and discrimination.

National Consortium of LGBT Resources in Higher Education

www.lgbtcampus.org/directory

Provides contact information for campuses with an LGBT resource professional.

Family Acceptance

www.familyacceptance.org

A website for parents of gay children presented from a Christian perspective. Helpful information for understanding, processing, and working through the thoughts, emotions, and realities many parents face when their child comes out to them.

Publications

Jennings, Kevin & Pat Shapiro. *Always My Child: A Parents' Guide to Understanding your Gay, Lesbian, Bisexual, Transgender, or Questioning Son or Daughter.* New York: Fireside, 2003.

Levithan, David & Billy Merrell. *The Full Spectrum: A New Generation of Writing About Gay, Lesbian, Bisexual, Transgender, Questioning, and Other Identities.* New York: Knopf, 2006.

Griffin, Carolyn Welch, Marian Wirth, and Arthur G. Wirth. *Beyond Acceptance: Parents of Lesbians and Gays Talk About Their Experiences.* New York: St. Martin's Press, 1996.

HEALTH: PHYSICAL AND EMOTIONAL

American College Health Association

www.acha.org

The American College Health Association is the principal advocacy and leadership organization for college and university health. This site provides links to specific college health topics.

Healthy Minds

www.healthyminds.org/collegementalhealth_new.cfm

An resource of the American Psychiatric Association. Contains facts, information, and resources related to college mental health.

Go Ask Alice

www.goaskalice.columbia.edu

An interactive question-and-answer website from the Columbia University Health Services. It includes an archive of lively answers to questions commonly asked by college students.

Virtual Pamphlet Collection

counseling.uchicago.edu/resources/virtualpamphlets

A virtual pamphlet collection from the University of Chicago with links to health-related resource pamphlets from universities across the country.

Publications

Kadison, Richard & Theresa Foy DiGeronimo. *College of the Overwhelmed: The Campus Mental Health Crisis and What to Do About It*. San Francisco: Jossey-Bass, 2005.

Marks, Andrea & Betty Rothbart. *Healthy Teens, Body and Soul: A Parent's Complete Guide*. Darby, PA: Diane, 2004.

LEARNING DISABILITIES AND ADHD

ADDvance

www.addvance.com/help/young_adults/index.html

A website specifically for young adults with ADHD and their parents. Contains resources for transition to college and the workplace.

Publications

Mooney, Jonathan & David Cole. *Learning Outside the Lines: Two Ivy League Students with Learning Disabilities and ADHD Give You the Tools For Academic Success and Educational Revolution*. New York: Simon & Schuster, 2000.

SECURITY AND CRIME PREVENTION

Campus Security Data

ope.ed.gov/security

A data search tool providing campus crime statistics for all postsecondary institutions that participate in federal student aid programs.

Security on Campus

www.securityoncampus.org

Contains information for parents and students about campus crime and prevention.

SEXUAL ASSAULT, RELATIONSHIP VIOLENCE, AND HARASSMENT

Rainn

www.rainn.org/get-information

Rape, abuse, and incest national network. Contains information on crisis response, statistics, reporting, risk reduction, and recovery.

Sexual Harassment Support

www.sexualharassmentsupport.org

Support and information for those who have experienced sexual harassment. Contains information, blog entries, stories, and support group information.

Publications

Ledray, Linda E. *Recovering from Rape*. New York: Henry Holt, 1994.

STUDY ABROAD

Council on International Educational Exchange

ciee.org

Provides information about international study, research and travel programs with a special section specifically for parents.

ESPECIALLY FOR PARENTS

College Confidential

talk.collegeconfidential.com/parents-forum

Discussion forum for parents about college life from application to graduation.

College Parents of America

collegeparents.org/cpa/index.html

College Parents of America is a fee-based national membership association dedicated to helping parents prepare for and successfully put their children through college. The organization provides a wealth of information for parents from the time they begin preparing for their children to go to college, through the complex admissions process, until their college graduation. CPA also serves as an advocacy organization for parents and higher education on Capitol Hill.

Publications

Damon, William. *The Path to Purpose: Helping Our Children Find Their Calling in Life*. New York: Free Press, 2008.

Raskin, Robin. *Parents' Guide to College Life: 181 Straight Answers on Everything You Can Expect Over the Next Four Years (College Admissions Guides)*. New York: Princeton Review, 2006.

GIFT BOOKS FOR THE NEW COLLEGE STUDENT

Cohen, Harlan. *The Naked Roommate: And 107 Other Issues You Might Run Into in College, 2nd Edition*. Naperville, IL: Sourcebooks, Inc., 2007.

Feaver, Peter, Sue Wasiolek, and Anne Crossman. *Getting the Best Out of College: A Professor, a Dean, & a Student Tell You How to Maximize Your Experience*. Berkeley, CA: Ten Speed Press, 2008.

Kennedy, David. *How to Ace Your Way Through College and Still Have a Life!* Denver: Wellness Research Publishing, 2007.

Light, Richard. *Making the Most of College*. Cambridge, MA: Harvard University Press, 2004.

Malone, Michael S. *The Everything College Survival Book: From Social Life To Study Skills—All You Need To Fit Right In*. Cincinnati: Adams Media, 2005.

Wider, Jennifer, M.D. *The Doctor's Complete College Girls' Health Guide: From Sex to Drugs to the Freshman 15*. New York: Bantam, 2006.

GIFT BOOKS FOR THE NEW COLLEGE GRADUATE

Fischer, Kristen. *Ramen Noodles, Rent and Resumes: An After-college Guide to Life*. Supercollege, Llc, 2008.

Patchett, Anne. *What Now?* New York: Harper, 2008.

Syrtash, Andrea. *How to Survive the Real World: Life After College Graduation*. Hundreds of Heads Books, 2006.

NOTES

Chapter Two

Some Things Never Change: The Search for Identity, Independence, and Intimacy

1. Margaret Mahler's pioneering research on the development of young children has provided countless insights into the preverbal period of childhood. Trained as a pediatrician, Mahler later became an eminent child psychoanalyst and researcher. As a result of thirty years of painstaking daily observation of children interacting with their mothers during the first three years of life, Mahler and her associates described a complex developmental sequence, which they named separation-individuation. These were seen as two separate but complementary interweaving themes. Separation referred to the young child's emergence from a symbiotic relationship with his or her mother. Through individuation the child develops unique personality characteristics and the ability to retain a consistent mental image of mother and self.

Mahler adopted the biological term symbiosis to describe the early bond between mother and infant. She suggested that the first signs of the separation-individuation process are the specific smiles that a baby reserves for its mother at about 4 or 5 months, signs of recognition of her as a separate and special person. Through the next two and a half years, the child goes through the sometimes exhilarating, sometimes painful process of moving away from mother to become a separate person in his or her own right. Mahler described the often contradictory behaviors of the separating child, from the practicing phase, when toddlers, who have just learned how to walk, feel all-powerful and in love with the world, to the rapprochement phase, when with increasing separation anxiety they become aware of their vulnerability and helplessness. An empathetic and helpful mother responds to her child's natural pull to venture forth with encouragement and support.

By about 3 years of age, healthy children will have the capacity to hold in their mind a loving, positive representation of mother as well as a consistent and clearly separate self-image. This positive internal mother image is available for comfort at those difficult times when mother is away or when she is frustrating or disappointing. It is a remarkable and complex achievement for a 3-year-old and one that requires both trust and confidence as well as a physical and cognitive maturity. A decade later, Daniel Stern, a highly respected psychoanalyst and developmental researcher, challenged Mahler's notion of symbiosis between mother and child, suggesting that infants experience a sense of emergent self from birth. He posits that while separation is going on, at the same time, and of equal importance, children are seeking and creating new ways to connect with their primary caretaker.

2. Psychologist Peter Blos has written extensively about the tumultuous years of adolescence. In his classic work *On Adolescence*, he borrows the term second individuation from Mahler to describe this chaotic time, which leads finally to a consolidation of individual identity. "The oppositional, rebellious, and resistive strivings, the stages of experimentation, the testing of the self by going to excess—all these have a positive usefulness in the process of self-definition. 'This is not me' represents an important step in the achievement of individuation and in the establishment of autonomy; at an earlier age, it is condensed into a single word, 'No'." (Peter Blos, *On Adolescence: A Psychoanalytic Interpretation*. New York: Free Press of Glencoe, 1962, 12).

3. Psychoanalyst and developmental theorist Erik Erikson points to this critical time as part of the natural evolution of human psychosocial development. His "eight stages of man" extend through the life cycle. Each stage is characterized by a crisis, or turning point, with polar opposite possible resolutions, one leading to growth and the other to difficulties: basic trust versus basic mistrust; autonomy versus shame and doubt; initiative versus guilt; industry versus inferiority; identity versus identity diffusion; intimacy versus isolation; generativity versus stagnation; ego integrity versus despair. At each stage, there is a crossroads, a shifting in perspective, which leads to disequilibrium and vulnerability. The positive resolution of one stage makes moving to the next one possible. The child who has successfully negotiated earlier stages of trust, autonomy, initiative and industry will have an easier time becoming a confident and self-reliant young adult, discovering the answers to the question "Who am I?"

Erikson's stages are not neatly packaged, clearly defined periods. Moreover, his clinical observations were based on a male model of development. The subsequent research of theorists Nancy Chodorow and Carol Gilligan pointed to significant differences between identity development for men and women. Whereas men's identity had been defined primarily through individual achievement and autonomy, women's identity is formed in the context of relationships. Gilligan's positive acknowledgment of the "woman's voice" of empathy, responsibility, and care added a provocative dimension to the study of human development.

Other theorists are examining the subtleties in the identity formation of specific minority groups. What is it like to be black in a white world? A homosexual in a world that values heterosexuality? A young man or woman from a culture that values close ties and obligations to extended family living in a Western society that promotes individualism and independence? All pose questions that challenge or may simply broaden Erikson's original observations.

4. Based on a study in the 1950s and 1960s involving a series of interviews with Harvard undergraduates across their college years, William Perry and his associates postulated a theory of intellectual and ethical development that has had a far-reaching impact on our understanding of the college student. Perry's scheme describes how students think in increasingly complex ways as they move through their college years. Many educators and researchers have found the material relevant and useful in tracing the development of critical thinking in the college student. Perry's research was done on male subjects. Subsequently, as an outgrowth of the work of Carol Gilligan, others have been expanding on Perry's original work to incorporate "women's ways of knowing."

Perry described nine positions, moving from an early stage of basic duality, when students see things in black-and-white terms, to a more complex, relativistic view of the world, and finally to a point at which they are ready to make personal commitments.

5. According to Erik Erikson, it is essential to develop a solid sense of identity before moving on to the next task in his developmental scheme, forming intimate relationships. He writes in *Identity: Youth and Crisis*: "It is only when identity formation is well on its way that true intimacy—which is really a counterpointing as well as a fusing of identities—is possible. Sexual intimacy is only part of what I have in mind, for it is obvious that sexual intimacies often precede the capacity to develop a true and mutual psychosocial intimacy with another person, be it in friendship, in erotic encounters or in joint inspiration." (Erik Erikson, *Identity: Youth and Crisis*. New York: W.W. Norton, 1968, 135.)

Chodorow and Gilligan challenge Erikson's assumption, claiming that his linear scheme is not representative of women's experience. For women, the formation of identity and a capacity for intimacy are much more likely to be intertwined.

Chapter Three

Some Things Do Change: College Life Today

1. John H. Pryor, Sylvia Hurtado, Victor B. Saenz, Jose Luis Santos, and William S. Korn, *The American Freshman: Forty Year Trends, 1966-2006* (Los Angeles: Higher Education Research Institute of UCLA, 2007), vii.

2. John Pryor, Sylvia Hurtado, Jessica Sharkness, and William S. Korn, *The American Freshman: National Norms for Fall 2007* (Los Angeles: Higher Education Research Institute of UCLA, 2007).

3. The representation of entering Latinos increased dramatically from less than 1 percent in 1971 to more than 7 percent in 2006. Asian and Asian American/Pacific Islander students enjoyed a sizeable increase as well, from less than 1 percent in 1971 to close to 9 percent of the entering class of 2006. The percentage of African American students rose throughout the '70s and '80s to a peak of 12.5 percent in 1980, but declined to 10.5 percent by 2006. American Indians who were less than 1 percent of entering freshmen in 1971 were more than 2 percent of the entering class of 2006.

4. Project on Student Debt from the National Center for Education Statistics. National Postsecondary Student Aid Study.

5. Helen Lefkowitz Horowitz, *Campus Life* (New York: Alfred A. Knopf, 1987), 289.

6. Mark Yim, Professor of Mechanical Engineering and Applied Mathematics, *Pennsylvania Gazette* (Nov./Dec 2007), p. 51

7. Joe R. Feagin, Hernan Vera, and Nikitah Imani, *The Agony of Education: Black Students at White Colleges and Universities* (New York: Routledge, 1996), 46.

8. Beverly Daniel Tatum, PhD., *Why Are All the Black Kids Sitting Together in the Cafeteria?* (New York: Basic Books, 1999), 80.

9. Wechsler, Henry, Jae Eun Lee, Tobin F. Nelson, and Meichen Kuo. "Underage College Students' Drinking Behavior, Access to Alcohol, and the Influence of Deterrence Policies: Findings from the Harvard School of Public Health College Study." *The Journal of American College Health* 50:5 (March 2002): 223-36.

10. Task Force of the National Institute on Alcohol Abuse and Alcoholism, A *Call to Action: Changing the Culture of Drinking at U.S. Colleges* (April 2002).

11. More than 18% percent of students reported that they did not drink at all and an additional 26% reported they chose not to drink at parties in the past year. American College Health Association—National College Health Assessment, *Journal of American College Health*, Vol. 56, No. 5 (Spring, 2007).

Chapter Five

Ready, Set, Go: The Departure

1. Gail Sheehy, *Spirit of Survival* (New York: William Morrow, 1986), 26.

Chapter Six

Orientation and Disorientation

1. Ellen Goodman, "When Students Fly from the Empty Nest," *The Philadelphia Inquirer*, September 17, 1986.

Chapter Seven

The Freshman Year: Academic Life and the College Scene

1. David Schoem as quoted in "An Early Start: First Year Seminars" by Leslie Stainton, *LSA Magazine*, University of Michigan, Fall 1996, 12.

Chapter Eight

In and Out of Your Life

1. Richard Kadison, M.D. and Theresa Foy DiGeronimo. *College of the Overwhelmed* (San Francisco: Jossey Bass, 2004), 100.

Chapter Nine

Sophomore Slump and the Years Beyond

1. Kenneth Keniston, "Youth, A 'New' Stage of Life," in *Readings in Adult Psychology: Contemporary Perspectives*, ed. Lawrence R. Allman and Dennis T. Jaffe (New York: Harper and Row, 1977), 133.

2. Hey-Kyung Koh Chin and Rajika Bhandari, *Open Doors 2006: Report on International Education Exchange*. New York: Institute of International Education.

BIBLIOGRAPHY

Apter, Terri. *Altered Loved: Mothers and Daughters During Adolescence*. Ballentine Books, 1991

Baxter Magolda, Marcia B. *Knowing and Reasoning in College: Gender-Related Patterns in Students' Intellectual Development*. San Francisco: Jossey-Bass, 1992.

Belenky, Mary F., Blythe M. Clinchy, Nancy Rule Goldberger, and Jill M. Tarule. *Women's Ways of Knowing*. New York: Basic Books, 1997.

Blos, Peter. *On Adolescence: A Psychoanalytic Interpretation*. New York: Free Press of Glencoe, 1985.

__________. *The Adolescent Passage*. New York: International Universities Press, 1979.

Bogle, Kathleen. *Hooking Up: Sex, Dating, and Relationships on Campus*. New York: New York University Press, 2008.

Bok, Derek. *Our Underachieving Colleges: A Candid Look at How Much Students Learn and Why They Should Be Learning More*. Princeton: Princeton University Press, 2006.

Bowen, William G., and Derek Bok. *The Shape of the River*. Princeton: Princeton University Press, 2000.

Boyer, Ernest L. *Campus Life: In Search of Community*. Princeton: Carnegie Foundation for the Advancement of Teaching, 1990.

__________. *College: The Undergraduate Experience in America.* New York: Harper & Row, 1987.

Cehn, Joan, Risa Nye, and Julie Renalds. *Writin' on Empty: Parents Reveal the Upside, Downside, and Everything in Between When Children Leave the Nest.* Oakland, CA: No Flak Press, 2008.

Chang, Mitchell J., Julie J. Park, Monica H. Lin, Oiyan A. Poon, and Don T. Nakanishi. *Beyond Myths: The Growth and Diversity of Asian American College Freshmen, 1971–2005.* Los Angeles: Higher Education Research Institute of UCLA, 2007.

Chodorow, Nancy. *The Reproduction of Mothering: Psychoanalysis and the Sociology of Gender.* Berkeley: University of California Press, 1999.

Coburn, Karen Levin. "Organizing a Ground Crew for Today's Helicopter Parents." *About Campus* (July-August 2006): 9-16.

Cohen, Harlan. *The Naked Roommate: And 107 Other Issues You Might Run Into In College.* Naperville, IL. Sourcebooks, Inc., 2007.

Combs, Patrick, and Jack Canfield. *Major in Success: Make College Easier, Fire Up Your Dreams, and Get a Very Cool Job.* Berkeley, CA: Ten Speed Press, 2007.

Damon, William. *The Path to Purpose: Helping Our Children Find Their Calling in Life.* New York: Simon & Schuster, 2008.

Daniel, Bonnie, and B. Ross Scott. *Consumers, Adversaries, and Partners: Working with the Families of Undergraduates.* San Francisco: Jossey-Bass, 2001.

DeBuono, B.A., S. H. Zinner, M. Daamen, and W.M. McCormick. "Sexual Behavior of College Women in 1975, 1986, and 1989." *The New England Journal of Medicine* (March 22, 1990): 821-5.

Dobkin, Rachel, and Shana Sippy. *The College Woman's Handbook: Educating Ourselves.* New York: Workman's Publishing, 1995.

D'Souza, Dinesh. *Illiberal Education: The Politics of Sex and Race on Campus.* New York: Free Press, 1998.

Erikson, Erik H. *Childhood and Society,* 2nd ed. New York: W.W. Norton, 1994.

__________. *Identity and the Life Cycle,* New York: W.W. Norton, 1994

__________. *Identity, Youth and Crisis.* New York: W.W. Norton, 1968

__________. "Youth: Fidelity and Diversity." In *Youth and Culture: A Human Development Approach,* edited by Hazel V. Kraemer. Monterey, CA: Brooks/Cole Publishing, 1974.

Feagin, Joe R., Hernan Vera, and Nikitah Imani. *The Agony of Education: Black Students at White Colleges and Universities*. New York: Routledge, 1996.

Feaver, Peter, Sue Wasiolek, and Anne Crossman. *Getting the Best Out of College: A Professor, a Dean, and a Student Tell Uou How to Maximize Your Experience*. Berkeley, CA, 2008.

Fiske, Edward B. *The Fiske Guide to Colleges 2009*. Naperville, IL: Sourcebooks Trade, 2008.

Fleming, Jacqueline. *Blacks in College: A Comparative Study of Students' Success in Black and White Institutions*. San Francisco: Jossey-Bass, 1984.

Gardner, John, A. Jerome Jewler, and Betsy O. Barefoot. *Your College Experience: Strategies for Success*. Blemont, CA: Wadsworth Publishing, 2002.

Gardner, John, Gretchen Van der Veer, and Associates. *The Senior Year Experience: Facilitating Integration, Reflection, Closure, and Transition*. San Francisco: Jossey-Bass, 1997.

Getz, Malcolm. *Investing in College: A Guide for the Perplexed*. Cambridge, MA: Harvard University Press, 2008.

Gilligan, Carol. *In a Different Voice: Psychological Theory and Women's Development*. Cambridge, MA: Harvard University Press, 1993.

Goodman, Ellen. "When Students Fly From the Empty Nest." *The Philadelphia Inquirer*, September 17, 1986.

Grayson, Paul, and Philip W. Meilman. *Beating the College Blues*. New York: Checkmark Books, 1999.

Greene, Howard R., and Matther W. Greene. *Greenes' Guides to Educational Planning: Making It Into a Top College*. New York: Harper Collins, 2000.

Griffin, Carolyn Welch, Marian J. Wirth, and Arthur G. Wirth. *Beyond Acceptance: Parents of Lesbians and Gays Talk About Their Experience*. New York: St. Martin's, 1997.

Hassan, Steven. *Combating Cult Mind Control*. Rochester, VT: Inner Traditions Intl. Ltd., 1990.

Historically Black Colleges and Universities. New York: Praeger Publishers, 1995.

Horowitz, Helen Lefkowitz. *Campus Life: Undergraduate Cultures from the Eighteenth Century to the Present*. Chicago: University of Chicago Press, 1987.

Howe, Neil, and William Strauss. *Millennials Rising: The Next Great Generation*. New York: Vintage Books, 2000.

The Institute for College Access & Success. "Student Debt and the Class of 2006." *The Project on Student Debt*. Berkeley, CA, 2007

International Student Handbook. Princeton: The College Board, 2009.

Jacobs, Lynn F., and Jeremy S. Hyman. *Professors' Guide to Getting Good Grades in College*. New York: HarperCollins, 2006.

Jennings, Kevin. *Always My Child: A Parent's Guide to Understanding Your Gay Lesbian, Bisexual, Transgendered or Questioning Son or Daughter*. New York: Simon & Schuster, 2003.

Kadison, Richard, and Theresa Foy DiGeronimo. *College of the Overwhelmed: The Campus Mental Health Crisis and What to Do About It*. San Francisco: Jossey-Bass, 2005.

Kaplan, Louise. *Adolescence: The Farewell to Childhood*. New York: Simon & Schuster, 1984

__________. *Oneness and Separateness: From Infant to Individual*. New York: Simon & Schuster, 1998.

Keniston, Kenneth. "Youth: A 'New' Stage of Life." In *Readings in Adult Psychology: Contemporary Perspectives*, edited by Lawrence R. Allman and Dennis T. Jaffe. New York: HarperCollins, 1982.

Kimbrough, Walter M. *Black Greek 101: The Culture, Customs, and Challenges of Black Fraternities and Sororities*. Cranbury, NJ: Rosemont, 2003.

Koh Chin, H., and Rajika Bhandari, Ph.D. *Open Doors: Report on International Educational Exchange*. New York: Institute of International Education, 2006

Kuh, George D., John H. Schuh, Elizabeth J. Whitte, and Associates. *Involving Colleges*, San Francisco: Jossey-Bass, 1991.

Ledray, Linda E. *Recovering from Rape*. New York: Henry Holt, 1994.

Levine, Arthur. "Hearts and Minds: The Freshman Challenge." *American Association of Higher Education Bulletin* (1986): 3-6.

Levithan, David, and Billy Merrell. *The Full Spectrum: A New Generation of Writing About Gay, Lesbian, Bisexual, Transgender, Questioning, and Other Identities*. New York: Knopf Books for Young Readers, 2006.

Light, Richard J. *Making the Most of College: Students Speak Their Minds*. Cambridge, MA: Harvard University Press, 2004.

Mahler, Margaret S., Fred Pine, and Anni Bergman. *The Psychological Birth of the Human Infant*. New York: Basic Books, 2000.

Marcus, Eric. *Is It a Choice? Answers to the Most Frequently Asked Questions About Gay & Lesbian People*, 3rd ed. San Francisco: HarperOne, 2005.

Marks, Andrea, M.D., and Betty Rothbart, M.S.W. *Healthy Teens, Body and Soul: A Parent's Complete Guide*. New York: Simon & Schuster, 2004.

McDougall, Bryce. *My Child Is Gay: How Parents React When They Hear the News*. Crow's Nest, NSW Australia: Allen & Unwin, 2006.

Mooney, Jonathan, and David Cole: *Learning Outside the Lines: Two Ivy League Students with Learning Disabilities and ADHD Give You the Tools for Academic Success and Educational Revolution*. New York: Simon & Schuster. 2000.

Nields, Nerissa. *How to Be an Adult*. Florence, MA.: Mercy House, 2008.

O'Sullivan, Marie, ed. *Passport: Academic Year Abroad 2008: The Most Complete Guide to Planning Academic Year Abroad*. New York: Institute of International Education, 2008.

Parrot, Andrea. *Coping with Date Rape and Acquaintance Rape*. New York: Rosen Publishing Group, 1995.

Patchett, Ann. *What Now?*. New York: Harper, 2008.

Pascarella, Ernest T., and Patrick T. Terenzini. *How College Affects Students: A Third Decade of Research*. San Francisco: Jossey-Bass, 2005.

Perry, William G., Jr. *Forms of Intellectual and Ethical Development in the College Years*. San Francisco: Jossey-Bass, 1998.

Pryor, John H., Sylvia Hurtado, Victor B. Saenz, Jose Luis Santos, and William S. Korn. *The American Freshman: Forty Year Trends, 1966–2006*. Los Angeles: Higher Education Research Institute of UCLA, 2007.

Pryor, John H., Sylvia Hurtado, Jessica Sharkness, and William S. Korn. *The American Freshman: National Norms for Fall 2007*. Los Angeles: Higher Education Research Institute of UCLA, 2007.

Raskin, Robin. *Parents' Guide to College Life: 181 Straight Answers on Everything You Can Expect Over the Next Four Years*. New York: Random House, 2006.

Reese, Deborah Frankel. "The Children Are Gone." Letter to the Editor, *The New York Times*, December 1985.

Richter, Laurie. *Put Me In, Coach: A Parent's Guide to Winning the Game of College Recruiting*. Riverwoods, IL: Right Fit Press, 2009.

Ross, Lawrence C., Jr. *The Divine Nine: The History of African American Fraternities and Sororities in America*. New York: Kensington, 2001.

Saenz, Victor B., Sylvia Hurtado, Doug Barrera, De'Sha Wolf, and Fanny Yeung. *First in My Family: A Profile of First-Generation College Students at Four-Year Institutions Since 1971*. Los Angeles: Higher Education Research Institute of UCLA, 2007

Seaman, Barrett. *Binge: What Your College Student Won't Tell You*. Hoboken, NJ: John Wiley & Sons, 2006.

Sheehy, Gail. *Spirit of Survival*. New York: William Morrow, 1987.

Shulman, James L., and William G. Bowen. *The Game of Life: College Sports and Educational Values*. Princeton: Princeton University Press, 2002.

Singer, Margaret Thaler, with Janja Lalich. *Cults in Our Midst: The Hidden Menace in Our Everyday Lives*. San Francisco: Jossey-Bass, 1995.

Stern, Daniel N. *The Interpersonal World of the Infant*. New York: Basic Books, 2000.

Tyler, Suzette. *Been There, Should've Done That: 995 Tips for Making the Most of College*. Lansing, MI.: Front Porch Press, 2008.

Wechsler, Henry. "Alcohol and the American College Campus: A Report from the Harvard School of Public Health." *Change* (July/August 1996): 20-25, 60.

Wechsler, Henry, Jae Eun Lee, Toben F. Nelson, and Meichen Kuo. "Underage College Students Drinking Behavior, Access to Alcohol, and the Influence of Deterrence Policies: Findings from the Harvard School of Public Health College Alcohol Study." *Journal of American College Health* 50:5 (March 2002): 223-236.

Weinstein, Miriam. *Making a Difference College Guide*. San Raphael, CA: Sage Works Press, 2000.

Wheeler, Dion. A *Parent's and Student Athlete's Guide to Athletic Scholarships: Getting Money Without Being Taken for a (Full) Ride*. New York: McGraw Hill, 2000.

Wider, Jennifer, M.D. *The Doctor's Complete College Girls' Health Guide: From Sex to Drugs to the Freshman 15*. New York: Bantam Books, 2006.

Windmeyer, Shane. *The Advocate College Guide for LGBT Students*. New York: Alyson Publications, 2006.

Wolensky, Robert. "College Students in the Fifties: The Silent Generation Revisited." In *Adolescent Psychiatry: Developmental and Clinical Studies*, edited by Sherman C. Feinstein and Peter Giovacchini. Vol.5. New York: Jason Aronson, 1997.

ACKNOWLEDGMENTS

We are deeply grateful to all the students, parents, and college faculty and administrators who have shared their insights and experiences with us. We have changed some of the identifying information to protect anonymity, but they are the heart of the book.

In addition, we would like to thank the following friends and colleagues who have listened, questioned, critiqued, and continued to give us their support: David Abel, Eliot Abel, Shirley Baker, Wendy Bashant, John Berg, Pat Book, Merle Brenner, Tom Brounk, Terri Brennan, Danielle Bristow, Kathy Brock, Justin Carroll, Dorothy Denburg, Steve Ehrlich, John N. Gardner, Alan Glass, Scott Granneman, Stephanie Habif, Kathy and Michael Jay, Delores Kennedy, Jane and Euan Kerr, Walter Kimbrough, Brenda Levin, Morgan Lewis-Smith, David Mahler, Dennis Martin, James McLeod, Melanie Osborn, Yogi Potini, Patricia Somers, Kathy Steiner-Lang, Priscilla Stone, Nanette Tarbouni, Martha Turner, Marc Wais, Ronnie Mae Weiss, Kristin Weyman, Rob Wild, and William Witbrodt.

A special thank you goes to our research assistant, Alicia Schnell, whose creativity, superb organizational skills, and sense of humor have been an enormous help and constant source of delight. Her patience and perseverance kept us on track and helped make it all happen.

We also thank our talented editor, Gail Winston, for her faith in our work and her knowledge, skill and good counsel. Thank you also to Shea O'Rourke, editorial assistant, for her attentiveness and steady support. And finally, we are particularly appreciative of our agent, Elizabeth Kaplan, who saw this project through from the kernel of an idea to its completion. Throughout all five editions we have been the fortunate recipients of her good advice, enthusiasm and encouragement.

INDEX